How the Saints Shaped History

HOW THE SAINTS SHAPED HISTORY

RANDALL PETRIDES

Our Sunday Visitor
Huntington, Indiana

Nihil Obstat
Msgr. Michael Heintz, Ph.D.
Censor Librorum

Imprimatur
✠ Kevin C. Rhoades
Bishop of Fort Wayne-South Bend
November 28, 2022

The *Nihil Obstat* and *Imprimatur* are official declarations that a book is free from doctrinal or moral error. It is not implied that those who have granted the *Nihil Obstat* and *Imprimatur* agree with the contents, opinions, or statements expressed.

Except where noted, the Scripture citations used in this work are taken from the *Revised Standard Version of the Bible — Second Catholic Edition*, copyright © 1965, 1966, 2006 National Council of the Churches of Christ in the United States of America. Used by permission. All rights reserved.

Every reasonable effort has been made to determine copyright holders of excerpted materials and to secure permissions as needed. If any copyrighted materials have been inadvertently used in this work without proper credit being given in one form or another, please notify Our Sunday Visitor in writing so that future printings of this work may be corrected accordingly.

Our Sunday Visitor Publishing Division
Our Sunday Visitor, Inc.
200 Noll Plaza
Huntington, IN 46750
www.osv.com
1-800-348-2440

ISBN: 978-1-63966-021-6 (Inventory No. T2761)

1. RELIGION—Christianity—Saints & Sainthood.
2. RELIGION—Christian Church—History.
3. RELIGION—Christianity—Catholic.

eISBN: 978-1-63966-022-3
LCCN: 2023930343

Cover design: Tyler Ottinger
Cover art:
Interior design: Amanda Falk
Interior art: AdobeStock unless otherwise noted

PRINTED IN THE UNITED STATES OF AMERICA

To my wife, Elizabeth

You are fellow citizens with the saints and members of the household of God, built upon the foundation of the apostles and prophets, Christ Jesus himself being the cornerstone, in whom the whole structure is joined together and grows into a holy temple in the Lord, in whom you also are built into it for a dwelling place of God in the Spirit.

— Ephesians 2:19–22

CONTENTS

PART IV: REFORMATION, REFORM, AND RENAISSANCE — AD 1500 TO AD 1700

PART V: ENLIGHTENMENT AND MODERNISM — AD 1700 TO AD 1920

PART VI: THE CHURCH IN MODERN TIMES — AD 1920 TO THE PRESENT DAY

HISTORICAL AND CHURCH TIMELINES

THE EARLY CHURCH

AD 1

c. 4–8 BC	Birth of Jesus
*unknown	**Saint Joseph**

12–68	**Saint Mark**, Evangelist
c. 16 BC–AD 48 or 57	**Blessed Virgin Mary**
30	Martyrdom of **St. John the Baptist**
33	Death and resurrection of Jesus; Pentecost
33–99	Missionary travels of the Apostles
c. 33–36	Martyrdom of **Saint Stephen**; conversion of **Saint Paul**
*unknown	**St. Mary Magdalene**
45–60	Saint Paul's missionary journeys
c. 46	Disciples called Christians in Antioch
48	Council of Jerusalem

50

c. 60	(d.) **Saint Barnabas**
64–67	Martyrdoms of **Saints Peter and Paul**
c. 65	(d.) **Saint Silas**
70	Destruction of Temple at Jerusalem

64–67
Nero blames fire in Rome on Christians; first imperial persecution

c. 81	Persecution under Domitian
c. 84	(d.) **Saint Luke**, Evangelist
c. 90	Rise of Gnostics
99	(d.) **Pope Saint Clement I**, Father of the Church

*mid to late first century
New Testament books written

100

100–165	**St. Justin Martyr**
c. 100	Didache written and assembled; writings of the first Fathers circulating
107	**St. Ignatius of Antioch** martyred

125–203	**St. Irenaeus of Lyons**, Father of the Church

150

c. 150–200	Most of New Testament accepted as Sacred Scripture
155	**Saint Polycarp** martyred
c. 161–180	Persecution under Marcus Aurelius

(d.) = death date only provided   (r.) = reign   Timeline images from AdobeStock

THE EARLY CHURCH

200

203	Martyrdom of **Saints Perpetua and Felicity**
235–270	Persecutions under various emperors; rapid growth of the Church

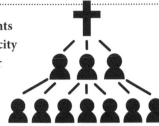

250

251–356	**St. Anthony of Egypt**
258	Martyrdoms of **Saints Lawrence and Cyprian**
292–348	**Saint Pachomius**
297–373	**Saint Athanasius**

300

c. 303–311	Persecution under Diocletian
304–305	Martyrdoms of **Saints Agnes and Lucy**
312	Conversion of Constantine

FROM CONSTANTINE TO CHARLEMAGNE

AD 313 TO AD 800

313	Edict of Milan
330	Constantine moves imperial capital to Byzantium, renamed Constantinople

325 Council of Nicaea; battles over Arian heresy continue

315–368	St. Hilary of Poitiers
315–386	St. Cyril of Jerusalem
316–397	St. Martin of Tours
329–379	Saint Basil, Father of the Church
329–389	St. Gregory of Nazianzen, Father of the Church
330–395	St. Gregory of Nyssa, Father of the Church
331–387	Saint Monica
340–397	Saint Ambrose, Father of the Church
342–420	Saint Jerome, Father of the Church
347–407	St. John Chrysostom, Father of the Church

350

354–430	Saint Augustine, Father of the Church
362	Council of Alexandria
366–384	(r.) Pope St. Damasus I
367	Saint Athanasius publishes complete list of New Testament books
376–444	St. Cyril of Alexandria
381	Council of Constantinople
389–461	Saint Patrick
397	New Testament canon recognized officially by Second Synod of Carthage

(d.) = death date only provided   (r.) = reign

Timeline images from AdobeStock

FROM CONSTANTINE TO CHARLEMAGNE

400

c. 400	Saint Jerome translates Bible into Latin, called Vulgate
410	Visigoths (Arian) sack Rome
428–431	Rise of Nestorius
430–461	Conversion of Ireland
431	Council of Ephesus
440–461	(r.) **Pope St. Leo the Great**

450

450	Beginning of the rise and spread of Western Monasticism
451	Council of Chalcedon
476	Fall of Roman Empire in the West
480–547	**St. Benedict of Nursia**
496	Conversion of Clovis, King of Franks

540–615	Saint Columban	**500**
590–604	(r.) Pope St. Gregory the Great	**600**
610	Beginning of Islam	
622–661	Islamic conquests in the Middle East and North Africa	
661–750	Islamic conquest of Spain	
672–735	Venerable Bede	
675–749	St. John Damascene	
680–754	Saint Boniface	

718–774	Frankish realm expands in Europe	**700**
c. 726–787	Iconoclasm controversy; teaching condemned at Council of Nicaea II in 787	
732	Battle of Tours; Charles Martel halts Muslim advance into Europe	
c. 754	Pepin, King of Franks, gives land to pope; origin of "Papal States"	**750**

(d.) = death date only provided   (r.) = reign   Timeline images from AdobeStock

CHRISTENDOM

800	800	Charlemagne crowned Holy Roman Emperor
	801–865	**Saint Ansgar**
	826–869;	**Saints Cyril and Methodius,**
	815–885	**missionaries to Slavs**

850	**846–902**	Muslim attacks in Italy
	863	Beginning of missionary efforts into Slavic lands
900	**909–929**	**Saint Wenceslaus of Bohemia**
	975–1015	**St. Vladimir of Kyiv**
	975–1038	**St. Stephen of Hungary**
1000	**c. 1000**	Kievan-Rus Slavs (pre-Ukraine and Russia) become Christian
	1001–1072	**St. Peter Damian**
	1024–1109	**St. Hugh of Cluny**
1050	**1030–1075**	**St. Stanislaus of Poland**
	1054	Great East-West Schism
	1077	Henry IV publicly apologizes to Gregory VII
	1073–1085	**(r.) Pope St. Gregory VII**
	1090–1153	**St. Bernard of Clairvaux**
	1096–1204	First Four Crusades
	1098–1179	**St. Hildegard of Bingen**
	1099	Capture of Jerusalem (First Crusade)

1100

1118–1170	St. Thomas Becket
1139	Second Lateran Council affirms priestly celibacy

1150

1170–1221	Saint Dominic
1174–1243	Saint Hedwig
1175–1275	St. Raymond of Peñafort
1181– 1226	St. Francis of Assisi
1187	Muslims recapture Jerusalem
1194–1253	St. Clare of Assisi
1195–1231	St. Anthony of Padua

1200

1204	Sack of Constantinople (Fourth Crusade)
1206–1280	St. Albert the Great
1207–1231	St. Elizabeth of Hungary
1209–1229	Crusade against Albigensians in France
1210	Pope Innocent III (r. 1198–1216) approves Rule of Francis; growth of Franciscan and Dominican mendicant orders
1217–1270	Fifth to Eighth Crusades, mostly unsuccessful
1221–1274	Saint Bonaventure
1225–1274	St. Thomas Aquinas

1250

1271–1336	St. Elizabeth of Portugal
c. 1291	End of Crusades in Holy Land

(d.) = death date only provided   (r.) = reign

Timeline images from AdobeStock

CHRISTENDOM

1300

1303–1373	St. Bridget of Sweden
1309–1377	Avignon Papacy
1337–1453	Hundred Years' War
1342–1423	Bl. Julian of Norwich
1347–1350	First and worst outbreak of Black Death; periodic outbreaks continue for centuries
1347–1380	St. Catherine of Siena

1350

1350–1419	St. Vincent Ferrer
1378–1417	Great Western Schism
1380–1444	St. Bernardine of Siena
1381–1457	St. Rita of Cascia
1386–1456	St. John of Capistrano
1390–1473	St. John of Kanty
1395–1455	Bl. Fra Angelico

1400

1412–1431	St. Joan of Arc
1414–1417	Council of Constance ends Great Western Schism
1415	Jan Hus, reformer, burned at stake
1416–1507	St. Francis of Paola
1447–1510	St. Catherine of Genoa

1450

1453	Constantinople falls to Ottomans
c. 1455	Gutenberg prints Vulgate Bible
1456	Battle of Belgrade; Ottomans repelled
1469–1535	St. John Fisher
1470–1540	St. Angela Merici
1474–1548	St. Juan Diego
1478	Spanish Inquisition founded
1478–1535	St. Thomas More
1491–1556	St. Ignatius of Loyola
1492	Columbus arrives in New World; Moors driven from Spain

REFORMATION, REFORM, AND RENAISSANCE

1500

1505–1551	**St. Francis Xavier**
c. 1506	Construction of St. Peter's Basilica in Rome begins
1510–1572	**St. Francis Borgia**
1515–1582	**St. Teresa of Ávila**
1515–1595	**St. Philip Neri**
1517	Luther posts 95 Theses in Wittenberg
c. 1519	Zwingli starts Swiss reforms
1521	Luther excommunicated
1521–1597	**St. Peter Canisius**
1524–1525	Peasants' Revolt
c. 1525	Anabaptist movement begins
1531	Marian apparitions at Guadalupe in Mexico
1534	Henry VIII declared head of English Church
1535	Munster Rebellion; slaughter of Anabaptists
c. 1536	Calvin starts reforms in Geneva; Calvinism spreads throughout Holland, Scotland, France, Bohemia
1538–1584	**St. Charles Borromeo**
1538–1606	**Saint Turibius**

1540s through 1600s Catholic Counter-Reformation

1540	Society of Jesus approved

(d.) = death date only provided   (r.) = reign

Timeline images from AdobeStock

REFORMATION, REFORM, AND RENAISSANCE

1540–1581	**St. Edmund Campion**
1541–1551	St. Francis Xavier's missions to Asia
1542–1591	**St. John of the Cross**
1542–1621	**St. Robert Bellarmine**
1545–1563	Council of Trent

1550

1552–1610	**Ven. Matteo Ricci**
1562–1597	**St. Paul Miki**
1562–1598	French "Huguenot" wars
1566–1572	(r.) **Pope Pius V**
1567–1622	**St. Francis de Sales**
1571	Naval victory over Ottomans at Lepanto
1572–1641	**St. Jane de Chantel**
1579–1639	**St. Martin de Porres**
1580–1623	**Saint Josephat**

1580–1654	St. Peter Claver
1580–1660	St. Vincent de Paul
1586–1617	St. Rose of Lima
1593–1649	St. John de Brebeuf
1607–1646	St. Isaac Jogues
c. 1640	Jansenism
1647–1690	St. Margaret Mary Alacoque
1656–1680	St. Kateri Tekakwitha
1673–1675	St. Margaret Mary Alacoque receives Sacred Heart visions
c. 1682	Gallicanism
1683	Battle of Vienna — Polish king John Sobieski leads victory over Ottoman Turks
c. 1685–1815	Enlightenment — major philosophers: René Descartes (d. 1650), John Locke (d. 1704), David Hume (d. 1776), Voltaire (d. 1778), Immanuel Kant (d. 1804)
1696–1787	St. Alphonsus Liguori

1600

1650

(d.) = death date only provided   (r.) = reign

Timeline images from AdobeStock

ENLIGHTENMENT AND MODERNISM

1700

1750

1800

c. 1700–1775	Catholic migration from Europe to Americas
1713–1784	St. Junípero Serra
1751–1816	St. Julie Billiart
1751–1820	St. Clement Hoffbauer
1769	St. Junípero Serra founds Mission San Diego
1773–1838	St. Elizabeth Bichier
1774–1821	St. Elizabeth Ann Seton
1769–1852	St. Rose Philippine Duchesne
1776	Declaration of Independence, United States of America

1786–1859	St. John Vianney
1789	French Revolution begins
1794	Compiègne Martyrs
1794	Laval Martyrs
1801–1890	St. John Henry Newman
1804	Napoleon becomes Emperor
1809	Mother Seton founds first school
1809–1882	Charles Darwin
1811–1860	St. John Neumann
1813	Mother Seton founds first American congregation of religious sisters
1815–1888	St. John Bosco
1818–1883	Karl Marx

1830s	Oxford Movement in England (John Newman)
c. 1834–1846	Asian martyrs, St. Andrew Kim Taegon (Korea), St. Andrew Dũng-Lạc (Vietnam)
1840–1889	St. Damien of Molokai
1844–1879	St. Bernadette
1844–1900	Friedrich Nietzsche
1845–1937	St. André Bessette

1850

late 1800s	Rise of biblical modernism
1850–1917	St. Frances Xavier Cabrini
1856–1939	Sigmund Freud
1858	Marian apparitions at Lourdes
1858–1955	St. Katharine Drexel
1869–1947	St. Josephine Bakhita
1870	First Vatican Council
1870–1957	Bl. Solanus Casey
1873–1897	St. Thérèse of Lisieux
1885–1887	Martyrdom of St. Charles Lwanga and Companions in Uganda
1887–1968	Padre Pio
1890–1902	St. Maria Goretti
1891–1942	St. Teresa Benedicta of the Cross (Edith Stein)
1894–1941	St. Maximilian Kolbe
1895–1979	Ven. Fulton Sheen

1900

1902–1975	St. Josemaría Escrivá
1903–1914	(r.) Pope Pius X
1905–1938	St. Faustina Kowalska
1910–1997	St. Teresa of Calcutta
1917	Apparitions of Our Lady of Fátima to Sts. Francisco and Jacinta Marto (1908–1919, 1910–1920) and Lúcia dos Santos (1907–2005)
1917–1980	St. Oscar Romero

(d.) = death date only provided   (r.) = reign

Timeline images from AdobeStock

THE CHURCH IN MODERN TIMES

1920

1922–1962	St. Gianna Molla
1927–1928	Martyrs of the Cristero War in Mexico
c. 1930	Rise of renewal movements throughout Christianity, — for example, Opus Dei (founded 1928), Focolare (founded 1943), preaching of Billy Graham (1918–2018)
1940–2006	Bl. Leonella Sgorbati

1950

c. 1950–1970	Rapid expansion of Church in Africa
1958–1963	(r.) Pope St. John XXIII
1960-1969	The "Sixties"— sexual revolution, anti-authority, civil rights & abortion rights movements
1962–1965	Second Vatican Council
1963–1978	(r.) Pope St. Paul VI
1967	Catholic Charismatic Renewal begins
1968–c. 1995	Rise and fade of Liberation Theology

1970s–present
Rise of Islamic terrorism

1978	(r.) John Paul I
1978–2005	(r.) Pope St. John Paul II
1980–1989	Solidarity movement in Poland
1989–1991	Fall of European Communism
1994	*Catechism of Catholic Church* published
1996	Martyrdom of Algerian Monks (Blesseds)

2000

2002–present Sexual abuse crisis

21st century trends continue:

- Biblical modernism
- Secularization of West and decline of Church in West
- Postmodernist rejection of truth, hostility to faith, exaltation of technology, and diversity
- Age of Martyrs — persecution in Middle East, China, Africa, etc.

INTRODUCTION

The history of the Catholic Church is an extraordinary drama of divine and human action.

At the center of that history are the saints — more influential than kings and nobles, often more so than popes and Church leaders. As Dorothy Day, twentieth-century American advocate for the poor, observed, "It is the saints that keep appearing all thru history who keep things going."[1] These men and women are not mere side actors in history, busy being "holy" while people in high places made Church history. The saints — those whom the Catholic Church has canonized, or recognized as especially holy — are the ones who have *led* the Church through her history.

In these pages, we will meet over 180 saints who shaped the history of the Church. As they confronted the issues of their day, they influenced history by their gifts and talents — but most importantly, by their resolute commitment to Jesus Christ. This commitment opened them to the grace of the Holy Spirit, acting in definite times and places. In a sense, this book is an effort not only to shine light on saints making history, but also to bring to light the role of the Holy Spirit as well. This is a daunting task — and may be considered presumptuous. But if we follow the actions of the saints, divine action becomes more evident. God works through individuals, and as they speak and act in commitment to him, divine as well as human action are manifest.

I have written this book with the eyes of faith. From this perspective, the Catholic Church and her history are different from other institutions, nations, civilizations, and their histories. The Church is not merely a human institution. She is the Body of Christ. Her founder and Head is Jesus himself. Jesus founded the Church to draw and lead God's human creation to union with him in eternity. To reduce her history strictly to human action is to miss the very nature of the Church. The saints understood this — that is why they are at the center of her history.

Many stellar histories of the Church have been written; I admire them and have consulted them in earnest. Many stellar lives of saints have also been written; I have drawn on them extensively in compiling this history. There is a place, however, for a history that puts primary focus on the role of the saints in making that history. And, since most collected saint dictionaries or biographies are organized either alphabetically or by feast day in the Catholic Church's liturgical calendar, I have presented here a study of saints, set chronologically in their historical context, that emphasizes their impact on the history of the Church.

This is not intended to be an academic work. I write for the ordinary person of any background who is interested in the Church's history and her saints. I will guide us through two thousand years of Church history, while bringing to light the pivotal role of certain men and women over the course of those years. Thus my focus is not on the saints' holiness for our inspiration — as evident and important as that is — but on how they are significant for Church history. For the reader interested in a more detailed study of particular saints, I direct you to the many excellent biographies of those men and women.

What we will see is that the saints, above all else, pointed to Jesus, to his command to love, and to his mission of salvation. Their singular focus on Jesus is what always inspired the Church to return to her first love, to her Head, to be open to renewal. When the Church seemed to lose her way, the saints pointed to Jesus, who *is* the way.

These are troubled times. The Catholic Church is under extreme duress in the twenty-first century. Loss of faith, secularization, and advancing persecution have grown to become grave threats. Internally, the Catholic Church is rocked by division, failures among many in leadership, and a virulent clergy sex abuse scandal that has shaken her to her core. Today's Catholic has good reason to feel deep concern.

With these challenges in mind, we can turn to the Church's history — where we will find that we have every reason for *hope*. Throughout her complex history, the Church has been in trouble more than she has not, and the present crises are not necessarily her worst. Each time the Church seemed to be defeated — as examples, the near triumph by the Arians in the fourth century and the trauma of the Reformation in the sixteenth — God raised up saints and holy people who helped to lift the Church up and out of the pit and into renewal. The distinguished Church historian Christopher Dawson observed that Church history tends to move recurrently through a fourfold cycle: trouble, crisis, decline, and then renewal. Where does that renewal come from, if not from the grace and mercy of God? Thus, in the midst of today's challenges, we can rest assured that the gates of hell will not prevail against the Church. As Pope St. John Paul II said, "Be not afraid." In God's time, whether we see it in our lifetimes or not, renewal will come. This is the lesson of history for our own times.

The Church came into being after the Resurrection, and that is where this history begins. Thus I consider the saints of the Gospels who died before the Resurrection to be "pre-Church," and not part of this narrative. Two, however, are worthy of mention: **St. John the Baptist**, who "prepared the way" for Jesus by his preaching of repentance and his ministry of baptism, and **Saint Joseph**, who, with the faith of Abraham, obeyed God's instructions, taking in Mary as his wife despite her mystifying pregnancy and, as husband and father, protected her and Jesus. Because of their vital roles in sowing seeds for the Church, they merit special admiration and gratitude.

This brings us to the greatest of saints, truly present in this narrative from beginning to end: the **Blessed Virgin Mary**, the Mother of the

Church for all time. We can rightly say that Mary initiated the history of the Church with her yes at the Annunciation. And, as Mother of the Church, Mary carries out for all history a perpetual ministry of intercession for the Church. Saints throughout the ages have been devoted to her and have looked up to her for inspiration and guidance. She is truly the Queen of Saints.

Let us begin our walk through the portals of history and "behold the works of the Lord" (Ps 46:8).

I

THE EARLY CHURCH

AD 30 to AD 312

The icon of *Christ's Appearance to Mary Magdalene* after the Resurrection from the Chiesa di Santa Maria Maddalena. AdobeStock

1

THE CONDITIONS WERE RIGHT

One of the most remarkable stories in history is how a small group of followers of a Jewish rabbi in a small corner of the Roman Empire grew to be five million — 10 percent of the Empire — in less than three centuries.[1] Imperial Rome was strong, pagan, and fiercely fortified against any threat to its authority. The first Christians were mostly poor, not well placed in society, and preached a new kingdom which seemed to be a threat to the established order. Despite these obstacles, a significant number of circumstances, conditions, and exceptional individuals — many of whom were great saints — contributed to the rise of the Christian Faith in the first three centuries after the earthly life of Jesus Christ. Before turning to the saints who lived and moved in these first centuries, we will look at these providential circumstances.

Caesar Augustus, called "the divine," even "Son of God,"[2] was the first and perhaps the greatest of the Roman emperors. During his reign from

27 BC to his death in AD 14, he oversaw a vast and powerful empire that surrounded the Mediterranean Sea and beyond. Peace had been achieved. Technological marvels abounded. Law and scholarship thrived. Yet, the life of his contemporary in backwater Palestine had so much greater influence that the calendar for much of the world for centuries would be based upon the time of *his* birth, not Augustus's. How did this come to be?

The first century was the time of Augustus's *Pax Romana* — the Roman peace. Except for military campaigns on the fringes, the conquests that created the empire were largely completed. The core area of the empire, though under the iron hand of Roman authorities, was at relative peace. One could move about in a mostly stable society with limited danger. Transportation was as good as the world had seen. Roman roads and sea-lanes were advanced and comparatively safe. Language was not a problem. Greek was predominant in the East, and Latin in the West. If a person knew one or both, he or she could be understood. The Good News could be communicated.

The culture was intellectually advanced and open to the exchange of ideas. Greco-Roman philosophy and literature were enduring influences on these times. Many theologians see the philosophy of Plato and Socrates as a foundation for the Christian message, and elements of this classical philosophy are even seen in the writings of Paul and John. Belief in the Greco-Roman gods was waning, and the prosperity of the time led to indulgence by the wealthy and slavery or hardship among the lower classes.

This created a receptivity to new religious ideas that offered meaning and direction to life. Thus Christianity had the possibility of a hearing. The new Faith competed not only with established Roman pagan beliefs, but also with other religions, including Judaism and a number of Egyptian mystery religions. Amid these competing religions, Saint Paul and others could be successful in missionary work because of the compelling nature of the message itself, the strong and unique moral code, and the example of love among Christians.

We can also point to God's providence that these circumstances were in place just as Christianity was born. The opportune timing of the Incarnation itself made the spread of Christianity possible. It was the right moment, chosen by God. Had the Incarnation occurred two hundred years before or after, these conditions would not have been in place. And, as we shall see, the new Faith spread and took hold primarily in the Roman Empire — not so much to the east or south. It was the Roman world that was most poised to receive the message. Wars, inferior roads, a lack of safety, instability in society, and less cultural receptivity were all obstacles outside the areas of the *Pax Romana*. This early surge of faith was due to the followers of Jesus cooperating with the grace of God, as the Holy Spirit paved the way for this new Body, a divinely ordained institution, to take hold and grow.

Yet most important among the reasons for the incredible spread of Christianity was the compelling nature of the message itself: The man Jesus, Son of God, rose from the dead. This was (and remains) an extraordinary claim. For many in the rough circumstances of life in those times, it was indeed "good news."

Christianity is an historical religion. It proclaims concrete historical facts as true. Whereas most other religions are human efforts to contact the divine, the Christian message is that the divine has contacted humans. The first Christians claimed that God, who had revealed himself in centuries past to the Hebrew people, entered human history in person through the birth of Jesus Christ in Bethlehem, a tiny village near Jerusalem in the eastern reaches of the Roman Empire.

If this claim is taken as true, then the history of the Church begins at the turning point of all human history: the Incarnation. God entered the world, and the world would never be the same. The early Christians taught — with conviction — that Jesus was the Son of God and that he carried out a ministry of teaching and miracles that culminated when he gave up his life as a universal sacrifice for the human race, by crucifixion under Roman authorities. They also made the astonishing claim that he rose from the dead — if true, the most extraordinary event in human history. This was a potent message, with significant evidence to support it.

The witnesses delivering this message were credible. People saw and experienced these events. They knew this Jesus of Nazareth. Some, most notably the apostles, were convincing in their claim to have seen Jesus after the Resurrection. Those hearing these accounts were in a position to evaluate the honesty and rationality of these eyewitnesses. What they saw and heard were witnesses who stuck to their claims despite obstacles. Many even went to their deaths as martyrs while maintaining their belief in the Resurrection. This mitigated any pie-in-the-sky sense to the "Good News." These firsthand witnesses were sober, resolute, and courageous. This was the witness of saints — known and unknown — and they made a strong impression.

The Good News about this Jesus, which these witnesses kept preaching with obvious conviction and sincerity, was that God loves us, came to save us from the ill effects of sin in this world, and offers the hope of eternal life in heaven to those who embrace this message and seek to follow Jesus. In other words, this Good News was not just geopolitical but offered to make a difference in individual lives. The greatest events in human history were applicable to each person who responded. This message was unique in the Roman Empire and appealed to many — primarily among the poor, including slaves. With the grace of the Holy Spirit flowing, thousands of people looking for meaning in life, for hope, or better circumstances, were drawn to this new message, presented by people who exuded love and concern — even for the poor. Yet it was also more than an individual religion. Christianity was a body of believers who formed communities and embraced the message of salvation together, as a people, linked together in God's grace. These communities of love were an attraction as well.

2

THE FIRST GENERATION

The Romans, urged on by the Jewish authorities in Jerusalem, had executed Jesus by crucifixion. The followers of Jesus were in mourning. Most had scattered out of fear. All the promise of Jesus' ministry looked hopeless. Something needed to happen; someone needed to step forward.

In the emerging light of dawn, outside of Jerusalem, something extraordinary did happen. Jesus rose from the dead. And it was our first saint, **St. Mary Magdalene**, who stepped forward. When the others were in hiding, she became the initial witness of the Resurrection. Jesus had changed her life, and for this she was grateful and devoted to him. She had come to the tomb where Jesus was buried to anoint his body. This put her at the turning point of human history, and it was this grieving woman who stirred the followers of Jesus into action.

St. Mary Magdalene had a mysterious past. Whatever her lifestyle (Scripture does *not* say she was a prostitute), she was drawn to Jesus, who had cast out seven demons from her (see Mk 16:9). She became a follower of Jesus, and, unlike all but one of the apostles, was present at the crucifixion. Because this devoted and grieving woman chose to return to the tomb, Jesus was able to appear to her, and she was the one to hear Jesus' first words after his resurrection. Through her vigil and her obedience, she became the first missionary of the Good News.

According to the Gospel of John, Mary Magdalene encountered Jesus soon after he had risen (see 20:1–18). Jesus gave her a task: Go tell the disciples, who were hiding in fear, that he had risen, that he was alive, and that he would soon meet them. She obeyed. The accounts vary in the other Gospels — including whether other women were with Mary Magdalene — but the Scriptures agree that Jesus appeared to Mary Magdalene and instructed her to inform the apostles that he had risen. At first, the apostles considered her tale to be nonsense. However, they did get beyond their initial disbelief, and tested Mary Magdalene's message. They encountered Jesus themselves, regained their courage, and began their own ministry of proclaiming the Good News. By Mary Magdalene's devotion and obedience, the history of the Church had begun.

As we will see with many saints, Mary Magdalene's role seems minor at first glance. Often, however, it is the small acts of devotion and obedience that make a major difference in "preparing the way" for more famous saints to follow. Simple acts of devotion can lead to extraordinary results, and such was Mary Magdalene's role in stirring the leaders of the nascent Church into action.

Jesus' appearances after his resurrection were mostly quiet visitations to his followers — not glorious shows to startle his enemies. To build his Church, Jesus worked through his disciples, like Mary Magdalene, inspiring them to put faith into action. Mary Magdalene's visitation to the distraught apostles with news of the Resurrection awakened **Saint Peter** and opened the door for the work of the other saints of biblical times. Peter, Paul, Barnabas, the Gospel writers, and their companions were now poised to set out on the task of building the Church.

At Mary Magdalene's news, Peter and John ran to the empty tomb, and Peter entered. He began to lead and to show the courage that Jesus had called him to. Jesus had been forming Peter well before the Passion and had anointed him to be the "rock" upon which he would build the Church (see Mt 16:17–19). After the Resurrection, Jesus sought out Peter at the shore of the Sea of Galilee, gave him the opportunity to be restored for having denied him during his trial, and exhorted Peter to feed his sheep. "Do you love me?" Jesus asked Peter three times — the eternal question for all Christians. Peter did, if imperfectly. Afterwards, Peter took on the role of leader in the early Church. Along with Paul, he was one of the two most influential leaders in the Church's formative years. Much of what happened in the ensuing years went through Peter, and it all started on Pentecost.

On a morning in Jerusalem, ten days after Jesus had taken leave of the apostles, Peter and a number of other followers of Jesus were gathered together in prayer. As they were praying, they experienced a powerful presence of God. Luke describes this experience as a supernatural descent of the Holy Spirit in "tongues of fire." They were changed and emboldened. As they prayed, they began to "speak in tongues," or other languages. A large cosmopolitan crowd had gathered outside, who heard the apostles speaking in various languages, and they were astounded. Peter then addressed the crowd with a passionate speech in a tongue that, miraculously, all could understand. Three thousand of the crowd were so moved at Peter's Spirit-inspired sermon that they chose to be baptized that very day.

Luke describes these events of Pentecost in Acts of the Apostles, chapter 2. The astounding events, striking in their incarnational blend of divine and human action, are impossible to explain by mere human action. The tongues of fire, Peter's bold speech, and the conversion of three thousand people all reveal the powerful movement of the Holy Spirit. God was still with them, as Jesus had promised.

FILLED WITH THE HOLY SPIRIT

Pentecost galvanized Peter and the other Christians in Jerusalem. No longer were they holed up in fear. The Holy Spirit not only energized their spirits, but also convinced them that the power of God was with them — knowledge they needed, since Jerusalem had become a hostile place for followers of Jesus. The Roman occupiers were wary of unrest in the aftermath of Jesus' crucifixion and reports of his rising from the dead. The Jewish authorities were resolute in their efforts to stamp out Jesus' followers whom they deemed to be a threat to their authority and an aberration in the understanding of their faith. The apostles' boldness in preaching the "Good News" brought them harassment and persecution. Peter himself was in and out of jail and of trouble with the authorities.

The apostles continued to preach in the Temple, attract converts, reach out to the people with compassion, and tangle with the authorities. Luke provides an example in Acts chapter 3. Peter encounters a crippled beggar on the street. Instead of giving him money, Peter tells him, in the name of Jesus, to stand up and walk. Peter takes his hand and raises him up. The man is miraculously healed and celebrates in the Temple. Not only did this miracle create a stir and raise the visibility and credibility of this new group, but it also gave Peter confidence that the Holy Spirit was indeed working through him.

Initial communities began to form, gatherings of believers who shared their possessions and listened to the apostles' preaching (see Acts 4:32–35). This development was significant. The evident question for the first believers was this: How exactly do we live out this new way? Living in community became the answer, and provided the template for the future. The elements of early Christian community — initiation by baptism, apostolic preaching, worship, sharing money and possessions, and partaking in the breaking of the bread as Jesus had directed — were present from the beginning.

The Church was taking shape, but did not continue to grow extensively in Jerusalem or even in Galilee, where Jesus had carried out much of his ministry. This must have been a surprise to the apostles and first disciples. Resistance from Roman and Jewish authorities took its toll. To be sure, a community of believers, which included Peter and James, was located and remained in Jerusalem, but it did not become the long-range center of the nascent Faith. This set the stage for two significant developments that defined the early Church in the ensuing years and beyond.

It was up the coast of the Mediterranean to the north that the Faith first caught fire. Numerous disciples also fanned out in missionary journeys in various directions — in response to Jesus' call to "teach all nations." The apostle **Saint Thomas** is said to have gone to India, where small Christian communities formed, but although they endured, they remained small. Arabia and other parts of the Middle East did not become fertile territory. The new Faith also spread along the African shore of the Mediterranean, from Egypt and westward, though still within the Roman Empire. But north into Asia Minor and eventually into Greece and further westward is where the Faith spread the fastest.

In addition to the advantages found within the Roman world, other factors contributed to the northern expansion. Persecution of the Church in Palestine drove many of the early believers north (see Acts 11). Jewish communities were in place up the coast, and it was common practice for the early missionaries — who were Jewish — to take the message first to these communities. That Jesus was the awaited Jewish Messiah was a part of the message.

Paul, the Jewish scholar who first persecuted Christians, was on his way north to Damascus in Syria to meet with Jewish authorities when he experienced his conversion. This is one sign that providence played a significant role in the pull to the north. God saw the future that his evangelizers could not. Several hundred miles north at Antioch, still in that first generation, the followers of Jesus were first called *Christians* (see Acts 11:26). Christian communities formed in various towns and cities, Antioch arguably being the most significant, and Gentiles were becoming attracted to this new Faith.

This attraction of Gentiles to the Faith — also not well-anticipated — led to the second significant development: the gradual separation of the new Faith from the Jewish faith and communities. While at first the disciples of Jesus sought to take the Good News to their fellow Jews, this did not bear nearly as much fruit as they had hoped. They experienced resistance and even hostility in many Jewish communities, and sometimes even persecution. A poignant example was the stoning to death of the deacon **Saint Stephen** (see Acts 7:54–60). This Jewish resistance challenged the thinking of the early believers who, as Jews, believed that the Jewish people, God's Chosen People, were to be a "light to the nations" (see, for example, Is 42:6 and Lk 2:32). And then word of Gentile converts arrived. What was God doing?

This was Peter's question, and the confusion came to a head near the year AD 50 at a meeting of Church leaders to address the issue of how to handle the increasing number of Gentile converts (see Acts 15:1–12). The Council of Jerusalem, as we now call it, was a turning point for the early Church. The leaders were divided over whether the Gentile converts should submit to circumcision and other aspects of Jewish law. This issue went to the heart of the early Church's self-understanding. Was the Church Jewish in nature, a prophesied "light to the nations," or was this new Christian way to somehow be independent of Jewish law and practice? The influx of Gentiles and hostility from many Jewish synagogues forced the question, and to the early Christians, the answer was not obvious.

At this Jerusalem gathering, Peter stepped forward and declared that the Gentiles should not be bound to circumcision and other Mosaic laws. His pronouncement — along with the ensuing letter of instruction from the body of Jerusalem elders — kept open the door for massive Gentile conversion. The Church quickly became predominately Gentile from this point forward.

This was Peter, beginning to act as the rock, "binding and loosing on earth" as Jesus had authorized him to do. The Council of Jerusalem was an early instance of the Holy Spirit using Peter to guide the Church to truth in a doctrinal matter — the beginning of the magisterial authority that was to reside with the Bishop of Rome, successor to Saint Peter. How this would work has confounded the Church for centuries, and still does today. Even at this council, as Peter is exercising authority, so is the body of elders — foreshadowing the issue for future generations.

This council also cleared the way for the ministry of the greatest missionary the Church has ever known: **Saint Paul**. The consequences of the decision cannot be overestimated. Had Peter and the elders decided to impose circumcision and Mosaic law on Gentile converts, the steady flow of their conversions would likely have fizzled. And it would have forced Paul into a horrendous dilemma. Paul believed that the Mosaic law should not be imposed upon the Gentiles. He would have been forced either to disobey the leaders and continue not to require Gentiles to follow Mosaic law, or obey and see his ministry effectively shut down.

Neither option was good. One can see the hand of the Holy Spirit in Peter's decision.

This issue of what to make of Gentile converts arose because of the enormous success Saint Paul was having. Even Jewish and secular historians attribute the dramatic explosion of growth of Christianity in large part to the work of Saint Paul. Just as God's providence worked through circumstances, he also raised up extraordinary people to move his plan forward.

THE CONVERSION OF PAUL

The conversion of Paul (described in Acts 9:1–9) stands as one of the most consequential events in all Church history. In one sudden divine intervention on the road to Damascus, Paul turned from a fierce and relentless persecutor of the young Church to a fierce and relentless missionary of the Christian Faith. Paul did not reach this earth-shattering change of heart on his own. This was a divine, miraculous event, God taking direct action to move human history. Paul's sudden conversion cannot be explained in any other rational way. To the surprise of Christians and Jews alike — no less to Paul himself — God had chosen his lead missionary. And this changed the world.

When God chose Paul for ministry on the road to Damascus, he chose a man well-suited for his calling. Consider these attributes:

- Paul was educated. He was a Jew who had become an expert on Mosaic law and Scriptures. He knew Hebrew, Greek, and most likely Latin as well. This facilitated his preaching and interactions on missionary journeys and his ability to communicate effectively in his letters.
- Paul was intelligent. His mind was sharp and analytical, capable of discerning courses of action. His letters, now a central part of the New Testament, are among the greatest expositions of Christian theology ever put to writing. Paul's insights into the nature and mission of Jesus, of the Eucharist, of faith, of grace and justification, of love and mercy, of the meaning of suffering, of the moral calling, and of Chris-

tian community, are extraordinary.

- Paul loved God. Before and after his conversion, Paul exhibited an all-encompassing devotion to God and a constant openness to grace. Undoubtedly, he spent countless hours in prayer and meditation, pondering the powerful realities of who Jesus was and what it means, drawing upon both grace and his own considerable understanding of Jewish theology.
- Paul was flexible. He was willing to learn and adapt to constantly changing situations.
- Paul was a Roman citizen. This gave him a greater ability to travel freely and a higher level of protection than if he had not been. Although he did speak of instances of shipwrecks and other travel woes, most of the time he was able to move freely about the Roman Empire.

All these gifts and talents, along with his relentless passion, enabled him to overcome constant obstacles and press on toward founding and supporting Christian communities all over Asia Minor and Europe.

As prodigious as Saint Paul was, if it was not for another saint, Paul may not have had a ministry at all. Like St. Mary Magdalene, **Saint Barnabas** was not a mover and shaker, but he humbly worked to get Paul approved for ministry and may also have had a hand in assuring that one of the Gospels would be written.

Barnabas was a Jew from the Mediterranean island of Cyprus. His real name was Joseph, but he was called *Barnabas*, which means "son of encouragement" — an apt nickname. He is introduced in Acts 4:36–37 as one who sold some property and donated the proceeds to the fledging Christian community. He is portrayed in Acts as respected, well-liked, and quietly effective in nurturing the faith of new Christians, a task whose importance cannot be underestimated.

Sometimes, extraordinary circumstances pull ordinary persons into important events. Such was the case with Barnabas. Even after Paul's conversion, fear of this persecutor of the Faith still lingered among the Church leaders in Jerusalem. When Barnabas introduced Paul to them and vouched for him, this was their first encounter with their former nemesis. They remained wary. They knew Paul had supervised the stoning of Stephen, and his alleged conversion had occurred a long way up the road. Whether Paul would be approved for ministry, whether he could be trusted, was at stake. Paul's future ministry hung in the balance.

Barnabas won the day. He persuaded the elders in Jerusalem — who were the leading Christian body at that time — to accept Paul as a disciple (see Acts 9:26–27). Plainly and simply, without Barnabas, we might not have had Paul. The confidence and respect the leaders had for Barnabas, which Barnabas had earned by his solid dedication as a Christian, convinced them that Paul was not a spy or a fake, but now a genuine Christian with great gifts to be used for spreading the Faith.

Barnabas traveled with Paul on missionary journeys, and may well have been a calming influence on the fiery Paul. There was one exception, which led to Barnabas's second crucial contribution to the development of the early Church. Barnabas and Paul had a falling-out and went separate ways (see Acts 15:36–40). Paul was dissatisfied with Barnabas's cousin John Mark for leaving them earlier at Pamphylia and did not want to take him on their next journey. Barnabas wanted to give Mark a second chance. Failing to resolve their dispute, Paul and Barnabas split up. Paul chose to travel with Silas instead, raising up a new missionary. Barnabas stuck with Mark: the same John Mark who eventually wrote the Gospel of Mark. Had Barnabas given in to Paul and abandoned Mark, what would have happened to Mark? Perhaps Mark would not have written his Gospel. It was Barnabas who held Mark together during what must have been a crucial time in his walk in the Faith.

Paul later reconciled with Mark, noting him as a companion when he was in prison (see Col 4:10), calling him "useful" to him (2 Tm 4:11), and even calling him his "son" (1 Pt 5:13). It would be no surprise if Barnabas played a role in their reconciliation.

THE GOSPELS

Saint Mark went on to write his Gospel, likely in the late 60s. It moves the reader quickly from one event to the next and offers numerous eyewitness details. Many scholars believe that Saint Peter is the source for much of Mark's narrative. A majority of scholars also believe it to be the first of the four Gospels to be written, and that it may have been a template for the Gospels of Matthew and Luke.

The reason that we know about Paul and Barnabas and the early Church at all is largely due to **Saint Luke**, who wrote the New Testament book Acts of the Apostles as well as the Gospel bearing his name. We know little about Luke's life except that he was a physician, literate in Greek, and a friend and sometimes companion of Saint Paul. One tradition tells us that Luke knew Mary, the mother of Jesus, and spent time with her, possibly in Ephesus. If this is true, then Mary herself is the source of Luke's infancy narratives — which do not appear in the other Gospels. One can picture Luke sitting at seaside with Mary as she reminisced on her early days, while Luke listened attentively and later chronicled them in his Gospel. In Acts, Luke narrates the early days of the Church in Jerusalem, Asia Minor, and beyond; the works of Peter and Paul; and the spread of the Christian communities throughout the Mediterranean world. We have no other comprehensive source for these accounts. It is hard to underestimate their significance.

No doubt Luke desired to write these accounts of Jesus and the early Church — but he was not forced. A question to ponder: What if Luke had not written them? Writing long expositions in his day was, by our standards, labor-intensive. The Holy Spirit inspired Luke, and no doubt prompted him to write; but Luke was free to choose not to write, or to simply not get around to it. He was human. A busy medical practice, heavy travel, other time pressures, doubts, or any number of other challenges could have interfered with his writing project. Unaware that his works would become part of Scripture for all time, he would not have realized the importance of writing these accounts. God can and does accommodate for our failures, and he would have worked around Luke's failure to write if that had happened — but it would not have been the same. We would have known less about the early Church. We would not have the accounts of the Annunciation, the Visitation, the parables of the prodigal son and Good Samaritan, or the account of the "good thief" at Calvary. Those come to us only from Luke. Perhaps a friend or relative of his encouraged him to write; perhaps it was Mary herself. If so, to this unknown person we owe a debt of gratitude.

Thankfully, Luke did in fact give the Church an extensive account of the life and teachings of Jesus, written primarily for Gentile Christians, and an account of the activities of the early Church. Limited as distribution was in those early days, Luke's and Mark's writings still circulated over time and became an important part of the formation of the early Church — as did the Gospel and letters of **Saint John,** the Gospel of **Saint Matthew,** and other pastoral letters later included in the New Testament.

ROME

The ministries of Peter and Paul — usually on separate tracks — evolved over the course of their lifetimes. What is remarkable, and crucial for Catholic Church history, is that both Peter and Paul ended up in Rome. It was in Rome, not Palestine or Asia Minor, where they spent their last days.

Paul always harbored a desire to take the Gospel as far west as he could. In his later days, he was arrested and held in Jerusalem. Using his status as a Roman citizen, he appealed to the emperor — a legal right he had as a citizen — parlaying his legal circumstances into a trip to Rome. While overcoming a shipwreck near Malta and declining a chance to escape, Paul got his wish. He spent his last days preaching, writing, supporting the growing community of Christians in Rome, and awaiting trial. Although Luke does not narrate the death of Paul, it is well understood that Paul died a martyr in the mid-60s in the city that was to become the center of the Catholic Church.

Amazingly, Peter also ended up in Rome. His path to Rome was separate from Paul's, was not recorded, and is subject to conjecture. Regardless of the circumstances, who would have thought that this fisherman from Galilee would travel to Rome? What compelled him? What ministry did he foresee for himself in Rome, as opposed to continuing to build the Church in Jerusalem or other places closer to home? These are fascinating questions for which we do not have answers.

The significance for the future of the Church is inestimable. Peter the rock, chosen by Christ, became the leader of the Church in Rome: in essence, the first Bishop of Rome. All future bishops of Rome would be deemed his successors. Again, the unpredictable action of the Holy Spirit is manifest in leading this Galilean fisherman out of Galilee to what would be the future home of the head of the Catholic Church. Had Peter declined the prompting to go to Rome, the Church today would be very different. He, too, was martyred in Rome in the mid-60s. His martyrdom was a seed for the Church, not only for growth but for securing her pastoral place in Rome for the ages.

3

THE NEXT GENERATIONS

As the second generation dawned, the Church stood at a crossroads. Would she survive and flourish, or would she wither away, as so many movements do after their first generation? The Church encountered four huge issues in the later part of the first century: the destruction of the Temple in Jerusalem; the deaths of the apostles and eyewitnesses of the resurrection of Jesus; the reality that Jesus had not returned as the Church had expected him to; and the beginnings of imperial Roman persecution. New leaders, new saints, would be necessary to shepherd the Church through these challenges.

In the 60s, Jewish patriots began a rebellion against Rome, triggering a war of independence against the imperial forces. It did not go well. Over one million Jews lost their lives in the ill-fated struggle. The Romans destroyed Jerusalem in the year 70 — and leveled the Temple. The Temple, center of Jewish worship, the only place where Jews could offer sacrifice, one of the most monumental religious structures in the world, was no more. This was a catastrophe the magnitude of which is hard to fathom today, most particularly for the Jews, but also for the Christians, whose roots were significantly Jewish. The Temple's destruction undoubtedly caused untold consternation among Christians. Jesus, a Jew, had spent important time in the Temple, preaching, worshiping, healing, passionately purifying it of moneylenders. It was the greatest physical monument to the living Judeo-Christian God in the world at that time. Now, under the might of pagan Roman power, it was gone.

One consequence of the Jewish War and destruction of Jerusalem and the Temple was the dispersal of the surviving Jewish community. This added to the competition and sometimes angst between the Jewish people who did not become Christians and the Christian communities, with their early mix of Jews and Gentiles. But Jew and Christian alike shared an unimaginable sense of loss.

Around the same time, the apostles died. Most were martyred — Peter and Paul among them. The first generation of disciples also died off, including the eyewitnesses to the Resurrection. This included most of the great leaders from the early days, leaving a huge void of leadership in the Church. What remained were Christian communities, now in a sense orphaned, led by disciples of disciples. None had as influential a name as the great biblical leaders; none had had direct contact with Jesus. Would the Church be able to move forward in the absence of its first leaders and those who knew Jesus personally?

To make matters worse, Jesus had not returned. Most of the first-generation Christians, including Paul and other leaders, had expected that Jesus would return during their lifetimes. No one had any inkling that thousands of years would pass without the return of Jesus. But decades passed without his return. It became more and more evident that Jesus might indeed not return anytime soon, or at least they could no longer count on his return as imminent. This forced the Christian communities to take careful stock of their interpretation of the apostles' teaching. Were they wrong? Was there a misunderstanding? What now? Their faith and perseverance were put to the test.

Times of imperial persecution set in. Starting with the persecution of Nero in 64, which claimed the lives of Peter and Paul in Rome, it became dangerous to be a professed Christian, if not at all times and places, then in many. Surviving Christians saw their friends and family put to death, often in the arena. Conflicts arose concerning those Christians who had renounced their faith or fled to avoid persecution. Persecution and its consequences became a formidable new challenge to the ensuing generations of Christians.

GROWTH IN A NEW ERA

Despite these trying times, the Church did survive and even continued to grow. How she did so is a question worth exploring.

First, it is vital to see the Church for what she is: not merely a human institution, but the Body of Christ. The Church was in need of divine assistance, and it was grace and providence — the echo of the Incarnation — that sustained the Christian people in the midst of these late first-century challenges. God raised up saints who played a vital role in nurturing and sustaining the Church, including those we now call Church Fathers, and he gave two powerful gifts to the post-biblical Church: the sacraments and Scripture. These leaders were not the only ones who sustained the Church, however. All along, in the time of the apostles and into these generations following, unsung local leaders, pastors, and devout yet ordinary believers toiled faithfully in their local communities to tend to their households and communities, teaching, giving example, and fulfilling the needs of the Christian faithful.

The apostles and Paul had laid a foundation for the structure of Christian communities and worship. Believers were gathering in cities and towns, meeting mostly in homes, on Sunday — in commemoration of Christ's resurrection — for worship and what we now call *the Eucharist*. The sharing of property, common in the earliest first-generation communities, had evolved to allow for more personal independence, but sharing and helping with each other's needs and commitment to loving one another remained consistent features.

As time passed, the structure of the Church developed and became more organized. The office of bishop developed. These early communities were headed by bishops, *episcopoi* in Greek, literally "overseers," successors of the apostles and early disciples. They were in touch with one another, often meeting to discuss issues. Some were well educated and became the first wave of theologians who helped the young Church recognize, preserve, and develop the teachings of the apostles. This was vital, because the Church was spread out over a vast area and prone to localized understandings of doctrines.

One of the sources of information about the early Church is the *Didache*, a first-century teaching treatise titled *Teaching of the Lord to the Gentiles by the Twelve Apostles*. It includes instruction on Christian morality, liturgical practice, disciplinary norms, and prayer — including the Lord's Prayer — references to baptism by immersion and confession of sins, and early forms of Eucharistic prayers. Noteworthy among its moral proscriptions is an admonition against abortion. It acknowledges bishops and deacons as leaders and servants in the Church, warns of the Antichrist, and, as was common in the early Church, asserts the belief that the end was coming soon. The *Didache*, lost for centuries but rediscovered in 1873, is available today for reading and study.

SUCCESSORS TO THE APOSTLES

Even as countless unsung local bishops and leaders carried on the work of the apostles in communities around the eastern Mediterranean, the need for Church-wide leadership to replace the apostles was still very real. And indeed, new leaders began to emerge: Among the most significant were St. Ignatius of Antioch, St. Irenaeus of Lyons, Pope Saint Clement, and Saint Polycarp. Each is considered among the early "Fathers of the Church" (whom we will discuss more in chapter 5).

St. Ignatius of Antioch (d. 107) was among the most influential of the early post-apostolic leaders. The bulk of his life spanned the later part of the first century, and he may have been a disciple of St. John the Apostle. He was the bishop of Antioch in Asia Minor for perhaps as long as forty years. Although little is known of his life and pastoral ministry, it is evident that he was beloved, well-known, and connected with the larger Church. In the year 107 he was arrested and traveled to Rome by ship, where he met his death. At each port where his ship docked on the way, large crowds of Christians were present to greet him.

Ignatius's life and ministry had a threefold significance: his pastoral leadership in the early Christian center of Antioch, the influence of his writings, and the witness of his martyrdom. On his sea voyage to Rome, he wrote a series of pastoral letters to affirm several seminal tenets of the Faith at this new post-apostolic time. These were so well received that they were later considered for inclusion in the New Testament. He wrote of the importance of the office of bishop, and also of the presbyters (priests) and deacons who assisted the bishops at a time when the ordained ministry was taking shape in the Church. Significantly, he noted the special emerging role and authority of the Bishop of Rome. This support was vital for the Church's understanding that the Bishop of Rome is the successor of Peter.

Ignatius also wrote in defense of the divinity of Jesus, a debate that would flare up a couple of centuries later; proclaimed the truth of the resurrection of Jesus; and wrote passionately on the Eucharist.

The very fact that he wrote these letters of instruction for the Church, and that they were preserved and circulated, indicates Ignatius's great pastoral influence in the early Church. And the letters offer us a window onto the Church's doctrinal formation in these early days. Ignatius was an important bridge from the apostles to the emerging post-apostolic Church, continuing their spiritual ministry as designated representatives of Christ himself. He certainly was a vital leader in his lifetime. His death by martyrdom also was significant; we will discuss it shortly when we look at the early martyrs in chapter 6.

Another early leader was **St. Clement of Rome** (d. 99), the fourth Bishop of Rome, whose name appears in the Roman Canon of the Mass after Linus and Cletus. He probably was a Roman convert and may have been baptized by Saint Peter himself. It appears that he succeeded Cletus as Bishop of Rome in about the year 91. The emperor Trajan exiled him to Crimea — on the Black Sea, the furthest ends of the empire — where he threw himself into evangelizing the prisoners who were working in the local mines. This earned him martyrdom.

While Bishop of Rome, Clement wrote a letter to the Christians at Corinth (as Saint Paul had done some years earlier), taking them to task for a schism that had broken out. This is a significant because it demonstrates that, as the Bishop of Rome, Clement was exercising authority over another Christian community. The preeminent role of Rome was already emerging.

Another of the leading bishops in the early post-apostolic period was **Saint Polycarp** (c. 69–155). He knew the apostle John and possibly Saint Peter as well, and thus is a true transition leader. He was bishop of Smyrna in Asia Minor, and Saint John himself may have consecrated him. He was a staunch defender of apostolic faith — opposing a growing number of unorthodox beliefs and movements — and was an influential leader in the Church at large, even consulting with the Bishops of Rome. The pursuit of orthodox, "apostolic" doctrine was crucial in these early days, as Church leaders sorted out truth on more and more issues. Polycarp and Ignatius were among the leaders in discerning, solidifying, and teaching apostolic doctrine. Like so many of the early leaders, Polycarp was also a martyr for the Faith.

St. Irenaeus of Lyons (125–203), a protégé of Polycarp who lived a few decades after Ignatius and Clement, was one of the most influential leaders in the second century. Although he was probably born in Asia Minor, he relocated to Lyons by the 170s, possibly sent by Polycarp. Lyons, today's Lyon, France, was over a hundred miles north of the Mediterranean, into the interior of Gaul. Just over a hundred years after the Ascension, a Christian community existed in the heart of France — over two thousand miles from Galilee.

Irenaeus was a pastor and the Church's first real theologian at a time in the young Church when these were especially needed. The Church was fragile. These Christian communities, scattered over the Mediterranean world, in an era of limited and difficult communications, were vulnerable to slipping apart. The Scriptures were still in formation, not yet codified and not easily accessible as they are today. The practice of pastoral care and the system of bishops, priests, and deacons were still in formation. And, as time passed, more and more individuals and groups began to propose new and different understandings of doctrine — some of which would become heresies. And many Christian communities — including in Lyons — began to experience persecutions, causing heroism and cowardice, bravery and discretion, and quarrels on what to do with

Christians who had denied their faith to save their lives. The Church was still active and growing, but needed saints and leaders to inspire and steer the faithful forward in truth and obedience to the Lord. Irenaeus was such a person. He was a deeply devout, well-educated priest, and eventually was made bishop of Lyons.

Most Catholics today take for granted that our bishops follow in a long line of apostolic succession. The early Church had to work this out after Jesus did not return in the apostles' lifetime. Irenaeus was instrumental in steering the discernment of Church leaders that bishops, ordained by laying on of hands, were successors to the apostles, with the same apostolic authority.

Irenaeus, like Ignatius of Antioch a few decades before him, was also one of the first leaders and bishops to assert that the Church of Rome was preeminent. Significantly, both of these men asserted their belief in the preeminence of Rome as bishops from places well away from Rome itself. The church of Rome, Irenaeus said, was the church of Peter and Paul. It had primacy.[1] His support of this preeminence, in conjunction with Ignatius and other key leaders, was vital to the recognition of Rome's authority. This took centuries to work out fully, but the advocacy of these early leaders was critical in setting the foundation for the papacy.

Irenaeus also composed a compendium of the Faith, an early "creed," often considered one of the first catechisms. His five-part *Against Heresies* refuted the Gnostics, who were among the most dominant voices against apostolic teaching in his day. It also is the first advanced treatise of systematic Christian theology. His writings are filled with references to Scripture and, as we shall see, he was instrumental in advancing the use and acceptance of the New Testament in the Church. Irenaeus also helped the Church grow her foothold in Gaul (France) by his missionary work. And, living up to his name (derived from the Greek word for peace), he was a peacemaker. He advocated for mercy for some repentant Donatists and helped patch up a dispute between the Bishop of Rome and some eastern communities. In 2022, Pope Francis declared Irenaeus a Doctor (teacher) of the Church, with the special title "Doctor of Unity."

Saint Irenaeus's ministries were prolific, and it is evident that he was an indefatigable defender and champion of the Faith. Without Irenaeus, the Church would have had much greater difficulty clarifying her teachings, fighting off heresies, remaining unified, understanding the special role of the Bishop of Rome, and growing in holiness.

In addition to the ministries of these saints and other leaders, two major developments were critical in securing the structure, doctrine, and life of the Church in the post-apostolic years. These were the emergence of sacraments — including liturgical worship — and of the Bible. This process unfolded over several centuries under the guidance of countless bishops, scholars, and leaders — some who were saints, many unknown to us today.

4

THE ORIGINS OF THE SACRAMENTS

In the Catholic Church today, we have the abundant spiritual blessings of the seven sacraments and the Bible. How did they get to us? The answer lies in the early centuries of the Church. What we see is the hand of the Holy Spirit working through numerous early Christians, including many saints.

In the first days of the early Church, neither sacraments nor the Bible were in place, nor even contemplated in the way they now exist. Yet, even though it took centuries for them to develop, the seeds of each were present from the beginning. The sacramental rituals and readings from sacred texts were an integral part of the life of Christian communities long before the theology, structure, and lists of sacred books and sacraments were finalized.

SACRAMENTS

Sacraments are incarnational rituals, portals of divine grace which flow through a material medium. Saint Augustine, whose writings advanced the early Church's understanding of sacraments more than any other theologian, defined them as visible signs of an invisible reality. They all have their roots in the practices within early Church communities, but it took centuries for their identities to be established. The Council of Trent in the sixteenth century confirmed and specified the seven sacraments as we know them today. In the first three centuries the Christians of the day developed and celebrated these rituals in their formative stages, in order to address their needs for community contact with God.[1]

Baptism was and remains the most foundational sacrament. Its origins are traceable to the ministry of John the Baptist and his baptism of Jesus himself, and Jesus' command to the apostles to go, make disciples, and baptize in the name of the Father, the Son, and the Holy Spirit (see Mt 28:19). Saints Peter and Paul note the significance of baptism (1 Pt 3:21 and Rom 6:3–4), and Saint Luke narrates the account of **Saint Philip** baptizing the Ethiopian eunuch (Acts 8:38–39). Baptism emerged from the earliest days as a rite of initiation of new Christians. The immersion in or pouring of water over the new Christian in the name of the Persons of the Trinity marked the flow of divine grace into the soul. The rite took form in the first decades of the Church and is even described in ways we can recognize today by Church Fathers, including the influential North Africans, Tertullian, and St. Cyprian of Carthage. The *Didache* also addresses baptism, prescribing the ritual of water and the Trinitarian formula.

As it is today, baptism was considered the means for the washing away of sins — including original sin. But baptism was a one-time event, and it took time for Church leaders to discern how to address sins committed after one was baptized. In light of this, there were times in the early Church when baptism was delayed until near the end of life, lest one sin again. Over many years, the Church came full circle and began to confer baptism on infants, for the sake of their salvation. This practice generated controversy at first, since it necessarily removed the act of individual decision and affected the catechumenate process. The late second- and early third-century Church Father, Tertullian, was one of the early critics.[2]

Baptism was (and remains) the first of the three "sacraments of initiation." *Confirmation*, which evolved as the middle initiation sacrament, was, at first, not a separate sacrament, but was part of the baptismal ritual. Called *anointing* in the early Church, confirmation eventually emerged from baptism as a separate sacrament because of its own characteristics: Holy oil was the sign, the bishop administered the "anointing," and the focus was on gifts of the Holy Spirit. In the East, these sacraments of initiation were usually conferred together. In the West, over time, the bishops began to confer confirmation via "laying on of hands," later in one's life as a completion of baptism, for strength to live out the Christian life. (This sense of "East" and "West" would become a major problem for the Church in future years.)

Celebration of what we now call *Mass* and the *Eucharist*, the third of the sacraments of initiation, was at the heart of Christian worship in the first centuries. Saint Peter and the apostles brought to the early Church communities their profound witness of the Last Supper, and Saint Paul spoke with authority of the bread and wine becoming the Body of Christ at the words of Jesus (see 1 Cor 11:23–26). This re-presentation of the Last Supper was the focal point of Christian worship from the beginning, and the Eucharistic ritual has continued through the ages in recognizable form. St. Justin Martyr describes this early "liturgy" in his *First Apology*, around the year 150, as he sought to assure nonbelievers that Christians were not practicing magic: The Christian communities gathered for prayer, listened to Scripture and the priest's interpretation, offered intercessions, and partook of the bread and wine together in thanksgiving as Jesus had directed, with the firm belief that the bread and wine truly became the Body and Blood of Jesus himself. This belief in the Resurrection and the Eucharist — certainly profound and unique — set Christians apart from other religions, drawing both converts and persecution.

Like many saints, St. Ignatius of Antioch preached on the True Presence of Jesus in the Eucharist. He called it "the medicine of immortality"[3] and the "flesh of Jesus Christ."[4] St. Irenaeus of Lyons taught that the bread and wine became the Body and Blood of Christ upon invocation of the

Word of God in Christian worship. These saints, and many other Church leaders and theologians, by their preaching and practice, guarded and preserved the vital doctrine of the Real Presence of Jesus in the Eucharist.

These early saints — and countless others throughout history — stood irrefutably on the belief that the Eucharist is truly the Body and Blood of Christ. The idea that the Eucharist is a mere symbol and not the Real Presence of Christ held little sway in the Church until the time of the Protestant Reformation. These early saints would strongly oppose this idea that it was a mere symbol.

In earliest times, these Sunday liturgical gatherings were in homes or other small places. As the Church grew, dedicated places of worship came into being, the first church buildings. This increased the visibility of the Christian communities — for good and ill.

Holy Orders, the sacrament of ordination of bishops, priests, and deacons, also dates to the early decades of Church history. The Church's understanding of priesthood and of the Eucharist are interconnected. The question of how the bread and wine become the Body and Blood of Christ was answered through their understanding of priesthood. Jesus presided over the first Eucharist at the Last Supper and instructed his apostles to do the same. Those who presided over "the breaking of the bread" in the early communities were considered to be successors of the apostles and endowed with the grace as Christ's representative among them. This included the divine authority to pray over the bread and wine at liturgies so that they become Christ's Body and Blood. They were ministers "set apart" for a special role *in persona Christi* — Christ present sacramentally among the communities of believers. St. Ignatius of Antioch made this clear in his Letter to the Church at Smyrna: "The sole Eucharist you should consider valid is one that is celebrated by the bishop himself, or by some person authorized by him."[5]

In the year 96, Pope Saint Clement wrote of the apostles' teaching that when the leaders die, "other approved men shall succeed to their sacred ministry."[6] These men were chosen from the community in light of their gifts, and were consecrated for service through the ritual of the laying on of hands, which is retained today in the ceremonies of ordination into the Sacrament of Holy Orders. The third-century theologian **Saint**

Hippolytus describes the rites of ordination of bishops, priests, and deacons in his work *Apostolic Tradition*. This was the origin of the doctrine of *apostolic succession*, that those consecrated for the priesthood were in a line of succession from the apostles. St. Ignatius of Antioch speaks of this in one of his letters.[7] In the time of Saint Paul, the position of bishop (*episkopos*) as liturgical and spiritual leader of a local community had already been established (see 1 Tm 3). In time, priests (*presbyteroi*) were associated with bishops as their coequal liturgical helpers. The ministry of deacons was focused not on liturgy, but on charity and care for the flock. Sts. Ignatius of Antioch, Irenaeus, Clement, and Polycarp all became influential bishops.

Like confirmation, the Sacrament of *Reconciliation* (formerly Penance) evolved out of baptism. It had an interesting development. According to Clement, public penitential practices were common by the end of the first century, and according to Hippolytus, bishops in the third century had the recognized authority to forgive sins. During the times of persecution, many Christians lost courage and fled to safety or renounced their faith rather than be put to death. When the persecutions subsided, some, called *lapsi*, sought to return to the Faith. This created controversy. Many who survived persecution or had seen loved ones give their lives were opposed to a reconciliation. Others observed that Jesus preached forgiveness. What to do? The early Church had to come to grips with the issue of whether she was a Church of saints or of sinners. In response to this dilemma, a method of reconciliation emerged that included public confession followed by severe penances. Sometimes this delayed reconciliation for years. As this process developed, it became clear that more than initial baptism was necessary to address the reality that all were sinners.

This public confession and penance gradually became less severe and more private, and evolved over many centuries into the Sacrament of Reconciliation as we know it today. It was in and near the sixth century that Irish and British bishops organized a practice of private confession and absolution.[8] This spread throughout the Church during the Middle Ages.

The Sacrament of *Matrimony*, as a covenant of fidelity before God, has rich roots in Scripture, beginning with Genesis, as Adam and Eve became one flesh in the creation narrative (see Gn 2:23–24). Christian marriage was celebrated from early times and was recognized as a sacred event. The early Church was mindful both of her Jewish roots and practice in the Old Testament, and of the affirmation of Jesus himself, who called marriage a divinely ordained coming together of a man and a woman to become one flesh (Mt 19:4–7 and Mk 10:6–8). Although the practice of a Christian blessing of a secular marriage bond was common, Ignatius of Antioch advised that Christians should marry with the assent of their bishop;[9] Augustine considered marriage a sacrament; by the eighth century, Church officials were themselves performing nuptials; and in 1139, the Second Lateran Council declared marriage to be a sacrament.

Praying for the sick was a natural and common practice in the early Church. At special times it took the form of ritual, as described in James 5:13–15 — presbyters would anoint the sick person with oil and pray for grace, healing, and forgiveness of sins. Anointings were considered a continuation of the healing ministry of Jesus himself, an occasion of grace. Healing was expected. By the eighth century, it was recognized as a sacrament of the dying, and the title *Extreme Unction* emerged. Today's Sacrament of *Anointing of the Sick* is derived from this ancient ritual, as modified by the Second Vatican Council, and it was once again opened up for the sick, and not just the dying.

Theological development followed the active practice of these sacramental rituals throughout the history of the Church. Rites, though ever evolving, were solidified. Theologians distinguished a difference between sacraments derived from Christ and those that were mere rituals. With this distinction, by the twelfth century, the considered number of sacraments shrank from over thirty to seven. A century later, theologian Peter Lombard and St. Thomas Aquinas were leaders in the process of discerning seven sacraments instituted by Christ. The Council of Trent, addressing the turmoil from the Reformation, officially declared these seven to be sacraments, and defined them and their attendant rituals.

5

THE BIRTH OF THE NEW TESTAMENT AND THE CHRISTIAN BIBLE

The formation of the Christian Bible is nothing short of incredible. It was a process that spanned nearly three hundred years, involved countless persons — including many saints — and, just as Christians hold that Scripture is inspired by the Holy Spirit, it is evident that the actual *process* of the formation of Scripture also was inspired.

First, Church leaders and theologians had to address the existing Hebrew Scriptures — our Old Testament. Though considered sacred by Jewish authorities, to the early Christians it was far from obvious that these writings should be adopted as sacred *Christian* texts. After all, Jesus ushered in the New Covenant that transcended the old covenants. And as every year passed by, the early Church became more Gentile and less Jewish. God, it seemed to many, was moving in a new direction, doing new things, and the old Jewish customs and writings could be set aside as part of an earlier, pre-Christian history.

Yet in the early decades of this post-apostolic generation, the leaders and bishops of the Church came to recognize the Old Testament as God's Word. They discerned that Jesus had fulfilled the old covenants, not replaced them. Jesus, a Jew, embraced the Hebrew heritage, knew and quoted the Hebrew Scriptures, and made clear that the Jewish law, given to the Chosen People by the Father, was not to be abolished. Jesus built upon the foundation of salvation history through the covenants with the Hebrew people. And many early Christians, including Saint Matthew, saw the Christian Church as rooted in salvation history, the covenants, and the promise of a Messiah. Saint Paul himself, who also quoted from the Hebrew Scriptures in his letters, taught: "All Scripture is inspired by God and profitable for teaching, for reproof, for correction, and for training in righteousness" (2 Tm 3:16). Since no New Testament yet existed when he wrote, Paul was obviously speaking of the Hebrew Scriptures. Saint Irenaeus quoted often from the Hebrew Scriptures in his writings as well, and defended their place in the Church as sacred.[1] So the early Church discerned that the Hebrew Scriptures had a proper place as sacred writings.

The creation and development of the New Testament was another matter. That twenty-seven texts composed by numerous Christians at different times and places in the several decades after the Resurrection would become what we now call the New Testament — sacred, divinely inspired writings for all time — was astounding.

The idea of a written "New Testament" of newly composed sacred writings could not even have dawned on the early Church leaders. Jesus never said, "Go therefore and compile a book." The Faith was passed down orally from the apostles in those early decades. Written material was not the primary way to learn or foster faith or knowledge; most Christians could not even read. A sacred book for posterity did not fit with the Church's expectation at that time of Christ's imminent return. In the earliest days of great missionary zeal, the books and letters of the New Testament were just beginning to be written, but they were targeted to specific communities and not at first even known or available throughout the wider Christian world. The notion that some of them were inspired sacred writings was not obvious at first, and even the idea of a body of sacred post-Resurrection writings, on par with the Hebrew Scriptures as the Word of God, had not yet been born.

In the first three centuries, the Church gradually moved toward the profound recognition that many of the newly written religious texts around them were sacred and inspired. This process was undoubtedly driven by the inspiration and guidance of the Holy Spirit, and unfolded in stages. First, there was the creation of the writings themselves; then the gradual recognition that many were indeed special (and that others were not); and finally, the eventual acknowledgment that these writings were the inspired Word of God. Pastoral leaders began to collect and copy these special writings for use in liturgy and teaching within the Church. As this was occurring, they discerned which writings were truly inspired and which were not.

It is noteworthy that no one or two or three saints or other persons were primary architects of this long process. It was an endeavor shared by numerous, often anonymous pastors and theologians, in dialogue with each other, starting locally where the writings first appeared, and proliferating from there. And one cannot forget that these writings would hardly have seen the light of day beyond their local community had they not been copied and shared from one community to another, and thus physically spread throughout the Christian world.

The books of the New Testament, starting with some of Paul's letters, were composed in the second half of the first century, starting near the year 50 — just twenty years after the Ascension of Jesus. Mark is usually deemed the first Gospel, possibly written as early as the year 60. The Gospel of John was the last, written perhaps in the 90s, maybe earlier. It must be kept in mind that these writings were composed for a particular purpose and reader. Their authors were not intending to write for a universal audience over time and place. None of them knew that they were writing something that would become part of the Christian Bible for all ages. That was decided by others at a later time.

It is important to note that it was *saints* who wrote most all the books of the New Testament. Open to the guidance of the Holy Spirit, Saints

Matthew, Mark, Luke, John, Paul, James, and Peter composed these Gospels, narratives, and letters. We have them to thank for listening to the Holy Spirit and writing. As these texts began circulating within the Christian communities, many began to take note of them. The Gospels and Paul's letters stood out as powerful expressions of the Faith with apostolic origins, and served the purpose of preserving the first generation of apostolic teaching.

By the end of the second century (between 150 and 200), most of our present New Testament, about twenty-two of the twenty-seven books, were generally acknowledged throughout much of the Church as sacred and inspired — particularly Paul's letters and three of the Gospels. Interestingly, the end of the Second Letter of Peter, likely written at the beginning of the second century, refers to the letters of Paul as "Scripture" (see 2 Pt 3:16). The Gospel of John, different in style and emphasis than the other three (*synoptic*) Gospels and written later in time, took more time — as did the Letter to the Hebrews (whose authorship was unclear) and some of the non-Pauline letters. By the 300s, they, too, were mostly accepted as part of the body of sacred writings.

At the same time, other writings were considered and rejected. Some were recognized as excellent Christian expositions (such as the letters of Ignatius of Antioch and Clement of Rome) and others, such as the *Gospel of Thomas*, were suspect as unorthodox or inaccurate. The Church leaders expected three things for acceptance into the *canon* (or official list) of sacred writings.[2] First, these writings had to be of apostolic origin — believed to be written either by the apostles or their close associates during the time that the apostles were active. Second, they had to be Christ-centered and faithful to the Christian message. And third, they must have attained pervasive acceptance and use within the Christian communities, especially in the liturgy. For instance, the letters of Ignatius and Clement — beneficial and revered as they were — were deemed not to be of apostolic origin.

Perhaps no other person had a more significant role in guiding the New Testament into the heart of the Church than Saint Irenaeus. He was the first to quote extensively from New Testament writings — over one thousand times in *Against Heresies* alone.[3] He repeatedly quoted from over twenty of the New Testament books in his writings, drawing from them a sense of apostolic authority and of pastoral guidance. Irenaeus also recognized four Gospels — Matthew, Mark, Luke, and John — and advocated for their authenticity as Scripture.[4] He was a forerunner in the use and application of the New Testament writings in the Church, just as these writings were being accepted as sacred. That such an influential theologian and pastor would draw from these writings at such an early date was crucial in normalizing the New Testament as Sacred Scripture and advancing its use within the Church.

St. Justin Martyr, who we will meet shortly, also acknowledged these same four Gospels, even earlier than Irenaeus. He is the first to use the word *Gospel* for what he calls the "memoirs of the apostles."[5] Justin describes Christian liturgy in his day as including the reading of the "memoirs of the apostles" and "the writings of the prophets."[6] As time passed, teachers, pastors, and theologians made more and more use of the New Testament in their writings and sermons. Saint Augustine, for instance, quotes both Old and New Testaments on almost every page of his *Confessions*, including, as we shall see, the passage from Saint Paul that prompted his conversion.

Even as the New Testament began to work its way into the consciousness of the Church as Sacred Scripture, the books comprising it were not made final until late in the fourth century. Saint Athanasius, the influential bishop of Alexandria, and also a prolific quoter of Scripture, proposed the New Testament canon of twenty-seven books as we know it in the year 367 in his *Festal Letter 39*. Pope St. Damasus I presided over a council in Rome in 382 that also published the same New Testament canon. Ultimately, a synod of bishops in Carthage in 397 declared this list of twenty-seven books to be the official "New Testament" Scriptures for the Church. Churches in the East followed suit shortly thereafter.

Remarkably, the Christian communities moved from first-generation apostolic preachers to a body of inspired sacred writings in about a hundred years. The baton of apostolic teaching and ministry had been passed to a new generation of leaders, supported by a growing sense of worship and sacrament and this new body of sacred apostolic writing. And saints were at the heart of each stage of this remarkable process:

composing; recognizing the sacred character of the texts; using them to teach, pastor, and to defend the Church's developing doctrines; and setting the canon of approved texts. The New Testament was born. The Word of God was passed from the apostles to their writings.

6

FATHERS OF THE CHURCH

As the Church found its footing in the post-apostolic age, a new generation of saints and leaders, bishops and scholars, and pastors and preachers rose up to lead and guide the faithful. These "next-generation" leaders made their presence felt throughout the Christian world in the early post-apostolic centuries, guiding the faithful toward holiness, worship, and prayer; advancing the Church's understanding of doctrinal truth — including the understanding of the nature of the Church and even of God himself; fighting heresies; and fostering the growth and understanding of Scripture. The most accomplished of them became known as Fathers of the Church. These were scholarly writers who left a legacy of written wisdom that has influenced not only their own generation, but the Church throughout history. Most (though not all) were advanced in holiness of life and prayer as well. They are called "Fathers" because they laid the foundation for the teachings and theology of the Church.

These Fathers included many bishops, some popes and laymen and, in most cases, saints. The title of "Father" is not an official, authoritative Church designation, so there is some variance in who is included, but a consensus of the main Fathers does exist. The era of Church Fathers was, loosely, the second through the seventh centuries. We will meet some of them later as well. Eight of the most influential Fathers in the first three centuries include four saints whom we have already met: Clement of Rome, Ignatius of Antioch, Polycarp, and Irenaeus of Lyons. The other four are Justin Martyr and Anthony of Egypt — both saints — and Tertullian and Origen, who, though they were important and powerful scholars, are not deemed saints.

St. Justin Martyr (100–165), born in Samaria to pagan parents, pursued the study of philosophy in his early years. A conversation with an elderly Syrian Christian led him to the study of the Christian Scriptures and ultimately to his conversion to Christianity. He spent his remaining life defending the Christian Faith — in writing and in numerous oral debates with nonbelievers. He is considered one of the leading expounders of the Faith in the second century, one of the first Christian apologists, and one of the most influential laymen in the early Church. He was an early proponent of the *Divine Word*, or *Logos* — God acting in history to plant the seeds of Christianity, even before the Incarnation. He was among the first scholars to explain that faith and reason are compatible and supportive of each other. While living in a culture that presented some of the same challenges to faith as ours today, Justin even challenged the Roman emperor who was persecuting Christians. Justin insisted that the emperor examine Christians and their contributions to society more closely, rather than merely accept the claim that they were hostile to the Roman order. In his last debate with a nonbeliever, he was perhaps too successful: The one he bested had him arrested — along with some of his students — for failure to sacrifice to the imperial gods. Justin and his companions were beheaded.

By his teaching and writing, Justin Martyr helped to deepen the still young Church's theological understanding. Integrating the word of the Hebrew prophets with the mission of Jesus, his expositions on the *Logos* and faith and reason, and his efforts to synthesize theology with philosophy were significant contributions to a Church moving from eyewitness accounts toward ever-deepening reflection on the meaning of faith. And Christians can be grateful to that anonymous Syrian elder for his role in inspiring the young Justin.

Tertullian (c. 160–240) and Origen (184–253), were both powerful scholars and theologians. Although neither is considered a saint, their contributions to the development of the Faith were significant. Tertullian, from North Africa — a vibrant Christian area in his time — is sometimes called the Father of Western Theology, even though some question his commitment to orthodoxy in his later years. His extensive and insightful writings have made him one of the more frequently quoted of the early Fathers. It was Tertullian who, in reflecting on why Christianity was attractive, made the immortal observation, "See how they love one another." It was also Tertullian who provided the oft quoted insight, "The blood of the martyrs is the seed of the Church."

Origen, another North African — from the renowned city of Alexandria in Egypt — was also a powerful theologian, and, like several Fathers, a great scholar of Scripture. He was a pioneer in the practice of *lectio divina*, a time-honored way of praying and contemplating with Scripture. Like Tertullian, his fidelity to orthodoxy was questioned, and the controversies over some of his beliefs — including the preexistence of souls — is likely why he also is not deemed a saint.

St. Anthony of Egypt (sometimes rendered *Antony*, 250–356), was one of the most admired and influential saints of the third and fourth centuries. His holiness of life and radical commitment to God, to the point of selling off considerable riches, were a powerful witness in his own time as well as throughout history. Anthony is often called the father of monasticism and the most well known of the oft-called "Desert Fathers." After selling off his property, he moved out into the Egyptian desert where he lived mostly in prayer, fasting, and seclusion. He experienced profound battles with temptation and Satan, and prevailed. In time, he attracted a number of other men whom he organized into what can be considered an early monastery. During a time of persecution in the early years of the fourth century, he left his seclusion and traveled to Alexandria to offer encouragement to the persecuted. Later, he founded another monastery, assisted his friend Saint Athanasius in the battle against the Arian heresy, and took residence in a cave. There Anthony became a popular consultant, offering Christian wisdom and advice to those who came to him. His reputation for asceticism, holiness, and wisdom was widespread across the Christian world. Athanasius was so impressed that he wrote Anthony's biography, the source of much of what we know of him.

Anthony's contemporary, **Saint Pachomius** (292–348) was also an influential monk from the Egyptian desert. Unlike Anthony, who, for the most part, fostered the practice of the monk as a lone hermit, Pachomius gathered his followers into small monastic communities. This practice was important for the development of monasteries in later centuries. He rightly shares with Anthony the role as father of monasticism. That both of these two "Desert Fathers" were contemporaries in time and place is a remarkable work of providence.

HERESIES

Many of the Fathers were called to undertake the task of countering heresy. As Christianity spread, the faithful heard the voices of scholars, pseudo-scholars, bishops, and charlatans reflecting on the Faith, defending it, explaining it, attacking it, proposing modifications or additions to it, or co-opting it for other philosophies. These voices forced the Church to grapple with the emerging issues of the nature of God and Christ and the Church. What was true about the Faith and what was not became a major issue. The Church Fathers, in union with most bishops, were instrumental in helping the Church clarify what was authentic apostolic teaching and how the truth was to be determined.

The word *heresy* does not roll off the modern tongue easily. In our age of relativism, the word sounds too strident, too judgmental. Yet in other times — perhaps most other times — the concept of heresy and use of the word was much more commonly accepted. Truth was much more valued than it is now. Even so, the battles over heresy have never left the Church, and each age — including our own — has its own unique struggle with truth and error.

Disputes in the early years were inevitable. Doctrine was in formation. The Church was comprised of imperfect people, and many were passionate. With the rapid spread of the Christian Faith over a vast distance and the challenges of communication, people could develop ideas that differed from others. In the early Church before the fourth century, three heresies reached a level of prominence and concern: Gnosticism, the teachings of Marcion, and Montanism.

Gnosticism was a mysterious blend of various beliefs which began to grow in influence early in the second century. Earthly, physical things were considered evil and only things of heaven were good. The path to salvation was to turn away from the evil physical world. To be truly human would make Jesus evil; thus Jesus only appeared to be human. The Incarnation was an illusion. In addition, there was a hidden Wisdom or Knowledge that is accessible only to certain special people, and it is this special knowledge that saves (thus its name — *gnosis* is the Greek word for knowledge). Gnosticism presented itself as an alternative to apostolic teaching and acquired surprising traction. Irenaeus's *Against Heresies* was aimed primarily at the Gnostics and, along with others, he helped to reassert the compelling nature of the Gospel message as handed down by the apostles and the eyewitnesses to the life, death, and resurrection of Jesus. The true special knowledge is the Revelation of God, through Jesus, now assured through the Holy Spirit. In time, the Gnostics faded from influence, though Gnosticism has reappeared in various forms throughout history, even to the present day.

The teachings of Marcion (c. 85–160), an influential leader from the eastern Mediterranean, were a variation on Gnosticism that created quite a stir in the second century. He, like the Gnostics, believed and taught that Jesus was divine but only appeared to be human. Marcion also taught that the God of the Hebrew Scriptures was incompatible with the Christian concept of God, and thus he rejected the Old Testament as not authoritative. He composed his own list, or *canon* of sacred writings, which consisted of his edited version of Luke's Gospel and ten of Paul's letters. This forced the leaders and bishops of the Church to begin identifying an accepted canon of Scripture. Thus Marcion, in a backhanded way, sped up the process of the creation of the New Testament.[1] But he was excommunicated for his heretical views, and his influence did not endure.

Montanism appeared in the middle of the second century. Although it did not espouse doctrines radically different from apostolic Christianity, its emphasis on ecstatic prophecy led to a cult of leaders who claimed to have a special prophetic connection with God. These leaders contended that they had prophetic word of the imminent Second Coming, something the early Church had been waiting for since the time of the apostles. This led to pastoral practices, including a call to a rigorous asceticism, that drew away from the apostolic message. Indirectly, this was also a challenge to the authority of the bishops. The Church condemned Montanism and its cult leaders as well.

As Christian doctrine grew into a more mature state, more heresies cropped up. We will meet some of the most powerful heresies in part 2. At the same time, another significant challenge arose that had a major impact on the life of the Church: persecution.

7

PERSECUTION

Persecution has been the ever-present companion of the Church. This reality stretches from the early days after the Resurrection (witness the stoning to death of Stephen and the jailing of apostles in Jerusalem and their eventual martyrdom) and continues to this day.

Perhaps nothing shaped the early Christian Church as did the waves of imperial persecutions from about the year 64 through the first decade of the fourth century. Various Roman emperors, at various times during the first three hundred years, turned on the empire's Christians with concerted pogroms. The lasting images of Christians being thrown to the lions in amphitheaters has a basis in fact.

Jesus warned that persecutions would happen. His kingdom was not of this world, as he said; his message was a "sign of contradiction" to the kingdoms of the world. His death is a witness to this. It was to be expected that many of his followers would also be seen as threats to the world order. Christianity, as it grew to be a visible religion in the Mediterranean, came into unavoidable conflict with the mores and religions of the Roman Empire.

As the Church grew and became more noticeable, she began to attract suspicions that her adherents were disloyal to the emperor, and perhaps dangerous to his authority. The Christian belief that bread and wine became the Flesh and Blood of Jesus was misunderstood by many as a radical, even disgusting form of cannibalism, further tarnishing the reputation of Christians.

These problems might have been overcome, but a fire destroyed much of residential Rome in or near the year 64, causing anger against Emperor Nero. He looked for a scapegoat to deflect blame — and chose the Christians. The Roman historian Tacitus, writing in the second century, is a primary source of information about this initial imperial persecution of Christians.[1] We do not know how many Christians lost their lives at Nero's direction in the several years after this fire, but it appears to be significant. This begs an incredible point: In Rome, no more than thirty years after the Ascension of Jesus, there was already a community of Christians of significant size. If the number of Christians had been just a few, they would not have been on Nero's radar. This illustrates how fast the Faith was spreading — even into the capital of the empire. Peter and Paul were both martyred between the years 64 and 68, during the persecution of Nero.

Persecution was not constant, but periodic under various Roman emperors. Many emperors directed or approved persecutions of Christians out of their perception that Christians opposed their authority or resisted calls to offer sacrifice to the Roman gods or to the emperor, who often was proclaimed as a god. The desire of rulers to maintain power at nearly all costs was as prevalent then as it is now. Often, the temperament of the emperor, instability in the empire, misunderstandings of Christian practices or beliefs, hostility of key advisors, or Christians' lack of popularity among many in the wealthy and political classes contributed to these persecutions.

Among the Roman emperors who authorized (or permitted) persecutions of Christians after Nero were Domitian in the late first century (probable but disputed, and sometimes considered the persecution referred to in the Book of Revelation); Trajan, in the early second century; and Marcus Aurelius in the late second century. Ironically, Marcus Aurelius was a cultured, civilized scholar and philosopher — not the type of emperor one would expect to approve violent persecution — while his cruel, paranoid, and egotistical successor, Commodus (popularly portrayed in the movie *Gladiator*), actually called off the persecution of Christians! Other emperors who authorized persecutions were Septimius Severus in the early 200s and Decius and Valerian in the mid-200s. The final persecution, and one of the most severe, was under Diocletian from about 303 to 311.

The number of Christian martyrs in these first three centuries is difficult to determine, but there were thousands. One historian estimates seventy thousand.[2] Most died in heroic obscurity, or at least their stories are lost to posterity. Some stand out as well-known saints, such as Peter and Paul.

Many heroic Christians have had the courage to embrace martyrdom. Ignatius of Antioch was on yet another level. He desired martyrdom, not as a death wish, but to make the ultimate witness to his faith in Jesus Christ and the hope of eternal life. He spoke openly about that desire. When Ignatius was thrown to the lions in 107, it was already four decades after the Roman killing of Christians had begun. He saw the crown that awaited and desired union with his Savior. Certainly, he had extraordinary faith in the truth of eternal life to fuel a desire for martyrdom. His witness made a huge impression on the Church, giving courage to his contemporaries and offering inspiration to the later Christians.

Both Sts. Polycarp and Justin Martyr died as martyrs. Polycarp was burned at the stake and speared to death at age eighty in the year 155, during the reign of emperor Marcus Aurelius, for his refusal to sacrifice to the gods and acknowledge the emperor's divinity. Justin Martyr was beheaded in 165 for the same reasons.

The Christian communities across North Africa had grown strong and vibrant, and inevitably ran into persecution. Among the noteworthy North African martyrs was **Saint Perpetua** (d. 203). She is enshrined in the Roman Canon along with other martyrs because of the admiration

for her in the Church. Perpetua was put to death in Carthage, a cosmopolitan North African city on the Mediterranean coast during the persecution of emperor Septimius Severus. Her death indicates that the authorities often did not spare women from death. Perpetua was a nursing
mother at the time, yet, when asked to renounce her faith — even by her
tearful father, who did not want to be disgraced by a daughter joining the
Christian Faith — she remained resolute and was tossed to wild beasts in
the town amphitheater. She survived, but was ultimately killed by sword,
along with her companion, **Saint Felicity** (d. 203), who had just given
birth. An account of their martyrdom still exists. Not much is known
about Perpetua's life save that she was from the nobility, but her death
created a stir of popularity in North Africa that endured for two centuries. Several generations later, Saint Augustine himself had to step in and
caution against an overly strong cult honoring Perpetua that thrived in
his area, near where she lived and died.

 St. Cyprian of Carthage (d. 258), also enshrined in the Roman
Canon (paired with Pope Saint Cornelius), was a lawyer who converted
to Christianity. In 248 he became bishop of Carthage. Cyprian became
embroiled in a controversy common in the early centuries — whether
and under what circumstances the Church should take back the *lapsi*,
those who had strayed from the Faith. He called a council in Carthage
in 251, which laid out terms for accepting them back. He endorsed and
defended the supremacy of the pope and authored several significant
doctrinal and pastoral treatises. Cyprian was caught up in the Valerian
persecution, and, when he refused to participate in the imperial sacrifice
to the gods, he was beheaded.

 Saint Lawrence (d. 258) was also put to death in the persecution
under the emperor Valerian. He died in Rome, where he served as a
deacon. Not much is known about his life but it appeared that he was
a leader among the Roman Christians. Legend and fact are difficult to
sort out, but the popular account is that the prefect of Rome confronted
him, demanding that he turn over the treasures of the Roman Christians.
In three days' time Lawrence gathered the poor, blind, crippled, and or-
phans of the Christian community and presented them to the prefect as
the treasures of the Church. This was theologically true, but also a direct

insult to the prefect. As the account goes, he was thereupon tortured and killed on a red-hot gridiron. His example and death helped to further the conversion of Rome from paganism to Christianity.

Saint Sebastian (d. 288) probably died under the rule of co-emperor Maximian, who sat in Rome while Diocletian ruled in the East. Much of Sebastian's life is legend, but that legend is an indicator of the impression his martyrdom had on the Christians of his day. Several Renaissance paintings depict Sebastian pierced with arrows. The legend is that Sebastian was a Roman soldier who was discovered to be a Christian. He was tied to a tree and shot with arrows, left for dead, discovered still alive, and nursed back to health. Later, the Romans caught him and finished the job. Legend aside, it is likely that Sebastian was a soldier put to death for being a Christian. Even before the fierce Diocletian persecution a decade away, Christians were being purged from the army. The loyalty of the army was crucial for the emperors, subjecting soldiers to special scrutiny. In 320, the **Forty Martyrs of Sebaste**, Christian soldiers in the Roman army, died for their faith near the city of Sebaste (in modern Turkey).

The Diocletian persecution was the last but the most fierce and comprehensive pogrom against Christians by any of the Roman emperors. It spanned the length of the empire, from Asia Minor in the East, where Diocletian himself reigned, to Rome, Spain, and other western areas. As in earlier times, women and children were not spared. Two of the more famous martyrs under Diocletian were the young women (or girls), **Saint Agnes** (d. c. 305) and **Saint Lucy** (d. c. 304). The accounts of each are steeped in legend, but most historians acknowledge that they did exist and were martyred for the Faith. Agnes was likely a girl of about thirteen who was put to death in Rome. Her courage in facing torture and death became an inspiration for her contemporaries and posterity. A basilica was built over the site of her death not long after her martyrdom. Even Saint Ambrose called attention to her in a sermon. Like Sebastian, Agnes is depicted frequently in Christian art, often with the symbol of a lamb, which signifies Christ. Also, the name *Agnes* is from the Latin word for lamb. Lucy was martyred under similar circumstances a year earlier in Syracuse, on the island of Sicily. Her parents erected a shrine in her honor, which helps to verify the truth of her martyrdom aside from popular legend.

Beyond these saint-martyrs were the thousands of ordinary Christians who suffered martyrdom as well. They were known only to their families, friends, and communities. We can fall into the trap of seeing martyrdom, like war, only as a glorious thing. All but the most courageous undoubtedly experienced fear, or even terror, as they faced death and often torture for their faith. For every Ignatius there were thousands of ordinary believers for whom martyrdom was not sought but something to be feared. Many, if not most, had an out if they chose to reject the Faith. Yet they kept the Faith and gave up their lives as witnesses to the truth of Jesus Christ. They remained faithful despite their fears. That is what courage is. In ways untold, the blood of these thousands of anonymous martyrs truly seeded the vast fields of the Faith.

Martyrdom was a witness to the reality of eternal life. It took great confidence in the truth of eternal life in heaven for one to give up his or her life on earth. No one would stake life on a guess or hunch or an uncertain belief. This is the key to understanding why the blood of martyrs seeded the growth of the Church, and why her persecutors could not destroy her. Seeing the "stake-my-life-on-it" faith of the martyrs as they were killed rather than renounce their faith left a tremendous impression on those who remained. Belief was serious. Heaven must be real. To remain in the faith of the martyrs had true value. Thus the martyrs — then and now — are profound builders of the history of the Church. Their blood was vital in seeding the growth of the Church in the first three centuries.

As the year 313 dawned, the stage was set for the next phase of Christianity. With a few exceptions, persecutions ended, Christianity became akin to a state religion, and massive, divisive theological issues raised their ugly heads. Just when it seemed that freedom and prosperity had arrived, instead great challenges arose.

II

FROM CONSTANTINE TO CHARLEMAGNE

AD 313 to AD 800

Saint Athanasius of Alexandria, fresco on the ceiling of the Saint John the Baptist church in Zagreb, Croatia. AdobeStock

8

THE END OF PERSECUTION

Everything changed in the year 313. The Diocletian persecution came to an end. The persecuted Christians suddenly were given a reprieve, and even protection. In an extraordinary twist of history — what many believers would call divine providence — the conversion to Christianity of the Roman emperor himself ended imperial persecutions.

Diocletian resigned as emperor in 305 due to illness, and died in 311. Constantine, sometimes called "the Great," became emperor (in part) in 306 but his rule was contested. At the Battle of Milvian Bridge, against the forces of his rival Maxentius in 312, Constantine secured his position of emperor over the entire Roman Empire. As the battle was about to begin, he claimed that he saw a vision in the sky: a cross with the words "In this sign you will conquer." After winning the battle, Constantine turned away from the Roman rituals and became sympathetic to the Christian Faith.

Whether it was at the Battle of the Milvian Bridge or a later time, it appears likely that Constantine did have a genuine conversion to Christianity. The level of his faith commitment is debated, but he clearly acted as a believer throughout his time as emperor. Constantine not only ended the persecution of Christians but ruled sympathetically toward believers and even participated in Christian affairs. He governed from the East, in the Roman city of Byzantium, renamed Constantinople in his honor, strategically located on the Bosphorus Strait, linking the Black and Mediterranean seas.

In the year 313, Constantine issued the Edict of Milan, also called the Edict of Toleration. This decree ended the persecution of Christians and declared a freedom to practice any religion in the empire. It was not limited to Christianity, but Christians, so recently subject to fierce persecution on a wide scale, had the most to gain. The edict also provided for the return of confiscated property. It did not declare Christianity to be the official religion of the empire, but was in essence a "free exercise" decree. It took some time to take hold: Witness the Martyrs of Sebaste, killed seven years later under Constantine's temporary co-emperor, Licinius, (who, ironically, coauthored the Edict of Toleration). Exceptions aside, this abrupt change was one of the most transformative moments in Christian history. Christians throughout the empire now began to practice openly. Although the religion was still short of favored status, the reality that the emperor himself appeared to be a Christian certainly aided the spread of the Faith. It even became somewhat fashionable or opportune to be Christian — which, of course, is a mixed blessing.

Nonetheless, this reprieve was welcome. But a monumental controversy quickly shook Christianity to the core. Just as Christians were coming out of the darkness of persecution and into the light of toleration, free to build a Christian society, they were met with the most serious challenge to apostolic belief in Church history.

9

WAS JESUS DIVINE? ATHANASIUS AND THE ARIAN CONTROVERSY

As persecution ended, five million Christians were living throughout the Mediterranean world and beyond, and not entirely in contact with one another. The Church enjoyed a remarkable unity, but inevitably, disagreements over doctrine began to arise. Apostolic teaching did not evolve into precise, detailed, analyses on every doctrine, and thus it was only natural that Christian thinkers would delve into the depths of these issues. As they asserted their ideas, debates ensued among bishops and scholars on matters such as the nature of Christ, the Trinitarian nature of God, the identity and role of the Blessed Mother, and how Christians should live their lives. The Church's efforts to address these disputes sharpened her ability to discern and promulgate doctrine. Leading the way were a number of saints who rose up to fight against heresies and inspire the Christian faithful to grow more deeply in the Faith. A number of these saints are now considered Fathers of the Church. Among the most prominent heresies of this era were Donatism, Pelagianism, Nestorianism, and Iconoclasm. But we will begin with the most serious one: Arianism.

Just as the ink dried on the Edict of Milan, Arius, a priest from Alexandria in Egypt — one of the great centers of the Christian Faith — began to preach that Jesus was not divine but a created being. For much of the rest of the fourth century, this proposition created a massive division among the bishops. As the Church began to wrestle with Arius's teaching, a number of bishops and scholars, many of whom are saints, took up the challenge to defend apostolic teaching. We will see that this is a pattern throughout all history.

The Church's greatest champion against Arianism, also from Alexandria, was Athanasius. If not for **Saint Athanasius** (297–373), we all might be Arians today. If not for Athanasius, his allies, and their tireless fight for a proper understanding of who Jesus was, today we might look back at the "divinity heresy" that claimed Jesus was God. Perhaps it would have been called the "Athanasian heresy." Truth hung in the balance for decades as bishops chose sides. This makes Saint Athanasius one of the most significant saints in Church history. In a real sense, he *made* history. Athanasius is justly deemed one of the great Fathers of the Church.

At the time that Arius came forward in the late 310s and 320s, the Church more assumed than defined the precise nature of Jesus. And the Church was not yet experienced in resolving deep issues through worldwide councils of bishops or other means. Often it took a controversy to force Church leaders to delve into an issue and seek the guidance of the Holy Spirit to resolve it. The Church to this point had understood Jesus to be divine; apostolic teaching held that Jesus was divine and human. But, before the advent of precise and thorough pronouncements, there was room for bright scholars such as Arius to speculate, and sometimes to drift beyond apostolic teaching.

Arius sincerely believed that Jesus was not divine, but was the first creature whom God created. He agreed that Jesus was supreme Lord, Redeemer, and Son of God, but disagreed that Jesus was divine. Arius preached that, as supreme as Jesus was, "There was a time when he was not." A gifted scholar and communicator, Arius and his many supporters (which included several emperors), were persuasive, and many bishops embraced this new teaching. This had major implications for the meaning of the Eucharist, the Incarnation, the Trinity, the Blessed Mother, and the relationship between God and the Church. These beliefs and practices, and devotion to Mary, were at the core of Christian life.

• • •

The Arian crisis led bishops to advance the practice of meeting in *councils* to work out doctrinal matters. In time, many of these councils took on special significance, and today, an *ecumenical council* — a gathering of bishops from the entire Church — holds a special place in the Magisterium, or teaching authority of the Church. The New Testament, though mostly identified, was still short of final formation, and the biblical texts did not fully spell out the precise understanding on these issues. That was not the purpose of the Scriptures. The Holy Spirit left it to the Church to work these matters out under his guidance. Hard feelings, exiles, interference from civil authorities, and genuine differences of opinion among Christian bishops — devout or not — made for a messy process. But when these councils were over, who Jesus was and the nature of God as Trinity were resolved for all time. Five crucial councils were held from 325 through 451, each one working to discern and define the nature of Jesus and the Trinity.

The emperor Constantine convened the first of these councils in Nicaea, a city near Constantinople in 325, to deal with the Arian question. At this Council of Nicaea, the gathered bishops and their assistants debated the issue of the nature of Jesus. Athanasius, a twenty-eight-year-old deacon and assistant to the bishop of Alexandria, took an active part. The "apostolic" or "orthodox" perspective prevailed and Arianism was condemned as heretical. The earliest version of the *Nicene Creed* originates from and is named after this council, although a later council modified and expanded this Creed, or statement of faith.

The key phrase, advocated by Athanasius, was that Jesus was "one in being" with the Father. A sidenote: In an earlier English translation of the Nicene Creed used at Mass, we used to say "one in being" with the Father.

This is a direct translation from the Greek *homoousios*, the word in the Greek text of the Creed from the Council of Nicaea. In the new translation of liturgical texts introduced in 2011, the English word we now use is *consubstantial*. This is a translation from *consubstantialis*, used in traditional Latin liturgical texts, and the Latin equivalent of *homoousios*. *Consubstantial* and *one in being* mean the same thing. Each is a rendering in English of *homoousios* from the original Creed.

According to Athanasius, over three hundred of the world's one thousand eight hundred bishops attended the Council of Nicaea. This was impressive given the difficulties of travel in that era; but with over 80 percent of the bishops not in attendance, numerous bishops clung to Arian belief. Declaring Jesus to be one in being with the Father, that is, divine, remained controversial. The historian and bishop Eusebius even criticized this formulation as "unscriptural." Aggressive bishops and secular rulers, including emperors (Constantius, the son of Constantine, and Julian the Apostate among them) remained a powerful force in support of Arianism. In the mid-fourth century, Arianism grew to claim the support of over half the bishops, particularly in the East. As Saint Jerome noted when he looked back on this crucial time, "One morning the Church awoke, groaned, and realized it was Arian."[1] The tenacity and burning commitment of Athanasius and several other key saints and scholars to the truth of Jesus' divine nature were vital in turning back the tide.

As the empire became more Christianized, the line between Church and state blurred. Emperors involved themselves in religious matters and many Christians — including bishops — were often attracted to Arianism not so much out of theological conviction but because embracing the emperor's view was a popular and career-enhancing thing to do. And, as Athanasius discovered, opposing the prevailing imperial theology was a career hazard. Athanasius was attacked and repeatedly banished from his diocese, enduring more polemics, exile, and personal attacks than any person could be expected to survive. But survive he did. His opponents once even trumped up a murder charge against him — until the supposed victim was confirmed as alive, something most people had known all along. (Fake news is not new.) Athanasius was a prime target because he was a brilliant, skilled, passionate, and influential theologian and a popular bishop from the renowned See of

Alexandria, the most formidable foe the Arians had to face.

Athanasius's most significant attribute was his resolve. He was successful in combatting the powerful and well-connected Arians because he never abandoned the fight. He became bishop of Alexandria in 327 and was immediately drawn into the fight with the Arians. Athanasius was forced out as bishop of Alexandria and sent into exile *five times* — to Germany, to Rome, and to the North African desert. Each time he was exiled, he could have accepted defeat. Despite the relentless attacks he faced and the efforts to silence and marginalize him, Athanasius continued to fight, using his considerable pastoral zeal and skills as a scholar and expert in Scripture. He stayed in contact with and fostered alliances with orthodox authorities, including popes, and continued to speak out and write. His *Orationes Contra Arianos* were his foremost treatise contesting Arianism. After each exile, he worked his way back — sometimes benefitting from the ever-changing winds of politics — only to be driven out again. Athanasius spent seventeen years in these five periods of exile as Arian and orthodox emperors and bishops fought for control. When he was finally able to spend his last seven years as bishop, Athanasius organized a "Nicene Party," an influential group of Church leaders who defended doctrinal orthodoxy and pressed the cause against the Arians. Although Athanasius died eight years prior, his Nicene Party was instrumental at the Council of Alexandria in turning the tide against Arianism.

Athanasius was active in other endeavors as well. He moved forward a correct understanding of God as Trinity, an endeavor which, as we will see, other contemporaries developed further. He advocated the monastic movement and greatly admired his friend, St. Anthony of Egypt. His *Life of Antony* was widely read and influential both in his own time and in the centuries following, helping to steer monasticism out of Egypt and into Europe. And, as we have noted, Athanasius was influential in defining the precise canon of the New Testament. Late in life, Athanasius, a devotee of Scripture, compiled a list of twenty-seven books that matches the canon we have today. This helped to set in motion the final affirmation of the New Testament a few decades later. He was a prolific writer. One of his treatises, *On the Incarnation*, arose out of his opposition to the Arians, and survives and circulates among Christian readers to this day. Athanasius was an engaged, beloved bishop to his flock, even when in exile, and wrote pastoral "Festal Letters" to his people each year.

Athanasius lived at a pivotal moment in Church history, as bishops were growing in influence, as the Church was digging out of persecution, rapidly expanding, and working out crucial doctrinal matters that would affect posterity. It is hard to overestimate the enormous influence Athanasius had on Church history. His appearance on the world stage at his time as a fierce defender of orthodoxy was providential.

The second of the five "Christological" councils, the Council of Alexandria, was held in 362 and hosted by Athanasius, who by this time was bishop of Alexandria. The gathered bishops continued the fight against Arianism but also addressed the related issue of the Trinity. Deepening the Church's understanding of the nature of God, this council declared that the Holy Spirit also was "one in being" with the Father. This brought the Church closer to discerning that God was a Trinity of Three Persons. The Church's Jewish heritage affirmed the truth of the One God; now the mystery of the One God as Three Persons was recognized. The origins of the doctrine of the Trinity are apostolic, but it took time to reach a full understanding, first of the divinity of Jesus as the Son, and then also of the divinity of the Holy Spirit. That process continued in the next council and in the reflections and writings of bishops and Church Fathers — including Augustine — in the following century.

Theologians were delving deeply into these matters, discerning such delicate theological points that the Son is "begotten" by the Father, while the Holy Spirit "proceeds" from the Father. In later centuries, the Western Church, in order to specify that the Holy Spirit also proceeds from the Son as well as from the Father, added the word *filioque* (Latin for "and the Son") to the Nicene Creed. This was *not* in the Creed as adopted at Nicaea or Constantinople, and this Western addition to the Nicene Creed would cause serious problems between East and West centuries later.

This council also declared that the Bishop of Constantinople (eventually to be called *patriarch*) was first in significance after the Bishop of Rome. This had the dual effect both of acknowledging the primacy of Rome and also challenging that primacy, setting up further controversies between East and West in the ensuing centuries.

⑩
ALLIES OF TRUTH

Athanasius was not alone. Although he could rightly be considered the leading opponent of Arianism, he could not have been successful without allies, including Church and sometimes civic leaders — and other saints.

St. Cyril of Jerusalem (315–386), one of two saints of this era named Cyril, was a Scripture scholar and an excellent preacher who became bishop of his home city of Jerusalem. Much like Athanasius, he had a stormy ride as bishop. Several times he was driven out as Arians exercised their power. Each time Cyril was able to return to his post as bishop, but nearly half of his years as bishop were spent in exile. Cyril was known for his pastoral and charitable approach to debates. This caused each side at times to accuse him of being sympathetic to the other. While others were fiery, Cyril remained conciliatory and did not break friendships with Arians. He remained a fully orthodox opponent of Arianism, however, even as he gave witness to the call to charity.

St. Basil the Great (329–379), a bishop in the East and a Church Father, was also among the most important opponents of Arianism in the East. Basil became a monk, and then a priest, and founded the first monastery in Asia Minor. He developed a *rule* for his monks that, like Saint Pachomius's, emphasized living in community more than isolation — a significant advance in the direction of monastic life. Due to his holiness of life, scholarship, and his leadership skills, Basil became a *metropolitan* in Caesarea in the area of the Holy Land — a title common in the East for a bishop over bishops. This brought him into conflict in the 370s with Valens, the last Arian Emperor (who was also behind one of Athanasius's exiles). In a great battle of wills, Basil stood his ground against Valens, and it was Valens who backed down. Basil was a leader at the Council of Constantinople in 381 — a few years after the death of Athanasius — and as such, instrumental in the condemnation of Arianism. This council and the death of Valens were crucial factors in the final demise of the Arian threat among bishops and rulers.

In addition to his holiness and scholarship, Basil was known for his great oratorical skills, as a great writer, and as an advocate for the importance of the Eucharist and good liturgy. As a bishop and pastor, he spearheaded efforts to aid the poor and strengthen the clergy. He also fought against prostitution.

If it were not for Basil's older sister, **Saint Macrina** (c. 327–379), Basil might never have entered religious life or followed a Christian path. Basil returned from university studies in Athens, proud and eager to embark on a secular career. Macrina, as perhaps only a big sister with a deep faith could, leaned on her younger brother and persuaded him to use his abundant gifts in service to God instead. They came from an impressive family: Their parents were also recognized as saints, and their brother was St. Gregory of Nyssa.

Two Gregories, both learned Fathers of the Church, were also opponents of Arianism as well as advocates for the divinity of the Holy Spirit. They are Basil's brother **St. Gregory of Nyssa** (330–395) and their friend, **St. Gregory Nazianzen** (329–389). These three are often called the "Cappadocian Fathers" from their origins in Cappadocia, an area in central Asia Minor. Both Gregories were effective in winning back many who had become Arian, and also suffered persecution from Arians. They, too, were active at the Council of Constantinople.

Basil appointed his brother Gregory as bishop of Nyssa with the expectation that he would fight the Arians. Gregory did not have the skills to be successful in this particular quasi-political task, but he became renowned as a scholar of Scripture and doctrine and as a powerful preacher, blending great scholarship with practical advice.

Gregory Nazianzen, whom Basil had met as a fellow student in Athens, was also a great scholar, considered a Doctor of the Church, and also a bishop. A group of fellow bishops urged him to go to Constantinople in 380, which at that time was heavily Arian. His efforts produced numerous converts from among the Arians, tipping the scales in favor of Trinitarian Catholicism, but brought down on him severe persecution and abuse as well. A newly converted emperor, Theodosius, came to power and decreed that his subjects be Catholic, and appointed Gregory as patriarch of Constantinople. It was from this position that Gregory presided over the Council of Constantinople in 381. Arianism was essentially defeated, but Gregory retired, exhausted from the stress of his many battles.

In addition to securing a consensus against Arianism, the Council of Constantinople also expanded and promulgated the Nicene Creed to a form close to what we have and use today, and reaffirmed the divinity of the Holy Spirit.

Arianism, defeated at last through much of the Church, did not disappear. It survived in small pockets for a few centuries — in areas such as Arabia and among several of the northern tribes who would eventually bring down the Roman Empire in the West — but by the end of the fourth century, it was vanquished as a force in the heart of the Christian world. In its stead, other controversies emerged.

ONE PERSON, TWO NATURES

A new issue concerning the nature of Christ was more complex than the Arian issue. The question was: Just how did this divinity work in light of the evident humanity of Christ? The Gnostics, among others, had already resolved this by denying Jesus' humanity — the other end of the spectrum. Jesus, they claimed, only *appeared* to be human. Irenaeus and others had worked to refute the Gnostics. But as the Arian influence faded by the end of the fourth century, other theories on the nature of Christ surfaced and grew in popularity. These were the subject of two fifth-century councils, the fourth and fifth of the series of councils on the nature of Christ and the Trinity.

The Council of Ephesus in 431 was called to address the *Nestorians*, followers of Nestorius, then the patriarch of Constantinople. This city, rapidly growing in size and influence both in the Church and the world, was the seat of the emperor in the East, and was also fast becoming the leading center of Eastern Christianity. This made Nestorius highly influential. Nestorius questioned how Jesus could be divine and human. He came to contend that Jesus' divine and human natures were separate, and thus Mary, the mother of Jesus, was only *Christotokos*, that is, mother or "bearer" of Christ — his human nature only. The council, however, declared that Jesus was one Person, with divine and human natures which were *not* separate. Thus Mary was *Theotokos*, Greek for bearer or Mother of God, not just mother of Jesus' human nature. This understanding is well known today, but the council fathers had to work their way through this at Ephesus.

St. Cyril of Alexandria (376–444) presided over the Council of Ephesus and was the most instrumental voice in leading the bishops to this determination. He was a brilliant theologian and is also a Father of the Church. At the council and beyond, Cyril was a strong advocate of Jesus as both divine and human. He had risen to become patriarch of Alexandria, and from there he had come into conflict with Nestorius in the years leading up to the council.

Cyril also defended and clarified the doctrines of the Trinity and Incarnation, and he was instrumental in advancing the apostolic nature of true doctrine. The Church does not merely discern a doctrine, he taught, but must identify its origin in the teaching of the apostles. The Faith is handed down from the apostles to their followers, and identifying that connection was vital to finding the truth. This is important for understanding the basis for the Church's teaching authority. Cyril also followed and advanced the teachings of Athanasius and identified those teachings as handed down from apostolic teaching.

Without Cyril's opposition to Nestorius, this matter may have come out differently. Nestorius, defeated, was deposed as patriarch and eventually forced into exile. Cyril, in charity, sought to find unity and common ground with the defeated Nestorians in the years after Ephesus. Although Nestorianism lingered in Central Asia for some time, it no longer held sway through most of the Christian world, and was deemed a heresy.

Still, there was uncertainty among bishops and theologians on the full understanding of precisely who Christ was. **Pope St. Leo the Great** (c. 400–461) called the Council of Chalcedon to address these issues. Held in 451, it was the last of the five great Christological councils. It declared that Jesus was one Person, with two natures, human and divine, but those two natures were not separate but closely united and without division. They chose the term *hypostatic union* to describe the relationship between these two natures. This is why Mary is called the Mother of God, and not just the Mother of Christ — Jesus' divine and human natures are in union, not separated. The Council of Chalcedon also gave final and official approval to what we know today as the Nicene Creed, first drafted at the Council of Nicaea and modified at the Council of Constantinople.

Pope Leo composed what is now called the *Tome of Leo*, a letter to the patriarch of Constantinople which paralleled the teachings of the council on the unified natures of Christ. Leo's leadership at the council, and the use of his Tome as an authoritative doctrinal explanation, advanced the universal authority of the Bishop of Rome — a key development of the still-emerging papacy. These Christological councils were held in the East and managed primarily by the bishops of the East. Leo's involvement as Bishop of Rome, the see of purported primacy and as a representative of the West, helped to enhance the level of unity and universality in the decrees of these councils.

Leo also met with the invading Attila the Hun in 452 and, remarkably, managed to persuade him not to sack Rome. Later, when the Vandals did sack Rome, Leo persuaded them not to burn the city. He ministered to those injured in the attack and helped to rebuild Rome.

The council fathers at Chalcedon also recognized **St. John Chrysostom**

(347–407) as a Doctor of the Church. (A *Doctor* is one whose teaching on doctrinal matters is considered especially important. John is also deemed a Father as well.) John's nickname of *Chrysostom* means "golden-mouth" in Greek. John was an extraordinary preacher and an accomplished scholar. His preaching had a major effect on the spiritual life in his home city of Antioch, and in 398 he was appointed patriarch of Constantinople. From there, his attention to the poor, his ascetical practices, and his firm commitment to moral standards benefitted his flock, but also made him enemies in high places. He suffered exiles, denouncements, and physical suffering in his later years, yet continued to write and defend the Faith until dying of exhaustion during a series of forced marches as part of his last exile.

The work of Chalcedon and the other councils was intricate theology, but these councils were works of the Holy Spirit to assist the Church for all time in gaining a deeper and more accurate understanding of the nature of God. Not all agreed; in addition to the remnants of the Nestorians, a sect called the *Monophysites*, who believed that Christ had only one nature — divine — held a presence in the East for many years. But in time this too faded from significance.

The Council of Chalcedon brought to an effective conclusion the Christological debates that had raged throughout most of the fourth and parts of the fifth centuries. After Chalcedon, the unified nature of Jesus as divine and human and the nature of God as a Trinity of Persons became accepted as revealed truth for most of the Christian world.

These five councils, and the saints who worked on behalf of apostolic teaching during and alongside these councils, did the heavy theological lifting to provide us the understanding that we have today of Christ, the Holy Spirit, and the Trinity.

11

A BRIDGE FROM ANTIQUITY: AUGUSTINE AND HIS CONTEMPORARIES

Saints Jerome, Ambrose, and Augustine, contemporaries and Fathers of the Church, were among the giants who shaped Church history both in their own time and down through the ages. And Saints Monica and Pope Damasus were instrumental in the lives of these great scholars and theologians. Together, they formed a bridge for the Church to move from antiquity to the Middle Ages.

"Ignorance of Scripture is ignorance of Christ" — this is the most famous saying of **Saint Jerome** (342–420) and flowed out of his life's vocation of making the Bible accessible to the Church. Jerome's contributions to enhancing the place of Scripture in the Church are of monumental importance, leaving their mark on the Church to this day. His greatest achievement was translating the entire Bible — both Old and New Testaments — from the original Hebrew, Aramaic, and Greek into Latin, the common language of the West. This made it possible for most of the communities of the West to have direct access to Scripture. We know this today as the *Vulgate*, the most used translation of Scripture for centuries, made official by the Council of Trent in the sixteenth century, and the basis for translations into modern languages until just decades ago. The Douay-Rheims English translation from Jerome's *Vulgate* was the standard for centuries and is still circulated today.

It is difficult today to fathom the tremendous value for the Church of a one-Bible, common-language collection of Sacred Scripture. Without Jerome's translation, the accessibility of the Scriptures throughout the Christian West would have been limited and delayed. In addition to its quality of scholarship, Jerome's translation was also quality prose — its readability helped Christians to read and understand the New Testament. Before his conversion, Saint Augustine turned up his nose at the poor quality of the then-existing Latin translation of the New Testament, delaying his study of the Scriptures. Jerome fixed that.

This was no small task. Jerome had to be a first-rate scholar to begin with — which he was. Augustine once quipped that "if Jerome doesn't know it, no one knows it." Jerome developed a scholar's knowledge of ancient Hebrew, Aramaic, Greek, and Latin. It took years to translate from the original languages to Latin, line by line, book by book. Errors or mistranslations were remarkably limited. Modern scholars, with many more tools to work with, have made improvements in today's translations, but Jerome's Vulgate still remains as a lofty work. And Jerome did his painstaking work in the late 300s and early 400s — just after the Church gave final approval to the canon of the New Testament.

Jerome was not involved in finalizing the New Testament canon, nor was he directly involved in the Christological debates that were occurring around him. He did get into a series of scholarly debates on numerous other issues, including on the Pelagian heresy, on celibacy, and on interpretation of Scripture, even once debating with Augustine; but his main contribution was spreading access to Scripture. He eventually was ordained a priest, but he never became a bishop.

Jerome immersed himself in Scripture. For him, this was not merely a scholar's task, but a personal connection with the Word of the Divine Creator. Thus his famous observation that ignorance of Scripture is ignorance of Christ — he meant it, and he lived it, if imperfectly. He cared about what God was communicating and burned to share it. As his work proceeded, he reflected on the meaning of what he translated and wrote Scripture commentaries from the fruit of his reflections. This was a scholar who loved God and sought him.

As devoted as he was, Jerome was not a perfect man. It seems that God used his flaws to help set up his life vocation. Jerome was cantankerous, hot-tempered, and had a sarcastic wit. He was combative and regularly got himself into scrapes — many of which he probably did not need to get into. This led him to move often, as he sought to get away from his opponents and to give himself a chance to start anew, repenting of his personal failings. Though flawed, Jerome was self-aware and struggled to overcome his weaknesses. He spent several years as a hermit, praying and fasting in the Syrian desert, and eventually settled in Bethlehem, where he founded a monastery. This is where he did much of his work on Scripture, and where he died. Sainthood does not require perfection, but a strong, devoted, repentant, and persistent faith. And charity — Jerome knew this and endeavored to practice the virtue. While he was working on Scripture in Bethlehem in the year 410, Rome was sacked by the Visigoths. A stream of refugees fled the city, many ending up near Jerome in Bethlehem. Jerome suspended his beloved Scripture studies to help tend to the refugees — his Christian duty of love. As he observed, "Today we translate the words of the Scriptures into deeds and instead of speaking saintly words we must act them."[1]

Saint Jerome might not have taken up the huge task of translating the Scriptures had it not been for the encouragement, even insistence of **Pope St. Damasus I** (305–384, r. 366–384). This pope took the young Jerome under his wing as his secretary, saw the tremendous potential in this brilliant but ill-tempered scholar, and appointed Jerome to the task. Damasus was himself well versed in the Scriptures and worked to settle the canon, particularly at the Council of Constantinople in 381. The canon and the translation worked together to solidify the New Testament as divinely inspired and at the heart of the Church.

Damasus was another key figure in defending doctrine from heresies, including Arianism. Also, he popularized the veneration of martyrs as a special class of heroic Christians. It was on his watch as Bishop of Rome that the Roman Emperor declared Christianity to be the state religion. This led to a large increase in the number of Christians — even to a majority within the empire. But, at best, that was a mixed blessing.

SAINT AUGUSTINE

If the Church were to list a "top ten" saints of all time, **Saint Augustine** (354–430) would surely be on it. His is the consummate sinner-to-saint conversion story. His *Confessions*, the heartfelt story of his early life and conversion, is one of the most powerful and insightful Christian works ever written. One of the most profound and well-loved quotations from Augustine is from the opening page of his *Confessions*: "Our hearts are made for you, O God, and they are restless until they rest in You."

Augustine was born in Tagaste, North Africa. His mother was Catholic; his father was not. He did not absorb his mother's faith, and rose from youth to become a pagan scholar in nearby Carthage. Seeking meaning and purpose in life, he joined the Manichaean sect, a dualistic religion similar to Gnosticism, which originated in Persia in the third century. For years Augustine had a live-in girlfriend and then a son, and moved to Italy in search of career advancement. He taught rhetoric in Milan, at that time the seat of the emperor. After a tortuous struggle in search of the truth, Augustine converted to Christianity. In the *Confessions*, he describes his gradual movement toward his conversion. It culminated one day when he took the Scriptures and went off by himself to reflect. He heard some children playing a game, and singing, "Tolle lege" (Take up and read). He "took up" the Scriptures and came upon Romans 13:11–14. This passage, which ends with, "But put on the Lord Jesus Christ, and make no provision for the desires of the flesh" (Rom 13:14, NABRE), was the final straw. Augustine saw the light of truth.

After his conversion, he returned to coastal North Africa, having first to bury his mother who died before they could sail. He later became bishop of Hippo, a coastal city in North Africa, and one of the greatest Christian scholars of all time. His expositions on faith, love, the nature of grace, the Trinity, and the relationship between the earthly and heavenly worlds, among many other topics, remain influential today.

Augustine is one of the most quoted and referenced saints in history. The *Catechism of the Catholic Church* quotes Augustine more than anyone beyond biblical times. This is not just because he was brilliant, although his brilliance informed his teaching, but primarily because of the depth of his faith and the insights that flowed from that faith. More than most, he understood the enormity of God's grace, flowing to us flawed humans out of his infinite, incomprehensible love. From his own life history, he waded into deep meditations on who God is and how he loves his human creation. Augustine is one of the best windows to the nature of the God of love. He came to understand that faith was not an abstraction or a mere set of rules for right living. Rather, it was a *relationship* with the eternal God of love himself. God was a personal Being who loved him and sought that relationship. Augustine pined to be in close relationship with God, and that understanding is behind all his brilliant theological writings. He wrote a significant explanation on the Trinity, assisting the Church in fathoming the coequal Triune nature of the Father, Son, and Holy Spirit. He realized that the key to understanding the Trinity is love: a relationship of love among the Persons of the Trinity, from which love flows to us.

Beyond the intimate relationship the believer may have with God, Augustine also reflected on the nature of society and how it relates to God's kingdom, particularly in his great work *The City of God*. And he was a fiery defender of orthodox faith, which led to multiple battles with and defense against heresies. He battled against the Donatists, a North African sect that broke away from the Church over issues on the clergy. *Donatism*, which grew in Augustine's time and lasted into the sixth century, alleged that priests must be faultless in order to be ministers of sacramental grace. Augustine enhanced the Church position that grace flows through the ministry of priests despite their shortcomings. This is a recognition that we all are sinful, and that God's grace overcomes our sinfulness. Augustine also tangled with *Pelagianism*, a heresy promulgated by a British monk who was a contemporary of his, and which denied the effect of original sin and asserted that the only way to salvation was strict moral living. Augustine argued that this denies the essential role of Jesus' sacrifice and God's grace. We are all sinners, damaged by original sin and our own sins, and we cannot save ourselves simply by being good. This was a major theological insight (and one which Luther drew from 1,100 years later).

The Church owes much to Augustine for advancing her understanding of what sacraments are and of their effect. It was Augustine who taught that sacraments were visible signs of the supernatural and portals of grace. The sacraments are at the center of Catholic Church's life, self-understanding, and pastoral practice. This emphasis on sacraments has served the Church well through her history, not only for the pastoral benefit of her members, but in preserving the connection to the divine and defending against the various spirits of the times.

Some say that the battle against the Pelagians may have pushed Augustine too far on the grace/works continuum and away from a proper appreciation of the human will and response to God with our works. Augustine offered brilliant insights on grace, faith, and works, but even the greatest of theologians and saints are not infallible. The beauty of the Catholic Church is that she is a universal family beyond time and place. Many admirers of Augustine have acknowledged his deep insights into God's grace but have added recognition of the cooperative role of our obedience to God through our works. This delicate dynamic of faith and works has challenged the Church throughout her history (especially at the time of the Reformation) as she has sought to reach a proper understanding that encompasses the role of each. We are saved by faith, as Saint Paul says, but we are called to follow Christ in right living out of that faith as well. Augustine laid a strong foundation for future theological reflections on the issue.

More than just a scholar, Augustine was a diligent pastor to the people in his diocese for thirty-five years. His influence was not just for posterity, but also in his own time. Saint Jerome said in a letter to Augustine in 418, "You are known throughout the world; Catholics honor and esteem you as the one who has established the ancient faith anew."[2] He died in Hippo, as bishop of his flock, with the invading Vandals about to take and burn the town. By the providential intervention of Augustine's friends and followers, his writings survived the mass destruction carried out by the Vandals, and these works, perhaps the greatest collection of Christian writing by one person in Church history, have been preserved for all posterity.

SAINTS MONICA AND AMBROSE

Augustine was one of history's greatest saints, but what if he had never converted? What if he did not have a mother so intent on his acceptance of the Christian Faith, to the point of hounding him? Augustine's mother, **Saint Monica** (331–387), was a North African woman surrounded by strong, non-Christian men — her husband Patricius and her son Augustine. She easily could have been dominated by either or both of them, but she held her own as a serious Christian woman. She could have dialed down her faith and just floated along, but she burned for the conversion of her family. No doubt the Holy Spirit was alive in her, and it appears evident that God raised her up to play a vital role for the conversion of her husband and son. Without Monica's obedient embrace of the Faith and relentless efforts to draw her son to conversion, we likely would not have had the blessing of Saint Augustine.

She pined for Patricius's conversion, and he did embrace the Faith as he lay dying. Not long after, Augustine left for Rome. Monica saw something in her son that led her to virtually heroic efforts to chase him across land and sea and press constantly for his conversion. She prayed for him constantly, sought to persuade him, even traveled after him to Milan where she helped connect him with Ambrose, bishop of Milan. She rejoiced when at last Augustine converted, and she died soon after, before reaching home. Her work, it would seem, was completed.

Augustine was inspired to pen his *Confessions* in part as a tribute to his mother's love and persistence. This book, while primarily Augustine's spiritual reflection on his personal path to Christianity, is also the source of our knowledge of Monica's life and her faith in action. His account of her fruitful efforts to lead him and his father to the Faith has given Christians over the centuries encouragement and reason to hope that prayer for their loved ones may well be answered. Like Barnabas, Monica was a saint in the background who loved and sought to obey God to great effect — for more famous saints and for the Church's benefit throughout the ages.

Along with Monica, the other key player in Augustine's conversion was **Saint Ambrose** (340–397). A powerful scholar who could speak to Augustine's intellect on equal footing, he was able to provide Augustine with the theological justifications for the Christian Faith. Ambrose brought Scripture alive for Augustine, demonstrating how to read the Old Testament as a "journey toward Christ" and he "enabled Augustine to solve the intellectual difficulties which he had wrestled with earlier in his life.[3] Ambrose baptized Augustine in the year 387.

But Ambrose was a significant figure in his own right. In 374 — while still a catechumen — he skillfully quelled a near-riot between Arians and Catholics. Such was the impression he made upon his community that he was made bishop of Milan — by popular acclamation, succeeding an Arian. During his more than twenty years as bishop, Ambrose was a formidable preacher and a fierce guardian of his flock. Ambrose served in the late 300s — a particularly turbulent time. Though fading, the Arians were still present and aggressive, the Empire was unstable, society was weakening, and northern tribes were flowing down to undermine the Roman world. Ambrose was the most powerful opponent of the Arians in the West, twice standing down the Arian emperor Valentinian who tried to force churches to be turned over to the Arians. At risk to himself, he faced down the emperor Theodosius in 390 over a slaughter of civilians in Thessalonica which the emperor had ordered, forcing the emperor to repentance. He also opposed the intrusions of secular authorities into the life and leadership of the Church. And he readily acknowledged the primacy of the Bishop of Rome — in one of his writings, he asserted, "Where Peter is, there is the Church."[4]

Ambrose was one of the most influential forces in the rise of the Catholic Christian Faith in the West. Within the Church herself, he fought for orthodox doctrine and holiness of life. And he was a persistent defender of the Church against her enemies. His ministry within and on behalf of the Church also had the effect of enhancing the significance of the office of bishop as shepherd, pastor, and leader. All these contributions were instrumental in preparing the Church for the post-Roman world.

12

THE EMPIRE COLLAPSES; THE CHURCH FILLS THE VOID

Since Rome had become unsafe and marked by faded glory, the remaining emperors in the fifth century had relocated to Ravenna, in northeast Italy. In 476, the army of the ethnic "barbarian" Odoacer defeated the army of the last Roman Emperor, ironically named Romulus Augustulus, at the battle of Ravenna. This marked the end of the Roman Empire in the West. The empire in the East, seated at Constantinople, continued on for a millennium, but was on a slow path toward demise as well.

The fall of the empire in the West was a long time coming. Since the time of Constantine, a century and a half earlier, the Christian population had grown to become a majority in the empire. However, this did not stem the steady march of social, political, military, and economic decline throughout Roman society. (This is comparable to American society today, in which a lingering Christian majority has not prevented a similar decline in the fabric of our own society.) Further, from the fourth century on, Germanic tribes from the north were pouring down upon the lands of the weakening empire, migrating, intermarrying, and especially invading, changing the face of society. The pagan Franks overran much of the western ends of the empire, particularly the area of present-day France. As we shall see, their paganism would later work to the benefit of the Church. The Vandals, recently converted to Arianism, moved through much of Spain and conquered North Africa. They were at the gates of Hippo as Augustine died. The Lombards invaded northern Italy, captured Milan, where the fourth-century Western emperors had taken up residence (including in Ambrose's day), and threatened Rome. The various tribes of Goths from central Europe, also Arian and themselves fleeing the Huns, poured into Italy, sometimes as invaders, other times as allies. In one of the biggest blows to Rome in its illustrious thousand-year history, Visigoth leader Alaric sacked Rome itself in 410, effectively ending the city's status as a capital. In the absence of a strong Roman military, these tribes were free to roam and pillage. The empire was in the state of near economic, social, and military collapse. Then came Odoacer's final blow in 476. Historians debate the timing of the Western empire's actual end, but with the demise of the last emperor and the effective end of the Roman government, the traditional date of 476 remains a compelling one. The Catholic bishops were left to provide the most effective semblance of structure and leadership amidst the chaos of the times. This was to be both a burden and an opportunity.

The fall of the Roman Empire in the West was one of the most consequential events in all of human history. The landscape of Europe was changed forever. The thousand-year reign of Greco-Roman civilization came to an end. Much was lost. The achievements of law, philosophy, literature, science, architecture, and agriculture, and the practices of reading, thinking, building, and living together in community all were severely impaired or suspended until a later time as political and social turmoil rolled over the lands of the erstwhile empire. Politically and socially, the next three centuries can be accurately called "the Dark Ages." Yet they also became a time of new growth for the Church.

The Christian people were as affected by this upheaval as everyone living at the time. But it was the Church which led the way out and toward a new civilization. In the short term, bishops and Church leaders were the most effective at picking up the pieces and helping the population through these times. And as we shall see, it was monks who emerged from the ashes of the empire, who helped to sustain and inspire faith and to preserve much of the Greco-Roman literature and learning. The Bishop of Rome grew in influence, almost of necessity, as various popes began to fill the vacuum in spiritual and temporal authority and made efforts to evangelize the peoples of the Germanic tribes. Remarkably, many in these tribes were open to the Faith, including some of their leaders. The gradual conversion of most of these peoples, through missionary activity, assimilation and intermingling, and at times by conquest, is one of the most significant developments in the centuries after Rome's fall. This marked a new phase of missionary expansion beyond the Mediterranean and to the north. By the dawn of the ninth century, both Church and state had recovered significantly. And numerous saints led the way.

The monastic movement in the Middle Ages is often credited with nurturing, stabilizing, and even helping to preserve and expand the Christian Faith. Monasteries spread from the deserts of Egypt and into the heart of Europe from the fourth century on and became places of faith and learning in and near towns and cities as well as the less Christian countryside. Their interaction with the local communities varied, but whether direct or indirect, monks and nuns were instrumental in supporting and expanding the Faith. The monastic movement was at its peak in the Middle Ages, but its origins were in the fourth to sixth centuries and traceable to two key saint founders: Martin of Tours and Benedict of Nursia.

A soldier from Hungary who converted to Christianity, **St. Martin of Tours** (316–397) is credited with founding the first monastery in Gaul (now France). Martin battled against Arians, and was driven from Italy by the then-Arian bishop of Milan, Ambrose's predecessor. Martin settled in Gaul and began to live as a hermit on land given to him by St. Hilary of Poitiers. He attracted others, and from this arose the monastic community. Martin later became an energetic and effective bishop of

Tours, fostering faith and fighting paganism. His ministry in drawing the people of Gaul to the Christian Faith was so effective that he remains one of the patron saints of France. His evangelism also created a foundation for the Christianizing of the Franks a century later.

St. Hilary of Poitiers (315–368) was not only influential in fostering the life and vocation of Martin of Tours, but in his own right was an important figure in the fourth-century Church. He was born in Gaul, and, although he was married, was elected bishop of Poitiers in 350. He became a supporter of Athanasius and a fierce opponent of the Arians, suffering exile at one time at the hands of Arian bishops. Ironically, he was so persuasive in refuting Arians at a council in the East in 359 that the Arian emperor sent him back home to Gaul to be rid of him. In all his polemics with the Arians, however, he never lost his sense of charity toward them. Hilary, a leading theologian of the day who earned the admiration of such luminaries as Jerome and Augustine, has been declared a Doctor of the Church.

The most influential monastic in all of Catholic history was **Saint Benedict** (480–547). Benedict, from Nursia in Italy, was well born and was sent to Rome to study. He found Rome to be a cauldron of vice. The empire had collapsed, the city's leaders were atheist or pagan, the Church was beset by schisms, and Christians and non-Christians alike had fallen into serious moral decline. Benedict was so appalled that he fled Rome to live in solitude. Eventually, as others came to him to follow his way of life, Benedict set up groups of monks to live in Christian community. In time he settled at Monte Cassino, south of Rome, where he built his main monastery. Benedict's personal holiness became well known, even drawing a marauding Germanic chieftain to meet this holy man. A number of charity-related miracles were attributed to him as well.

Benedict's most significant contribution to the growth of monasticism was to draw up a *Rule* for his monks to live by. His Rule, which was to be modeled by other monastic orders for centuries, included moderate asceticism, work, prayer, and charity. It was *Benedict's Rule* that was the catalyst in the spread of monasticism, particularly his order of monks whom we now call *Benedictines*. Although today we might consider the Rule of Saint Benedict strict, it was a much more reasonable set of rules to follow than preexisting ones, and made a call to the monastic life more attractive and doable.

Benedict's legacy continues to this day, but it was built on the foundations of many monastics before him and by his ministry in his own time. His work helped to change the face of Europe. While Martin of Tours got monasticism started in the West, Benedict became the true father of European monasticism. Two hundred years earlier, Saint Pachomius had pioneered the formation of monks living together in community at what we now call *monasteries*; but it was the fruit of Benedict's work that fostered the spread of the monastic movement throughout much of the West. Ironically, Benedict himself never left Italy. Benedict gave his life to prayer and devotion to the will of God; the Holy Spirit took what Benedict started and graced its spread throughout the Christian world in the decades and centuries after Benedict died. What Benedict started became, in a real sense, a lifeboat for Christianity — and scholarship as well — in a time of extreme change and challenge for the Church.

Benedict's sister, **Saint Scholastica** (d. 543), founded an abbey for women, opening the door to monastic life in Europe for women as well as men. Early growth was mostly, if not exclusively, on the men's side. Few convents for women monastics were in place before the year 1000, but over the following centuries, convents of Benedictines, Cistercians, Poor Clares, and others proliferated across Europe.[1]

Holy Spirit-inspired Benedictine monasticism was among the most profound responses of the Faith to these post-imperial times. Aspiring monks founded hundreds of monasteries and many thrived. They became a source of faith and scholarship for their larger communities as they attracted prospective monks by the thousands. Even secular historians recognized that the monastic movement, led by the followers of Saint Benedict, in large part developed and preserved European civilization and culture in the Middle Ages, not to mention Christianity itself. Benedictine monasteries, though not as numerous or influential as in the early Middle Ages, still exist around the world to this day.

For more than a thousand years, Ireland sent missionaries throughout the world. Much of the English-speaking New World can trace its Catholic growth to the influence of Irish missionaries. It started with the missionary work of **Saint Patrick** (389–461). The American custom of beer-drinking and partying on his feast day aside, Patrick holds a major place in Church history. Patrick lived about a century earlier than Benedict and about a thousand miles to the north.

Patrick was likely born in present-day Britain, another remote northern island at the time, into a family that was Christian. Christianity, though far from entrenched, had already reached across the English Channel. As a teenager, Patrick was kidnapped and taken to pagan Ireland where he was forced to work as a shepherd. The country and its people left an impression on this young man. He escaped and eventually ended up back in Britain, studied at a monastery, and showed signs of spiritual awakening. In time, he was ordained a bishop and sent back to evangelize the rough and pagan peoples of Ireland. There, over the next three decades, Patrick worked to spread the Christian Faith. He traveled all over the island, and ran into constant and fierce opposition from pagan chieftains and Druids who felt threatened by Patrick's preaching of this foreign religion. Through all the challenges, Patrick said, "I cast myself into the hands of the Almighty God." In the end, most all the inhabitants of Ireland embraced the Faith, and over the centuries until recently, Ireland was a shining light of Catholic Faith to the world.

It is worth marveling that, through the work of Patrick, such a wild, primitive, remote island in the Atlantic Ocean, far north and west of Europe, became Christian. But Patrick's success was the fruit of another wave of missionary evangelism. As the Roman Empire in the south of Europe was crumbling, the Faith was spreading north among the various "tribes" that inhabited north and central Europe. The Faith had reached the northern shores of what is now France, and beyond, reaching Patrick himself in the 400s.

A significant event in the midst of this centuries-long wave of evangelism was the providential conversion of the Frank chieftain Clovis. He had been a pagan warrior and a nemesis to Christian settlements in Gaul. But he married a Catholic princess, **Saint Clotilda** (474–545) and, in 496, primarily due to Clotilda's efforts, Clovis himself became Catholic. Three thousand of his Frankish compatriots were baptized with him. The fact that Clovis was pagan may well have contributed to his conversion.

Many of the other Germanic tribes had become Arian and had temporarily spread Arianism back into the territory of the empire during their conquests. But the Franks were not Arian. Had they been so, Clovis may not have seen the attraction of Catholicism. And it was likely the work of St. Martin of Tours in spreading the Faith in these parts which gave us Saint Clotilda as a Catholic, positioning her to evangelize the king of the Franks. Providence was at work. The conversion of Clovis changed the dynamic in Western Europe and helped to facilitate the steady Christianizing of the region in the ensuing years. The Franks rapidly became Catholic, and militarily, they also became the dominant force among the Germanic tribes. This spread the Catholic Faith and blunted the reemergence of Arianism. These developments also laid the foundation for the Frankish-led Holy Roman Empire three centuries later.

Patrick's work in converting the people of Ireland helped to extend the reach of Benedictine monasteries in the years after Benedict's death. In the centuries after Patrick, monasticism flourished in Ireland. Irish monks, whose faith can be traced to missionaries from the south, returned the favor, traveling to the European mainland, carrying out missionary activity and founding monasteries.

Among the most noteworthy monk was **Saint Columban** (540–615). In the late 500s, he and several other monks were sent from Ireland to Gaul, where he founded three successful monasteries. Columban was strong-willed, feisty, and sometimes irreverent — traits that are both gifts and flaws which God can use. This led to a number of scrapes and conflicts with bishops and rulers suspicious of his Irish ways that sometimes rocked the continental boat. He was kicked out of several areas and suffered a shipwreck once while fleeing, but was not deterred in his missionary efforts. Columban and his followers founded sixty to perhaps more than one hundred monasteries all over Europe[2] — as far south as Italy. Columban himself ended up in Italy where the monastery he founded at Bobbio in northern Italy became one of the leading monasteries on the continent for both faith and culture. It was there that he died.

Pope St. Gregory the Great (540–604, r. 590–604) was the most influential Bishop of Rome of his time and one of the most significant leaders in all of Church history. He holds the honorable title of "Great" due to a vast array of reform and evangelizing endeavors. In 593, Pope Gregory persuaded the invading Lombards to spare Rome, much like Leo the Great had done two hundred years earlier with Attila the Hun — an astounding feat. He enhanced discipline and practice among the clergy and removed unworthy priests. He was active in numerous works of charity, and helped to feed and rebuild Rome after the destruction from invasions in the previous two centuries. He expanded the temporal holdings of the papacy in central Italy (for worse as much as better), and fought to enhance the authority of the Bishop of Rome, particularly against the competing Eastern Church. He was a pivotal leader in the ongoing process of enhancing the position of the papacy as the central authority in the Church. Gregory was an effective preacher, writer, and an evangelist of the Germanic peoples. He was a strong supporter of Benedictine monasticism and most likely played an instrumental role in the development of liturgical music. The birth and spread of *Gregorian Chant*, which leavened the Church in liturgy and worship for centuries, are attributed to him, (although it is difficult to discern his actual role). No one did more to lay the groundwork for the Church of the Middle Ages than did Gregory.

Gregory was a monk, and his monastic background contributed to the conversion of Britain. He was fascinated by this exotic northern island with its smattering of fair-haired Christians, some of whom he had seen in Rome, and, as pope, he dispatched a group of forty monks to evangelize Britain. These included **St. Augustine of Canterbury** (d. 604), often called the "Apostle of the English." Augustine is credited with facilitating the conversion of thousands of the English, despite difficulties. He is considered the first archbishop of Canterbury.

One of the fruits of Gregory's efforts to evangelize Britain was **Saint Bede** (more commonly known as "Venerable Bede," 672–735), an influential English monk. Bede was the leading scholar, literary analyst, and historian of his day and a particularly learned Scripture scholar. He was the inventor of the designation *Anno Domini*, or AD, for the years after the birth of Christ. He has been declared a Doctor of the Church.

Saint Boniface (680–754) is another son of Britain. He studied in English monasteries as a youth but did not settle in as a monk. His desire was to be a missionary. He traveled to the continent and became the "apostle to Germany." A key moment was when he cut down the "Oak of Thor," a tree sacred to local pagans. When this did not bring him the expected wrath from their gods, a wave of conversions to the Christian Faith ensued. Boniface became an effective leader, interacting with popes and kings as he sought to evangelize the German peoples. Eventually he was named a bishop and structured the Church in German lands with new bishoprics and monasteries. Like so many of the Benedictines, Boniface supported the papacy and considered himself an agent of the pope in his ministries to the German lands. In that role, he accepted an invitation from the king of the Franks to reform the struggling Church among the Franks. Boniface called a series of councils to that end which not only helped to bring renewal, but also helped to create links between the Franks and the papacy. This culminated in an alliance between the pope and the Franks in 754. Boniface died a martyr in that same year at the hands of a roving band of pagans.

13

THE CHURCH IN THE EAST AND THE RISE OF ISLAM

As the "eternal" Roman Empire came crashing down in the West, the empire hung on in the East at Constantinople. Known until its final demise a millennium later as the *Byzantine Empire*, it thrived for a century or so after the fall of the West. Its peak was under the emperor Justinian, who ruled from 527 to 565. Among his accomplishments were the capture of much of North Africa from the Vandals, temporarily rescuing Rome from the occupying Ostrogoths, and the building of the massive and magnificent Byzantine church of Hagia Sophia, completed in Constantinople in 537. The Eastern Church was intact and included the influential patriarchates of Constantinople, Antioch, Jerusalem, and Alexandria, which had inherited a rich theological tradition from the times of Athanasius, the two Cyrils, and John Chrysostom, among others.

However, the stability of the Church and empire in the East was not to last. The following century brought catastrophe.

The seventh century witnessed a monumental historical event. Out of the sands of Arabia, a new world religion was born: Islam. It transformed the history of the Church and the world. Its founder, *Mohammed* (570–632), claimed divine revelations and declared himself to be Prophet of God. He advanced his religion amidst the mixture of various religions in Arabia (primarily pagan, Jewish, and remnants of Arianism), and in time sought to spread it via the sword. Although Islam professed a belief in the one God, called *Allah*, and adopted some of the Old Testament heritage of the Jews and Christians, Mohammed and his followers considered Islam to be the ultimate true faith, worthy to be fought for. Its form of monotheism led to a deep aversion to the Christian belief that the One God was a Trinity of Persons, which Islam considered to be polytheism.

Mohammed and his followers quickly embraced military conquest as a way to spread the Muslim faith, first in Arabia and then beyond. By the time of his death, Mohammed's armies had set out across Arabia and into the Levant, conquering much of Palestine and Syria. This new threat to the world order at first was not recognized as serious. After all, they began as a band of Arabian fighters out of the desert. How could they endanger major cities and civilizations? Yet the danger turned out to be real.

The Battle of Yarmouk in 636 was a crucial moment in world history. A large Muslim army, led by Mohammed's followers soon after his death, faced off against a Byzantine Christian army at Yarmouk, east of the Sea of Galilee. The Islamic army won a surprising and decisive victory at Yarmouk, and set the stage for widespread Muslim conquest in the Christian world.

In less than a hundred years after the battle of Yarmouk, Muslim armies conquered the rest of the Holy Land and much of the Middle East — Jerusalem fell in 638, and within decades all of Saint Athanasius's and Saint Augustine's North Africa, and much of Spain. Half of Mediterranean Christendom fell to the Muslim armies. Few of these lands have ever returned to their Christian roots. Most of the Christian East which had not fallen remained under constant threat of attack. The great city of Constantinople itself endured a series of sieges and nearly fell in these early centuries. The Western Christian world, which had been expanding throughout most of Europe, now had shrunk to areas north of the Mediterranean. The Byzantine East was limited mostly to the Balkans and western Asia Minor, and was under constant pressure from Muslim armies.

The military conquests of so much Christian territory quickly created a new normal in the Christian world. Almost overnight, Islam became a strong religious competitor — one with few qualms about military advancement. For the first time in centuries, Christianity was on the defensive. The Muslim threat of future conquest has been present ever since.

One of the noteworthy saints in this era was **St. John Damascene** ("from Damascus," 675–749). He spent his entire life in a land under Muslim rule. It must be said that, in this place, under the specific rulers in place at his time, he was able to function as an educated Christian (although he did have to resign from a government post and move to a monastery in order to compose his religious writings). Others were not so blessed. Conversion to Islam in conquered territory was either forced or encouraged. Those allowed to maintain their Christian faith (and at times there were some) were designated as *dhimmi* — second-class residents with limited rights and subject to special taxation.

Specifics of John Damascene's life under Muslim rule are not clear. Educated by a monk, he was one of the great scholars of his day, and an early pioneer of what later came to be called *Scholasticism*. St. Thomas Aquinas admired John Damascene's writings and studied them daily five centuries later. Through Aquinas, John Damascene's theological insights took on a new life.

John Damascene is best known for stepping into the controversy of that time, called *iconoclasm*, the practice of banning use and veneration of images, statues, and art in churches, and often in opposition of ornate churches themselves. Under certain Byzantine emperors and some Eastern Christian leaders in the early eighth century, icons and other religious images were forbidden and often destroyed. This was under a strict interpretation of the commandment not to worship graven images.

John Damascene disagreed with the iconoclasts and became a champion of the more Western practice of using religious images to foster worship and faith. At the behest of the patriarch of Jerusalem, John wrote a series of treatises against iconoclasm. "Paintings are the books of the illiterate," he argued, "and the heralds of the honor of the Saints; they instruct those who look at them with a silent voice and sanctify life."[1] The iconoclast emperors wanted to silence John but could not — he was out of their reach because he was a resident of Damascus, in Muslim territory. John Damascene's defense helped to shore up openness to use of religious images and make more likely the building of beautiful churches in the centuries ahead. The Second Council of Nicaea, held in 787, condemned iconoclasm. After this council, Christian leaders in the East backed off strict iconoclasm, as a witness to the long and beautiful history of icons in the Eastern churches.

Iconoclasm resurfaced as an issue during the Reformation eight hundred years later as the Calvinists among others set out to destroy religious images in churches. This iconoclastic sense of keeping church architecture plain and simple, with no statues and minimal religious décor, continues today in many Protestant denominations and even some modern Catholic circles.

In addition to his involvement in the iconoclast controversy, John Damascene was a gifted theologian who wrote a number of influential texts of theology. But he is one of the few faithful Christians who was able to function from behind Muslim walls. Saints who helped to shape history from behind Muslim lines in the East are sorely lacking.

However, monasticism flourished in the East as well as in the West. Anonymous monks clustered in monasteries throughout Egypt and the Levant supported the Church as did their western counterparts. Justinian directed the founding of one of the most significant monasteries in the East, St. Catherine's monastery at Mount Sinai, in Egypt. Built between the years 548 and 565, it is the oldest continuously inhabited monastery in the world.[2] It is named after **St. Catherine of Alexandria,** a young woman who suffered martyrdom in her teens. Much of the story of her life and death is cloaked in legend, so it is difficult to know how much is true. This monastery, whose fortunes flowed with the tides of history, is now Greek Orthodox.

The year 732 also witnessed a critical moment in Christian and European history: yet another crucial battle. The Muslim conquests encompassed not only the areas around the eastern Mediterranean and its southern African shore, but also, by the eighth century, much of modern-day Spain in the West. For nearly eight hundred years, the Moors, as they were called, held much of Spain and built a thriving culture. Church-supported armies, often with papal encouragement, sought to drive the Moors out of what was once Christian land, with limited success before 1492. These efforts became known as the *Reconquista*.

By the 700s, the Moors were entrenched in Spain and, like their counterparts in the East, had their eyes on the belly of Europe and the goal of spreading Islam throughout the continent. In 732, a Muslim army of tens of thousands invaded southern France and moved north, sacking the city of Bordeaux on the way. In October 732, near Tours, in north-central France, this Muslim army joined battle with the Catholic Frankish forces under Charles Martel. According to many historians, had the Muslims been successful, Christian lands in Europe would have been hard-pressed to avoid further advances. Even if just the Franks had fallen, Christianity in Europe would have been severely impaired. It was the Franks who were to become the engine for Christian expansion in the following century. At the Battle of Tours, Charles Martel's forces defeated the Muslim army and drove them back over the Pyrenees. The heart of Europe was safe for Christianity — for the time being. Even so, the threat remained.

Charles Martel's victory at the Battle of Tours solidified the Franks as the military and cultural heirs of the Romans and paved the way for the "Carolingian Empire" in the next century. This would lead both to great benefits and great challenges for the Church. Charles Martel was Catholic but also a power-hungry warlord who persecuted the Church when it suited him. His son, Pepin, as we shall see, was more friendly to the Church, and Charles's grandson, Charlemagne, would, a few decades later, take his place as a transformational figure on the European stage.

In the five hundred years through the end of the eighth century, the Christian Faith had spread from the Middle East throughout much of

Europe and North Africa. It grew from persecutions and internal struggles to become in many places a state religion. Germanic tribes to the north and Muslim armies to the east were pinching Christian peoples as the empire in the West languished and ultimately collapsed. Much of the Middle East and North Africa eventually was lost to the advances of Islam, a threat that would persist for centuries to come. Yet conversions abounded, and the conversion of the Franks in Western Europe would prove pivotal for the Church. The world was in an unsteady place by the eighth century's end, but as the ninth century dawned, things would take a major turn.

CHRISTENDOM

AD 800 to AD 1500

St. Hildegard von Bingen. zatletic/AdobeStock

14

MISSIONARIES, MONKS, AND KINGS

On Christmas day, in the year 800, Pope Leo III crowned Charles, king of the Franks — thereafter known as *Charlemagne* — as the first "Holy Roman emperor." This ushered in a profound change in the Church. Christendom was born — a de facto convergence of Church and state in the West. In these "Middle Ages," the culture of most all of Europe became Christian to the core. But this became a mixed blessing. One consequence was a deepening of the ongoing conflict between East and West. The Byzantines of the East saw this new Holy Roman Empire as a rival force, at a time when Muslims were pressing their advances further into the Byzantine East. Another consequence was the immediate interference of state authorities in the affairs of the Church. Charlemagne, and his successors and underlings, truly believed that it was incumbent upon them to be involved in leading the Church, as had many of the Christian Roman emperors before them.

Much of the Middle Ages saw a flowering of piety, devotion, and belief, making this era one of the most "religious" eras in history. A majority of the people were sincere Catholics, though often they were ignorant of the specifics of the Faith, and moral shortcomings were widespread. Popular devotions flourished, traveling preachers enriched faith life and understanding, and pilgrimages to holy sites (such as the shrine of Saint James in Spain) were common, creating an entire industry of road building and hospitality. And some of the Church's greatest saints stepped onto the scene.

This was a time of missionary zeal. Those areas of Europe still not yet influenced by Christianity — mostly to the north and northeast — saw streams of missionaries. At times they also saw crusading kings invade and seek to force the Faith on an area. For instance, Charlemagne, in misplaced zeal, was known to attack an area and give the conquered the choice between baptism by water or by blood. But primarily the Faith spread through the work of dedicated religious missionaries.

Among the monastic missionaries early in this era was **Saint Ansgar** (801–865), known as the "Apostle of the North" for his tireless efforts in northern Germany and Scandinavia. Ansgar rose from monk, to abbot of New Corbie in present-day Germany, to archbishop of Hamburg, to missionary in Scandinavia. He built the first church in present-day Sweden. For much of his life he worked to establish the Faith in Scandinavia, only to see his initial efforts wiped out by pagan invasions. He went back to work to reestablish a Christian presence in this volatile region but, after his death, the pagans invaded again. However, the seed was planted and bore fruit again in later times.

Two brothers, born in the Balkans, became one of the most notable missionary teams in Church history. **Saints Cyril** (826–869) and **Methodius** (815–885) spent their lives evangelizing the Slavic peoples in east-central Europe, especially in and near Bohemia and Russia. They interacted directly with the people in their own languages, and worked to bring the Scriptures into the native tongues, even to the point of developing an alphabet — the forerunner of today's Cyrillic alphabet, named after Saint Cyril. In their labors, Cyril and Methodius had to overcome obstacles within the Church, including a need to defend to the popes and their advisors their unique approach of using local languages and their Scripture translations, and persistent interference from German bishops who resented their work in lands near their own. These popes, to their credit, did give approval for their mission work and the use of the local languages. The brothers were even consecrated as bishops, though Cyril died before he could return to his mission fields as bishop. Methodius resumed their work for many years after Cyril's death. The efforts of these two saints expanded the Faith into large areas of Europe outside the Empire, making the Church more universal and also bringing aspects of Slavic culture into the Church at large.

A number of kings and rulers were instrumental in advancing the Faith in central and northern Europe in the first centuries after Charlemagne. **Saint Wenceslaus** (909–929), of Christmas carol fame, is patron of Bohemia. In his short life, he became king in Bohemia, near and around Prague, and worked to enhance the Christian Faith in his realm. His brother, with an eye on the throne, had him killed while he was still a youth. **St. Stephen of Hungary** (975–1038) worked as king to foster the Christian Faith in his realm, founding bishoprics and monasteries, pushing to establish Christian culture, worship, and morality. He sought to assist the poor in his kingdom as well, often incognito. As king, **St. Olaf of Norway** (995–1030) worked to grow the Faith in the far Scandinavian north of Norway, sometimes by force. He has been the patron saint of Norway for a thousand years. (His influence in medieval Norway is brought to life in Nobel prize winning Catholic novelist Sigrid Undset's early twentieth-century novel *Kristin Lavransdatter*.) **St. Stanislaus of Krakow** (1030–1079) was bishop of Krakow, in Poland. He was a powerful preacher, a reformer of the clergy, and a benefactor of the poor. He stood up to King Boleslaus of Poland over his injustices and immorality, eventually excommunicating him. This enraged the king, who sought him out and, when his guards refused his order to kill Stanislaus, the king himself killed him. Stanislaus is the patron saint of Poland.

St. Vladimir of Kyiv (975–1015) is noteworthy today in light of Russia's 2022 invasion of Ukraine, as well as for his contribution to the growth of Slavic Christianity. Vladimir became a king of the "Kievan Rus," a Slavic people who inhabited parts of the areas of modern-day

Ukraine, Russia, and Belarus. He was a violent warlord who established numerous pagan shrines, and collected over eight hundred concubines and several wives. Vladimir killed his own brother in order to ascend the throne as king of the Kievan Rus in their capital of Kyiv and he conducted a series of military raids on neighboring realms to expand his own. But in 988, Vladimir converted to Christianity, by one account in order to marry the Christian sister of the Byzantine emperor. His conversion was one of the very few in all Christian history of an influential leader, well advanced in living a nefarious and immoral life, who then became a saint. Vladimir became a changed man. He turned the same intensity from his pagan days toward supporting the Faith as a ruler, tearing down his pagan shrines, making peace with the neighboring realms, sending away his concubines and wives, and building numerous churches. Vladimir's efforts contributed mightily to the spread of Christianity in what is now Russia and Ukraine. The Catholic and Orthodox churches of both Russia and Ukraine — and even their societies — honor Saint Vladimir as their patron saint. Numerous churches and cathedrals dedicated to Saint Vladimir stand tall in the cities of both nations. He is a worthy intercessor for conversion and an end to the war which began in 2022.

We hear little of Russia after Saint Vladimir from the Catholic perspective because, after the **Schism of 1054**, the Kievan Russian churches joined with the Eastern Orthodox. The Catholic Church has never established a significant presence in Russia, but several Slavic national churches are in union with the Catholic Church. Perhaps the most prominent is the Ukrainian Greek Catholic Church, which has had a difficult history. Both the Soviets and the Russian Orthodox Church have persistently sought to absorb the Ukrainian Catholics (*uniates*, or those united with Rome). Soviet dictator Josef Stalin even tried to wipe out the Ukrainian Catholics as part of a horrendous genocide of the Ukrainian people in the 1930s. Today, twenty-three Eastern churches are in union with Rome, enriching the Catholic Church with beautiful liturgies, a rich theological tradition, and as custodians of beautiful religious art, particularly icons.

MONASTERIES IN THE WEST

Building on the work of Benedict and others in the preceding centuries, monasteries flourished. As the Middle Ages progressed in the next few hundred years, thousands were built. They were spread out over most of the continent, in or near most of the cities and towns as well as in the countryside. They attracted thousands of men and women. These monasteries and their monks helped to preserve scholarship and develop theological understanding of the Faith, interacted with and served the local populations, offered hospitality to thousands of pilgrims, travelers, and people in need, and helped to inspire believers to grow in their faith. Fierce, destructive raids by Vikings in the two centuries before the millennium wrought destruction on both monasteries and towns, but still the monasteries spread and endured. The impact of the monastic movement on society was incalculable.

In 910, **Saint Berno** (850–927), a monk bent on reform, founded a monastery in Cluny, a town in east-central France, applying a stricter variation of the Benedictine Rule. Berno's passion for God moved him, but he did not know what was about to happen out of his passion. This Cluny monastery grew into a monastic order that sparked spiritual renewal throughout Europe. **Saint Odo** (879–942), Cluny's second abbot, was particularly instrumental in the growth of the Cluny monasteries throughout Europe. Over one thousand five hundred monasteries in the Cluny tradition sprang up and many of the best abbots became bishops who led renewal in their areas. The Cluny monasteries flourished in number and spiritual energy for the next two centuries.

The Benedictines also flourished. One of the most illustrious Benedictines in the eleventh century was **St. Peter Damian** (1001–1072), born in Ravenna, Italy. He sought the life of a hermit and entered a Benedictine monastery, eventually becoming abbot and founding several other monasteries. Peter Damian was a gifted reformer who collaborated with several popes, including Pope St. Gregory VII, in advancing reforms. He attacked corruption in the Church with ferocity — especially among the clergy. He specifically targeted simony and sexual immorality. In 1050 he authored a scathing attack against sexual abuse of minors by clergy and efforts by high clergy to cover it up. (Alas, not much is new in the

Church.) Clerical celibacy was becoming the norm in his time — it became official in the following century — and Peter fought for an open embrace of celibacy. For his insights, influence, and scholarship, he has been proclaimed a Doctor of the Church.

Saint Anselm (1033–1109), another influential Benedictine saint from Italy in this time, was one of the great biblical and theological scholars of his day. Anselm harbored a fire for God and for truth that was behind his varied undertakings on behalf of God and the Church. After living as a worldly youth, he entered a Benedictine monastery in Normandy when he was in his late twenties and, as a sign of his precociousness, became prior in only three years. Later, he was named Archbishop of Canterbury and sought to implement numerous reforms, but immediately came into conflict with the English kings. With the pope's help, Anselm fended off two kings' attempts to force him into exile and confiscate Church property. Anselm also prevailed in a dispute with the English throne over lay investiture, preserving the Church's right to name English bishops. Ahead of his time, Anselm denounced the English slave trade and, as a prominent scholar, assisted the Western Church in defending the insertion of *filioque* into the Nicene Creed. Anselm is often called the "Father of Scholasticism" and was one of the greatest thinkers in the Medieval Church. His scholarly work, which included harmonizing faith and reason, and arguments for the existence of God, opened the door for Sts. Albert and Thomas Aquinas to advance the Scholastic tradition in the following century. Anselm was a precocious writer and has left a legacy of Christian thought that has influenced many subsequent thinkers. Anselm is a Doctor of the Church.

CHALLENGES IN THE EAST

The Church in the East continued to evolve — separately from the West. It faced different issues and developed a different structure. Still, as the Middle Ages dawned, East and West remained united, though a sense of rivalry, traceable back to early centuries, was growing. The East was mostly Greek-speaking, the West Latin-speaking (though many other languages were spoken in both East and West). The Church in the East was closely associated with the Byzantine Empire, the successor to the

Roman Empire which had been centered in Constantinople since the fourth century. The Church in the West became tied to the Holy Roman Empire beginning in the ninth century. The East perceived itself as the more theologically sound, and this came with a measure of arrogance. The West, led by the see of Peter in Rome, considered itself the protector of true doctrine, and this came with a measure of authoritarianism. The primary sees in the East, with a long rich history of leadership in the early Church, developed into *patriarchates*, or high-level bishoprics. These included Antioch, Alexandria, Jerusalem, and, what became the "first among equals," Constantinople.

The Muslim invasions in the seventh century, a major threat in the West, were near-catastrophic for the much more exposed Church in the East. The Holy Land, Syria, and Egypt had all fallen to the Muslims and these territorial losses had severely impaired the once-influential patriarchates. Although Constantinople held out for centuries, it was under continuous pressure from the Muslim caliphates pushing through Asia Minor. Byzantine lands of the Eastern Church were squeezed and shrunk. Even the West was not immune from Muslim invasion — in 846, a Muslim army invaded Italy and attacked Rome. By 902 the Muslims had conquered Sicily.

Still, the Church in the East maintained spiritual vitality. Its divine liturgy was rich. Its art — including iconography — flourished after Church leaders put iconoclasm to rest. And its theological traditions remained strong. The missionary activity of Cyril and Methodius in the Balkans enriched the mostly eastern traditions in this area, and the Church was expanding into and near Russia. A number of monastic saints helped to strengthen the Church in the East. **St. Anthony of Kyiv** (983–1073), a contemporary of Saint Vladimir, is the father of the monastic movement in the Kievan Rus area, founding numerous monasteries. **St. Athanasius the Athonite** (920–1003) was a Byzantine monk credited with founding the monastic community on Mount Athos in Greece. This monastery, now under the auspices of the Greek Orthodox Church, is one of the most famous monasteries in the world. Athanasius founded other monasteries, served as an effective preacher, and even fought against the Saracens (Arabian Muslims). **St. Gregory Palamas** (1296–c. 1357) was a monk at Mount Athos and later archbishop of Thessaloniki in Greece. He was a leading theologian in the Greek Byzantine world and, although Orthodox, some Eastern Catholic churches recognize him as a saint, and Pope John Paul II has lauded him as a great theologian.

The missionaries and rulers, saints and anonymous Christians in the East and West sustained and expanded the imprint of the Christian Faith in the early Middle Ages. It was the Holy Spirit who was the primary missionary force behind the activities of these saints. The spread of the Faith was God's providential project of salvation. And the unseen daily faith and devotion of countless Christians everywhere, in the fields and villages, monasteries and churches, was real, and a sign of the grace of the Holy Spirit. The Body of Christ, though filled with flaws, was alive and growing.

But it was not all roses. Daily life was hard and it took a toll. Many, if not most leaders and ordinary people had but a nominal faith, unlearned in its teachings, or they were great sinners. The age-old battle between grace and original sin, between love and the flesh, played out each day. Institutionally, the line between Church and state was blurred and uncertain. Popes became rulers as well as pastors, and kings became Church leaders as well as secular rulers. This led both to conflict with rulers and a weakening of the clergy, and to one of the most profound issues of contention between popes and rulers in the Middle Ages.

LAY INVESTITURE

When Pope Leo III placed a crown on the head of Charlemagne, the leadership structure of the Church in the West was altered. Charlemagne was a genuine, if imperfect, Catholic, and that was the beginning of the problem. He viewed his role as emperor to include authority over the Church. In this was a mixture of sincerity and desire for power. He truly thought that Church governance was part of his job. Charlemagne — and his successors — sought the power to appoint bishops, who would then be subject to him. "I appoint, the pope prays," he once said. The popes did not see it that way.

What followed were centuries of power struggles over who appoints bishops: pope or ruler. Historians call this the issue of *lay investiture*.

When the emperors were stronger, they had sway to make appointments. When the popes were stronger, they appointed bishops. At times there were compromises. When rulers were successful in appointing bishops, those bishops were beholden to the rulers who had given them their appointment. This often included a grant of land or another temporal benefit, along with an oath of loyalty. This changed the nature of the office of bishop, impairing the independence of the bishop and distracting him from purely pastoral duties. It is no surprise then that the popes resisted this — lay investiture reduced their own authority and ability to pastor the Church. The popes did not accept Charlemagne's idea that their role was merely to pray and to lay hands on the king's chosen bishop to preserve apostolic succession. Battles between pope and ruler raged throughout the Middle Ages. Blood was spilled, excommunications were wielded, and political maneuverings were constant. Church and state battled for supremacy as two rival brothers in a family.

Stepping into this fray, and in essence following in Saint Anselm's recent steps, came **St. Thomas Becket** (1118–1170), a close associate of King Henry II of England. In 1161, Henry nominated Thomas to be archbishop of Canterbury. Thomas grew spiritually into this position and began to oppose Henry's efforts to assert greater control over the Church. Henry grew frustrated at this "interference" and mused, "Will anyone rid me of this troublesome priest?" Some of his knights took this to be a command, and assassinated Thomas in his cathedral. (The movie *Becket* and the play *Murder in the Cathedral* dramatize this conflict.)

Worse, emperors were at times even able to control the papacy itself, appointing or influencing the selection of new popes. In 963, Holy Roman Emperor Otto I even succeeded in removing Pope John XII, one of the Church's most immoral popes, and replacing him with someone better. Otto and John battled each other for another year until John died. As was often the case, Otto's motives were mixed. John was truly a terrible pope, but his removal served to increase Otto's power as well. Over large swaths of the Middle Ages, kings, nobles, princes, and other political leaders had a hand in choosing the popes.

Worse than the conflicts themselves was the effect on the clergy. When a bishop is beholden to a benefactor, he is not free to serve the

Church as he sees fit. His king is looking over his shoulder with his royal agenda. This often led to bishops sharing in the exercise of political power, becoming agents of their king and sometimes even rulers themselves. Often, these secularly appointed bishops were not really men of the Church but political allies of kings or princes given a Church appointment. Unsurprisingly, many of these secular choices behaved in secular ways, with a limited expression of faith and little appreciation of the true role of bishop as successor to the apostles. This was the beginning of popes and bishops as "princes of the Church," with worldly prestige and authority — a far cry from the time of the apostles, or even the time of Augustine and Ambrose.

Late in the eighth century, Charlemagne's father Pepin had given the pope a swath of territory in central Italy, and from this — which evolved into the Papal States — the papacy added military and land ownership to its spiritual responsibilities and became like another secular state. Political and diplomatic intrigue, purchase of the papacy by well-placed rich families, and significant loss of spiritual focus typified the papacy throughout several stretches of the Middle Ages. This lack of spiritual focus and ofttimes corruption affected the clergy at all levels. It seemed that there were two parallel churches: the power-hungry hierarchy and the pious, ordinary people and priests, who in large part held the Church together. Parts of the tenth and eleventh centuries particularly saw a string of immoral and corrupt popes. By the grace of God, good men eventually helped to pull the Church out, but future periods of bad popes would follow as well.

15

THE GREAT SCHISM

One of the greatest tragedies in Christian history was the splitting of the Church into two — East and West — in the eleventh century. The date attributed to the Great Schism is 1054, but it was a process that began before this date and continued in the years that followed.

The causes are many, but it could have been avoided. Both East and West lacked focus on the common vision of the Church as the instrument of salvation and on the unity for which Jesus prayed (see Jn 17). Human frailties, the sense of rivalry and separation going back centuries, and an array of political and (mostly minor) theological disputes created a momentum that neither "side" was able to stop. No one really wished for a schism; nevertheless, it happened.

When the Holy Roman Empire emerged in the ninth century, a new political rival in the West stood opposed to the Byzantine Empire in the East. Two empires; two languages; differing cultures, histories, and liturgical practices fueled the divisions. And each had different challenges based upon geography.

The Church in the West spent centuries contending with the Germanic tribes which had overcome the Roman Empire by the end of the fifth century. Over time the Christian peoples intermingled with them and in large part the various tribes had become Christian. But it was a long, messy, often violent process. The Bishop of Rome, who by the millennium was known as *papa* (in English, "pope"), successor to Saint Peter, grew in stature and universal authority in the West despite the demise of the city of Rome itself. And he claimed authority over the East as well.

The Church in the East had different issues. The Roman emperor had moved to Byzantium in the fourth century. This city, renamed Constantinople, grew to be the most illustrious city in Europe. After Rome fell, it was the capital of the Byzantine Empire, and a close relationship between the Empire and the Eastern Church developed. The see of Constantinople, headed by the patriarch, became the most important bishopric in the East, but it faced the greatest challenge to the Eastern Church: the threat of Islamic conquest. Much of the eastern Mediterranean had fallen to Muslim armies in the seventh century. Most of the major eastern patriarchates fell, including Antioch, Jerusalem, and Alexandria. Despite the richness of the Eastern Church in theology, liturgy, and art, the constant Muslim advances in the ensuing centuries squeezed the Church and Empire into smaller areas.

As the papacy grew in importance, and as many accepted the Bishop of Rome as the leader of the worldwide Church with universal authority, others were not so quick to agree. The strong episcopal sees that had grown in the East in the first several centuries gave some measure of acknowledgment to the primacy of Rome, but resisted Rome's claim of *exclusive* primacy. After the Muslim conquests and the consolidation of authority in the East to Constantinople, the challenge to the exclusive primacy of Rome was more pronounced. The main bone of contention over the centuries leading into the eleventh century, then, was Church authority, and whether or not the Bishop of Rome, as successor to Peter, held universal primacy over the Church above any other see or patriarchate.

The authority issue manifested itself in a debate over a technical doctrinal point in the Nicene Creed. Centuries earlier — as we have seen — the councils of Nicaea and Constantinople (held in the East) worked out the nature of Christ and the Holy Spirit, and the Nicene Creed was drafted in the Greek language. The Creed declared that Christ is *eternally begotten* from, and consubstantial with the Father, and that the Holy Spirit *proceeds from the Father*. In time, many theologians and Church fathers, including Saint Augustine, noted that, from a study of Scripture, the Holy Spirit proceeds from both the Father *and the Son*. Eventually, this was added to the Creed in the West, in its Latin version. The word added was *filioque* — Latin for "and the Son." The bishops and theologians of the East protested this, claiming — accurately — that this was a centuries-later addition to the text of the Creed approved by the councils. The emphasis on the doctrinal authority of councils in the East fueled their reaction to the "tampering" with such a significant conciliar document as the Creed itself. An irony here is that *filioque* has made no practical difference. The Eastern Church — then and now — was and is fully committed to the doctrine of the Trinity and expresses a strong devotion to the Holy Spirit. In a real sense, the *filioque* issue was a theological technicality. Although there were ways out of this dispute and it needn't have become as big an issue as it did, *filioque* became a stubborn sticking point between East and West. The emotional rivalries and the authority disputes exaggerated the importance of the *filioque* issue.

The conflict came to a head in the middle of the eleventh century. As so often happens in history, something small triggered the blowup: in this case, a dispute over territory. The Byzantines held territory in southern Italy, south of the Papal States. This did not sit well with papal officials, and the dispute escalated. As tensions increased, Patriarch Michael of Constantinople closed the Western churches in his city, angering the Western church leaders. Pope Leo IX sought to resolve the dispute, so he sent a legate, Cardinal Humbert, to Constantinople to negotiate. He chose the wrong man. Humbert was much more pugnacious than Leo intended and, instead of working for peace, he engaged in disputes with an equally pugnacious Patriarch Michael. This climaxed when Humbert defiantly marched up to the altar in Hagia Sophia and pronounced an excommunication upon the patriarch — *in his home church*. Naturally, Michael made the excommunications mutual. The Schism was born.

Efforts by both sides to heal the split began immediately. These efforts never reached fruition. One great irony was that Pope Leo had died before Humbert pronounced the excommunication, calling into question whether he even had the authority to pronounce it. Opportunities during the time of the Crusades a few decades later were missed, including the failure of the crusaders to help the patriarch and Eastern emperor in their battles against the Muslim Turks in Asia Minor in return for a pledge of reunification. (Imagine what might have been.) A later pope even agreed that the churches of the East could use the original Creed without *filioque*. Efforts to reunify what Pope St. John Paul II called "the two lungs" of Christianity have continued even to the present, but have yet to be successful. This has included the mutual lifting of the excommunications in 1965, when Pope St. Paul VI met with Patriarch Athenagoras. It remains one of history's greatest tragedies that we now have separate Catholic and Orthodox Churches.

As tragic as this Schism between East and West has been, it is important to note that the Byzantine churches were a federation of patriarchates, each having a certain independence. This independence, as opposed to being under the authority of a higher bishop — an intrinsic feature of the Eastern churches' self-understanding — was a key to understanding the East's reluctance to acknowledge the primacy of the Bishop of Rome. But that same sense of independence led several Eastern patriarchies to choose association with Rome even after the Schism. Though the majority of the Eastern churches remained in the federation with Constantinople, "the first among equals," a few did not. Those who remained loyal to Rome formed the foundation for an array of Eastern Catholic churches that are alive and well today. Many of the twenty-three Eastern Catholic churches are rooted in the formerly Byzantine areas (and their diaspora throughout the rest of the world) — Lebanese, Syrian, Greek, and Melkite Catholic churches among them — and they bring the richness and traditions of eastern spirituality into the whole Catholic Church. The Catholic Church is universal. It is not just a "Western" Church.

Certainly, God did not will the Schism. He is a God of love and unity.

It was the absence of these virtues, a turning away from grace, that fueled the split. Human factors, no doubt encouraged and even incited by Satan, caused this devastating Schism that would immeasurably weaken the Church and impair the Church's witness to the world for centuries.

We might ask: Where were the saints? Might not holy men and women of the time have acted to head off this tragedy? What if Cardinal Humbert or Patriarch Michael had been saints, and fully open to God's grace? These are questions worth pondering, but they are difficult to answer. The mix of grace, sin, evil, Satan, free will, and providence, as applied to events such as this, are cloaked in mystery. History shows that so often evil happens. *Why* is a question for all ages. This is a fallen world and the best of Christians cannot know fully the mind of God, the path of providence, or the depth of evil's influence. But whenever evil triumphs, grace later abounds.

The long history of the Orthodox Churches includes a rich tradition of worship, pastoral practice, liturgy, and politics, but sadly, from 1054 on, it is the history of a fellow Christian Church separated from the Catholic Church. From this point, we will return to the history of the Catholic Church and the many saints who shaped her history in the second millennium.

16

THE MIDDLE AGES

By the turn of the millennium, the Catholic Church, with her strengths and weaknesses, devotion and dissolution, was established as part of the fabric of life in much of Europe. Kings and peasants were mostly all Catholic. Society was primarily rural and feudal, and life was hard. The Church and her practices were built into daily life, resulting in strong observance even if knowledge and piety varied widely. And the Holy Spirit raised up saints.

One of the greatest popes of the era — even of all Church history — was **Pope St. Gregory VII** (1021–1085, r. 1073–1085). He would likely be called "the Great" had not the sixth-century Pope Saint Gregory already attained that title. Gregory was pulled into major geopolitical matters and handled them in a way that strengthened the Church. The century or so before Gregory had been marked by numerous ineffective, and too often even immoral or corrupt popes. Gregory was early in a line of reform popes, as the pendulum (as it always does) swung back for the better. Named Hildebrand, he had been an effective reformer while serving under several of the previous reforming popes, and was regarded as the most significant prelate in the Church at the time he was elected. The College of Cardinals elected him by acclamation in 1073. A few years earlier, Gregory himself had been instrumental in establishing the College of Cardinals as electors of the pope — a move intended to limit the ability of kings to choose or influence the choice of a pope.

As pope, Gregory set out to attack corruption and decadence in the Church. He deposed the archbishop of Milan for simony, replaced most of the bishops in France, and fought fiercely to end lay investiture (although some kings, including William the Conqueror, resisted).

Gregory is perhaps most famous for standing down Holy Roman Emperor Henry IV. After one of their clashes, primarily over lay investiture, Henry declared that Gregory was deposed. Pope Gregory responded by excommunicating Henry and even proclaiming that Henry's subjects were free of allegiance to him. This was a test of power for each, the ever-present question in the Middle Ages. Sometimes the key was military power or political influence. Sometimes it was moral authority. The question was, who would the subjects of the empire and Church — the same people — respect more?

The German nobles, for their own reasons, backed the pope, forcing Henry into one of the most dramatic acts of the Middle Ages. In 1077, Henry, the emperor of most of Europe, went to the pope at Canossa in northern Italy, and, barefoot in the January cold, knelt before the pope and begged forgiveness. Gregory was not naïve, but despite his suspicions of Henry's possibly-mixed motives, the pope lifted the excommunication. This had twofold consequences for history. First, it demonstrated that the papacy had recovered its lost influence and, when strong, could stand up to kings. The increase of moral authority allowed for renewed power. Second, Gregory carried out a genuine Christian act of forgiveness in lifting the excommunication, choosing service in the name of Christ over the exercise of power politics. This had long-range significance, helping the papacy to recapture much of its lost pastoral significance.

Sure enough, Henry did not stay repentant for long. Another political crisis a few years later led Henry to set up an antipope and declare Gregory deposed again. Once again, Gregory excommunicated Henry. This time, Henry invaded Italy and forced Gregory out of Rome. Political intrigue continued to engulf the standoff and Gregory died before it was resolved. Despite not prevailing in everything he set out to do, Gregory did much to right the state of the Church, both in internal reform and in independence from the interference of kings. This became a turning point in Church history.

Although Gregory was a skillful diplomat, his faith was the driving force in pointing the Church in the right direction. He did not seek personal power, as previous popes had, but fought for the Church to be free from secular interference. He sought unity with the Churches of the East but was unsuccessful. Lay investiture was mostly put to rest in Europe just a few decades after his death, but it has never disappeared. Periodically, civil rulers have used their influence to appoint Church leaders — even today, this issue lives on, particularly with China.

As so many of the Church hierarchy turned secular and so many kings and nobles acted with self-interest, it was the monastics who continued to fortify the Faith. Two gifted and devout monks in the eleventh and twelfth centuries fostered an explosion in the growth of monasticism throughout Europe. The first was **St. Hugh of Cluny** (1024–1109). First a monk, then ordained a priest, in 1049 Hugh became abbot of the monastery at Cluny, in France. As we have seen, Cluny had already become a center of monasticism. Through Hugh's efforts and administrative talent, the Cluny monastery family grew even more in this, its second century — to about two thousand centers throughout the continent. In 1095, a massive church-monastery was dedicated — one of the largest structures in Europe at the time. Hugh was a sought-after consultant, an advisor to nine popes, and was committed to enacting the reforms of Pope Leo IX and Pope St. Gregory VII.

St. Bernard of Clairvaux (1090–1153), a monk of the Cistercian order, was one of the most influential monastics, not just in the twelfth century but in all Christian history. One overriding aspect of his life explains his place in history: He was a holy man. Bernard burned with the love of God. Many of his spiritual writings, filled with profound wisdom and exuding a powerful devotion to God, are still read today. They also show his deep devotion to the Virgin Mary, a devotion strong in the Catholic Church throughout the Middle Ages. Bernard was able to accomplish all that he did because he was rooted in prayer and fostered a close relationship with Christ. He let the Holy Spirit work through him and enough people recognized that this was a special man to whom they should listen. Holiness attracts.

Foremost, Bernard invigorated monasteries. About the time Bernard was born, the Cistercian order was founded in the Benedictine tradition in the French town of Citeaux. This was in part as a counter to the Cluny monks, who had begun to drift from the fundamentals of monasticism — work and prayer — that Hugh of Cluny had worked so hard to establish several decades earlier. Among his own monks, Bernard helped to address this drift away from Hugh's original vision. Bernard founded several Cistercian monasteries early on, attracting men to become monks by his holiness. In time, he and his monks founded sixty-eight monasteries in Europe. As his reputation for holiness and wisdom spread, popes and rulers consulted with him. He took up a ministry of preaching to great effect, and many miracles were attributed to him. He was instrumental in challenging several heretics, helped to settle disputes among nobles to keep the peace, and preached the Second Crusade. (As we shall see, this was his greatest failure, for this Crusade was ill-conceived and a disaster). Bernard was considered the preeminent spiritual figure in Europe for over forty years, and his influence lives on. Two centuries later, the great Italian poet Dante gave Bernard a prominent place in the climax of his *Paradiso*, the last book of the *Divine Comedy*.

A contemporary of Bernard was the remarkable woman **St. Hildegard of Bingen** (1098–1179). This multitalented German nun led a devout and yet colorful life, and had her hand in an amazing array of pursuits: theology, music, poetry, art, church politics, administration of women religious, and medicine. She also received visions. Early on, these visions were a cross for her; later, she sought to turn them into a good for the Church. In time, she recorded her visions and, despite controversy, the substance of her visions eventually received papal approval, in part on the recommendation of Saint Bernard. Among her most significant writing was mystical theology — especially her reflections and interpretations of her visions, which reflected upon the meaning of salvation history and God's love for and relationship with his people.

Hildegard became an abbess of a community of Benedictine nuns, which, under her leadership, outgrew their convent. She moved and began reforming a number of convents. She composed music, including a musical morality play and many liturgical songs, and wrote scientific works on botany, medicine, and healing. Her insights gave her a deserved reputation as well-accomplished in healing arts. She traveled widely and, like Bernard, was a consultant to many in Church and monastic leadership and often would attract huge crowds. She could be outspoken and would at times reprove corrupt or underachieving Church and civil leaders. Once, she got into ecclesial trouble for approving the burial on convent grounds of a man who had been excommunicated.

Hildegard has become popular in recent times, sometimes even with feminists and New Age adherents. She was a woman of great accomplishment who is worthy of admiration, but her genuine devotion to God and service to the Church is the true substance of her legacy. For her contributions, she has been named a Doctor of the Church.

CATHEDRALS AND CLERGY

Art and architecture, present in the life of the Church throughout most of her history, blossomed in the Middle Ages. The parish church was the preeminent architectural feature of most every town, and, along with hundreds of monasteries — large and small — these edifices dotted the landscape.

Transcending these, from the beginning of the twelfth century, was the rise of spectacular Gothic cathedrals. Growing out of the Romanesque style that preceded them, these massive, soaring churches, with their flying buttresses, ribbed vaults, pointed arches, abundant statuary, and stained-glass windows, rose to dominate the landscape of numerous cities — first in France, then throughout much of Europe over the next several centuries. Some of the most famous include Notre Dame in Paris and the cathedrals at Chartres, Canterbury, and at the Duomo in Florence. Although to be sure there was a human sense of pride and "keeping up with the Joneses" in building these magnificent cathedrals, a true spirit of honoring God was present as well. They also stand as a testament to the popular devotion to the Virgin Mary in this era. A number of these cathedrals, not only at Paris, but at many other cities as well, are named after Mary, or Our Lady, (*Notre Dame* in French). The people themselves came together as laborers to build these cathedrals out of their faith and devotion to God, and to honor Mary. These monumental churches, with their extraordinary height and luminosity, were intended to lift the worshipers' minds and hearts to God and heaven. A visit to one today can make evident how true this is. As Pope Benedict XVI said: "The upward thrust was intended as an invitation to prayer and at the same time was itself a prayer. Thus the Gothic cathedral is intended to express in its architectural lines the soul's longing for God."[1] Their very existence is a testament to the Catholic sense that created beauty in art and architecture can be something holy and uplifting, the very opposite of the spirit of iconoclasm. This was no less true in the East as well. The patriarch's magnificent church of Hagia Sophia ("Holy Wisdom") in Constantinople, though not Gothic but Byzantine and built centuries earlier, was arguably the most spectacular in all the Christian world. Alas, in 2020, for the second time in its history, Hagia Sophia was turned into a mosque.

During this time the clergy, too, had its strengths and weaknesses. The investiture battles continued. Many of the higher clergy continued to be "plants" from kings with mostly secular goals. Yet many others were devoted to pastoring their congregations and dioceses as best they could.

One clergy issue that garnered attention in this era was *celibacy*. Many of the clergy in this era and before did not have wives, and some did. Others, without wives, were not celibate, even maintaining mistresses. In the early centuries, celibacy was not legislated, and many, including some of the apostles, were married. However, celibacy grew in significance and in practice, even without being required. By the third century, bishops were not permitted to marry after being ordained. Many of the Church Fathers, including Jerome and Augustine, praised the virtue of celibacy. Over the centuries, celibacy became the preferred choice for priests; but since it was not universal, confusion grew — especially during the times when the moral state of the clergy waned. Of the clergy who had become priests via civil appointments and not as a religious calling, most had little interest in celibacy. And, as many had children, issues of inheritance arose. The Second Lateran Council met in 1139 to address both the concern of ownership of Church property and the integrity of the priesthood. It made celibacy a requirement, clarifying expectations and codifying the prevailing practice. However, some high-placed clergy over the next few centuries, especially those appointed by civil authorities, still kept mistresses — often without even trying to conceal it. Despite the failings of some, thousands of dedicated clergy remained faithful to the thousand-year practice of celibacy.

17

THE CRUSADES

The Crusades are complicated, both in theory and in action. But first and foremost, and beyond the specifics of their military history, they constituted a *spiritual movement* of the Christian people of the West. They grew out of the personal faith and piety of popes and priests, kings and peasants. Few known saints were directly involved, but this spiritual energy, so common among saints, is what lay behind the Crusades, even as we are mindful of the sins and shortcomings of many crusaders.

The idea of a holy war (*bellum sacrum* in Latin) appears throughout much of history and among a multitude of religions. The idea tends to mean a war in the name of God for a spiritual purpose, whether justifiable or not, such as spreading a faith or rescuing coreligionists. Wars in the name of Islam are prime examples. The Catholic Church came late to the idea of a holy war. The many wars involving Christians in the first millennium had either been defensive or led by civil princes for secular reasons such as expanding their realm, even if some sense of spreading the Faith might have been part of a warrior's motivation at times. The Catholic concern about any war (even if not always followed in practice) was the demands of charity and the commandment not to kill. Centuries earlier, Saint Augustine had advanced what is called "just war theory," which endeavored to balance the needs of self-defense with the call not to kill. Just war theory (*bellum iustum*) was accepted through the Middle Ages, if not always followed, and included strict limitations on the conduct of war for it to be considered a moral undertaking. Augustine's just war theory remains an active though debated theological concept to this day.

The eleventh century saw an evolution in Church thinking from just war to holy war. From this thinking, the idea of *crusades* was born. Simply declaring a holy war and proceeding to fight it does not create automatic justification. Some holy wars have been wrongly called, and others, at least in part, wrongly fought. Yet, under the right circumstances and motivations, a holy war can be just and justifiable.

The word *crusade* is derived from the Latin word for cross: *crux*. Soldiers of the Crusades often wore a red cross on their breasts to signify the holy nature of the endeavor. In the broadest sense, crusades were Catholic Church–commissioned holy wars against heretics or infidels in the Middle Ages. These included the "Northern Crusades" against pagan Slavs near the Baltic Sea, the *Reconquista*, or a long series of military expeditions with the aim to drive out the Moors from Spain, and, as we shall see, a Crusade against the Albigensians in southern France. However, our focus will be on the more popular understanding of the Crusades, the series of Church-commissioned military expeditions from the late eleventh through the thirteenth centuries to free the Holy Land from Muslim control.

The notion of sending a crusading army to the Holy Land caught fire during the eleventh century in the West with reports that the Muslims in the Holy Land were attacking both Christians living in the Holy Land and pilgrims to the Christian holy sites. In the early eleventh century, thousands of Christian churches in the Holy Land were burned or pillaged, including the Church of the Holy Sepulcher in Jerusalem.[1] These reports caused great concern and advanced the idea of a holy war to aid Christians under Muslim rule and to recover these lands. Pope Urban II "preached" the First Crusade in 1095, formally raised at the Council of Clermont. He gave a speech urging that an army be sent to the Holy Land and promised forgiveness of sins to soldiers who took up the call to arms. This had the effect of the Catholic Church embracing the concept of a holy war. Thus began the Crusades.

The rightness of the Crusades has been subject to fierce debate. The truth lies well between the old Catholic ideal of holy, noble knights fighting to take back the Holy Land from the clutches of Muslim usurpers and the modern secular narrative of bloodthirsty westerners who raped and pillaged their way through cultured Byzantine and Muslim lands. And the truth is still debated, though the parameters of the debate have narrowed from the extremes.

First, it is imperative to emphasize what many current secular historians often ignore or minimize: The Crusades were efforts to *take back* lands conquered by the Muslim armies in the seventh century. The ethics of this can be debated, but to call the Crusades an effort to grab lands which Muslims peacefully and rightfully held is simply inaccurate. The Muslim invasions in the seventh century were expansionist conquests, not provoked or rooted in historical claims to these lands, with the primary purpose to spread the new faith of Islam. The invaders uprooted the existing Jewish and Christian cultures and tried — with great success over time — to convert to Islam the surviving local inhabitants. Jerusalem and Palestine had been Jewish-Christian territory. North Africa, with its great cities of Alexandria and Carthage, was a thriving Christian area — the land of Athanasius and Augustine and other Church Fathers and saints.

The treatment of Christians in these conquered territories varied in time and place. In many instances Christians were severely persecuted, even made slaves. At other times, they were allowed to live their lives and keep their religion (witness St. John Damascene). The eastern patriarchates were allowed to continue, but with much more limited pastoral influence. Even so, Christians and other non-Muslims were designated as *dhimmi*, second-class citizens subject to extra taxes and burdens. The ultimate goal of the Muslim rulers (often called at the time *Saracens*) was not religious tolerance for its own sake but conversion to Islam. Tolerance, when it was employed, was out of practicality, not any innate commitment to religious freedom. And indeed, as in the eleventh century, the Muslim rulers in the Holy Land would often subject Christians and Jews to severe persecution and violence. Reports of the violence toward Christian pilgrims and residents is what prompted Pope Urban's call for the First Crusade.

The number of Crusades to the Holy Land varies by historian. It is usually considered to be at least eight, through the late thirteenth century. Our focus will be on the first four Crusades over a period of just more than a century — from 1096 to 1204. They are the most consequential.

Pope Urban II was able to form an army led by wealthy knights to lead the First Crusade. This Crusade, which embarked in 1096, was the most successful. It was a marvel of technical achievement, as armies of thousands — with thousands of followers — made their way across the plains of central Europe to Constantinople.

Despite Pope Urban's admonition that the Crusade was a noble and holy endeavor which required the highest moral standards, some of the crusaders did not live up to that calling. One appalling example: On the way to the East, advance crusading armies raided several Jewish villages in Germany, killing thousands of "infidel" Jews. Jews had coexisted with Christians in Europe in an uneasy peace for centuries, but anti-Semitism worsened in the eleventh century throughout Christendom and periodically reared its ugly head with persecution and attacks.

The crusaders, who had hoped for cooperation from their fellow Christians in Constantinople, bickered with the Byzantine emperor, who in turn had hoped for the crusaders' cooperation in fending off the Muslim Turks who were threatening Constantinople. The crusaders declined, turned south, and eventually attained their goal, taking Jerusalem in 1099. They pillaged the city, killing hundreds of residents, unaware that many were Christian. However, they were unable to establish a new, secure state either in Jerusalem or in the surrounding territory of the Holy Land. They were forced into a defensive position for decades, trying to ward off Muslim efforts to recapture Jerusalem, with ever-shrinking garrisons as soldiers returned home. That was to be the fate of the remaining Crusades.

The Second Crusade, conducted in the middle of the twelfth century, was a military failure, and opened the door for the Muslim warrior Saladin to recapture Jerusalem. Two points about the Second Crusade: First, it represents the reality that the entire crusading enterprise was fraught with an array of difficulties and was not destined to reach the goal of capturing and retaining the Holy Land. Just as in modern times, Western efforts at "nation-building" are much harder to achieve than initial military success. Holding Jerusalem and surrounding areas proved to be too difficult in the long run. Second, even with the failure, the spiritual aspect of the Crusades as legitimate holy wars is underscored by the role of St. Bernard of Clairvaux. This influential and deeply devout saint preached the Second Crusade. Bernard believed that a crusade was indeed justifiable and even necessary to carry out the will of God. He gave an impassioned speech in support of this Crusade at Vezelay in France in 1144. As a spokesperson for the Church, he renewed the promise of an indulgence to remit punishment for sin for those who participated and described the impending Crusade as a holy calling to defeat the Muslims and deliver the holy places from them. Bernard's speeches at Vezelay and elsewhere had the desired effect. They stirred the spiritual zeal of many, leaders and peasants alike, to form and join the armies of this Crusade. However, a sense that a crusade is God's will (even if indeed it is true) neither guarantees success nor assures the infallibility of saints preaching the crusade. Human and military weaknesses still exist, the enemy still fights, and God's providence is mysterious. Despite Saint Bernard's appeal, the Second Crusade was not a success. One is reminded of Mother Teresa's observation that God calls us to be faithful, not successful.

Saint Bernard also gave crucial support to the *Knights Templar*, a monastic military order founded in 1119, between the first two Crusades. This order of "fighting monks" represented the religious zeal behind the crusading movement. Devout, committed to serving God and the Crusades, the Templars built their headquarters on the Temple Mount in Jerusalem, then under crusader control. As armored cavalry, the Templars became skilled warriors in many of the battles in subsequent Crusades, even once defeating an army led by Saladin. Most of their members were not soldiers, however, and the Templars also built fortifications and supported the cause behind the scenes. They also became influential back home, and for two centuries they were heavily involved in charity and finance throughout Europe.

The great Muslin warrior Saladin had recaptured Jerusalem from the crusaders in 1187. The goal of the Third Crusade, conducted in the late 1180s, was to retake Jerusalem again. Despite its illustrious leaders, Holy Roman Emperor Frederick Barbarossa, Richard Lionheart of England, and Philip of France, this Crusade fizzled without success. Jerusalem remained in Muslim hands and the position of the remaining territory still held by the crusading armies became more precarious.

During this Third Crusade, a number of hermits inhabited some caves at Mount Carmel. In 1209, their leader, **Saint Brocard** (d. 1231), requested the assistance of **St. Albert of Jerusalem** (1150–1215) to write a rule for them. He did so. This was the founding of one of the most noteworthy monastic orders in Church history, the *Order of Carmelites*, the order of Sts. Teresa of Ávila, John of the Cross, and Thérèse of Lisieux, an order that thrives worldwide today. Albert was a gifted Italian bishop, who once mediated a dispute between the pope and Emperor Barbarossa. The pope appointed him the patriarch of Jerusalem in 1205, a dangerous assignment since Jerusalem was back under Saracen control and persecution was rife. Albert courageously agreed, but providentially, he had to relocate to the crusader-held town of Acre, which happened to be close to Mount Carmel. The Carmelites consider Saint Albert to be their patron.

The Fourth Crusade, commissioned by Pope Innocent III, was a tragedy. Its objective was to engage the Muslim military forces in Egypt, making it possible to recapture Jerusalem from the south. Lured by a would-be king of Constantinople with a bevy of promises, the leaders of the Crusade redirected the army while on route and, in one of the darkest moments in Christian history, the crusaders invaded, captured, sacked, and plundered Orthodox Christian Constantinople in 1204, including the magnificent church of Hagia Sophia. Pope Innocent had not authorized this and was furious. Constantinople was the seat of Eastern Christendom and by no means a target for crusaders. Western forces held onto Constantinople for several decades until the Byzantines were able to regain their capital. The sack of Constantinople created deep and understandable bitterness and effectively ended the efforts to reunify the Christians of East and West. Despite profound apologies given by Pope St. John Paul II, this tragic event remains today an emotional impediment to efforts to reunite the Catholic and Orthodox churches.

Several succeeding Crusades followed over the next hundred years, none of them effective. Even the leadership of St. Louis IX, King of France, who led the Seventh and Eight Crusades into Egypt, failed to find lasting success. The difficulty of sending armies long distances, the tendencies of the leaders to make bad decisions on their own, and military weakness so far from home all combined to result in their failure to hold onto the lands captured in the First Crusade. By 1291, the crusading enterprise to the Holy Land was over, and the Holy Land was back in the hands of the Muslims.

Were the Crusades, then, a failure? At best, they were only partially successful in retaking the Holy Land, and then only for a time. But even if they were not military successes in the long run, their spiritual dimension cannot be ignored. Despite the moral failures of some, most of the leaders and soldiers were motivated by genuine Christian piety and fought honorably. The effort itself, even if not militarily successful, was, as John Vidmar, quoting historian Henri Daniel-Rops, notes, "the manifestation of a spiritual impulse, springing from the depth of man's soul."[2] Vidmar continues: "Recent historians maintain that the Crusades simply make no sense unless they are understood spiritually, or at least that a spiritual dimension was active. They were, if ever there was one, a holy war."[3] Such spiritual energy, messy and imperfect as it was, cannot fail to bear fruit. Without much doubt, the spiritual energy flowing from the crusading spirit penetrated Christian society and became a contributing reason for the flowering of Christian faith and civilization in the thirteenth century. This century that followed the first four Crusades is often considered the high point of the Faith in the Middle Ages, perhaps even of all Church history.

18

A RESURGENCE OF CHRISTIAN FAITH AND CULTURE

Often in God's providence, a springtime will follow a period of darkness. The tenth and eleventh centuries were trying times for the Church, but seeds of spiritual renewal began to emerge within Christendom in the late eleventh century and through the twelfth. The ensuing thirteenth century — though far from perfect — would bring renewal, like springtime after winter. It was home to some of the greatest saints the Church has ever had. And it started with Francis of Assisi.

St. Francis of Assisi (1181–1226) is one of the greatest saints in history. He had tremendous influence both in his own time and for posterity. What made Francis stand out so powerfully was, down to his very core, his radical, total, and often literal commitment to follow God, as much as anyone in Church history. It is evident that God chose to provide Francis a special measure of grace, not just for himself but so that Francis could inspire the world to turn to God. Francis may well be considered one of the greatest icons of Jesus Christ in the history of the Church. His primary charism — then and throughout history — was to reflect the very Person of Jesus Christ. He did so by his total commitment to the Gospel. Francis was no "hippy" who danced among the flowers, but a highly intelligent and intentional man consumed with following Christ to the point of suffering.

Francis grew up in a well-to-do mercantile family in Assisi, then a city-state in north-central Italy. He was a free-spirited socialite in his youth, yet he showed signs of sincere compassion. As was common, he entered the military, and fought in one of the frequent small wars between city-states in Italy. He was captured, and while sick in prison, began to question the direction of his life. Not long after, he experienced a profound conversion which occurred in a series of encounters with God, effecting in him a strong desire to love and serve God. Family members and friends could not understand the radical change in Francis, but their efforts to persuade him to "come to his senses" failed. One of the events in his conversion process occurred as he visited the church of San Damiano outside Assisi. There he heard a voice asking him to "rebuild my church." At first Francis assumed God meant the building, which indeed was in disrepair — and which he began to rebuild — but in time he understood that God was calling him to a larger mission of "repair" within the Church at large.

He set himself to it with a radical willfulness. Inspired by the Gospel accounts in which Jesus sent out his disciples to preach (see Mt 10:5–15), telling them to take nothing, not even a second coat, Francis set out to preach. He followed this Gospel passage literally — retaining no possessions, begging for provision, trusting in God for all his needs.

Francis exuded an uncommon and extraordinary joy no matter how difficult the circumstances. It may well not be everyone's calling, but at that time and place, with all the needs of a weak Church, this was Francis's calling. Whether embracing lepers, getting robbed and beaten or turned away, or being disinherited by his furious father, Francis never lost his joy in the love of God. This spiritual fruit of joy came not by life's circumstances, but by knowing God's love. That insight is one of his enduring legacies. Perhaps lost in the popular understanding of his exuberance was his tremendous wisdom, his profound insight into the divine plan. His radical new lifestyle was rooted deeply in prayer.

As Francis traveled the roads and preached God's love, he began to attract followers. He had tapped into a hunger for life's meaning, felt by many in his day. He settled with his followers at a small chapel near Assisi called the *Portiuncula* or "Little Portion."

By the year 1210, Francis, who remained an obedient son of the Church, traveled to Rome to seek the pope's approval of his newly drafted rule of life and permission for his followers to travel the roads and preach. Always thinking big, he chose Rome instead of his local bishop. In one of the most significant moments in Church history, Pope Innocent III, at first reluctant, decided against the advice of his advisors and gave Francis approval. Francis and his band of followers were then able to take to the roads and preach the love of God and the need of repentance. He and his followers became highly popular and effective at stirring the flame of faith among the populace. As the number of followers grew, he organized his *Franciscans*, as his order came to be known, into three groups, or orders: the first order, the friars, or the Order of Friars Minor, both priests and brothers; the second order, women religious, who became known as the Poor Clares; and a third order, known as the Third Order Regular (TOR), those who still lived in the world but were formally associated and agreed to live by the rule. Poverty (owning nothing), trust in God, obedience, and radical charity were the foundations of his rule.

The women followers were led by **St. Clare of Assisi** (1194–1253), who was inspired by the preaching of Francis to leave behind a well-to-do life and follow Jesus radically. Her family also resisted mightily, but she stuck with her vocation, in time even attracting her mother and sisters. She founded the women's branch of Franciscans, the Poor Clares, and led them for forty years under a rule that included Franciscan poverty, and which Pope Innocent also approved. Clare outlived Francis by twenty-seven years, and thus was able to step outside Francis's shadow and grow in her own unique ministries. She became an influential consultant to Church leaders and a powerful prayer warrior. Her order and her influence continue to this day.

Francis attracted so many Third Order Regulars that the princes of the Italian city-states were less able to conduct wars because they could not find enough men to join their armies. This is typical of the strategy of Francis — not so much to confront evil and corruption directly, but simply to preach and carry out the love of God so that the love spreads and swallows up much of the evil and corruption around him. The Franciscan "movement," if it can be fairly called that, created a profound stir on the Italian peninsula and beyond, and led to a noticeable return of thousands to the active practice of the Catholic Faith.

Francis popularized the nativity crèche, and tried to convert the Sultan of Egypt (nephew of Saladin) when he visited the front lines of the Fifth Crusade. In 1224 he received the stigmata, visible wounds that corresponded to Christ's wounds on the cross. He and his Franciscans were among the most influential force in rebuilding the Church of the Middle Ages and reigniting the spark of faith. The Franciscans remain active today — eight hundred years later — and continue to foster faith and renewal in the Church.

One of the most effective of the early Franciscans was **St. Anthony of Padua** (1195–1231). He was born in Lisbon, ordained a priest, and probed around for his vocation until joining the Franciscans, possibly moved by accounts of Franciscan martyrs in Morocco. He may be known today mostly as the patron of lost articles, but in fact he was one of the greatest preachers in the history of the Church. He traveled the roads of Italy as a friar, eloquently preaching repentance, conversion, and the love of God to great effect. Thousands listened to him and returned to the Faith. He settled in Padua where he preached against corruption, leading to a full revival of faith in the city. Francis himself admired the learned Anthony and appointed him to be a teacher to the friars. He is a Doctor of the Church.

A contemporary of Francis from Spain, **Saint Dominic** (1170–1221), embarked upon a parallel ministry. Dominic was a gifted scholar — particularly of Scripture — a Benedictine prior, and a reformer in his early career, helping to reform the Cistercians. He was a man of deep prayer and faith, who, like so many saints, saw the call to charity. Once during a famine, he sold his precious Scripture parchments to aid the hungry, reasoning that he should not study with dead skins when living skins were going hungry.

As Dominic's career was unfolding, a notable heresy was taking hold in southern France — *Albigensianism*. This was a dualist neo-Gnostic belief system. Albigensians (also known as *Catharists*), believed that there was a good (the spiritual) and an evil (the physical, including the body). Thus, like the Gnostics, they believed God could not have become man. Their spiritual goal was to escape the captivity of the body. Their practices were radically ascetic, with the goal to escape the influence of the physical. It was a denial of grace and of the Incarnation. Pope Innocent III authorized a Crusade against them. Church-sponsored and secular French armies carried out this Crusade from 1209 to 1229. It was successful militarily but it took more time for this sect to fade. It also resulted in the deaths of thousands of people and opened the door for military opportunism by secular rulers, prompting the Church to begin to doubt the wisdom of crusading.

The rise of the Albigensians affected the direction of Dominic's missionary activity in his later years. Called to evangelize them and filled with zeal, he preached to the wayward Albigensians, first in the wake of the Crusade, but to limited effect. His concern for their return to the Catholic Faith led him to found an order of evangelists in 1214. He and his followers became known as the Order of Preachers, later called *Dominicans*. They grew in number, and traveled mostly throughout Spain, France, and Italy. Dominic tended to the growth of the order, and obtained papal approval in 1216. He and his followers founded new houses and sought to harmonize the intellectual life with the needs of the people through their preaching. These Dominicans were highly successful in this traveling ministry of conversion and reform, drawing thousands back to or deeper into their Faith, including many of the Albigensians. Dominic's order practiced a strict asceticism, especially as compared to the regular clergy, and this attribute played a key role in attracting the ascetical Albigensians.

These two orders, Franciscans and Dominicans, began to be called *mendicants*: traveling, begging friars, unlike parish clergy or cloistered monks. They crisscrossed the roads and villages of Europe for centuries with their preaching, and were instrumental in fostering the faith of thousands of Christians throughout Medieval Europe. That these two orders, with so many similarities, exploded onto the scene independently but at the same time, is markedly the work of the Holy Spirit. God raised up these two great saints to foster a two-pronged revival of faith in the thirteenth-century world, and beyond — even to the present day.

One of the most powerful and important popes of the Middle Ages, **Pope Innocent III** (r. 1198–1216), was a contemporary of Francis and Dominic. He is not canonized as a saint, but still he was a dedicated man of faith. In addition to approving the rule and ministries of Francis, Innocent fought hard to obtain papal supremacy over the kings of Europe, believing that the pope ought to have civil as well as spiritual authority. This is not the ideal model for the papacy, but it was rooted in a genuine desire to enhance the Church's spiritual mission in the world. Innocent had the force of personality to advance papal authority and to garner independence from the interference of kings. His efforts to overcome lay investiture by the kings were largely successful. One instance was standing down King John of England (of Magna Carta fame) over whether the pope or the king appoints the archbishop of Canterbury. Innocent prevailed.

Innocent was also a reformer. He fought heresies and other challenges to Church teaching, sought reform of the clergy, and presided over the consequential Fourth Lateran Council in 1215, which addressed doctrine and Church order and is considered the most significant council of the era. This council affirmed that Christ is fully present in the Eucharist, defined the doctrine of transubstantiation, and made a rule of Church discipline that all Catholics make a confession to a priest at least once a year. It addressed Church and clergy discipline and how to respond to heresies. It asserted the primacy of the pope but also gave a succeeding order of primacy. Interestingly, the patriarch of Constantinople (who was present at the council) was given first order after the pope. Efforts to heal the division with the Eastern Church, however, were not successful.

Before and after the ill-fated Fourth Crusade, Innocent made efforts to heal the Schism between East and West. The devastating sack of Constantinople in 1204 by his crusading army — which infuriated Innocent — dealt a fatal blow to his efforts. The Byzantines recaptured their capital in 1261 from the occupying crusaders, but Constantinople and the Byzantine Empire were weakened.

The thirteenth century saw the growth of scholarship and theology in the monasteries, among a number of saints, and in the new universities that emerged in places such as Paris, Bologna, and Oxford. The modern-day university system traces its beginnings to these original medieval Catholic universities. The value placed upon knowledge and education by the Catholic Church laid the foundation for the advancement of science and culture, as well as faith, in the Western world in the centuries hence. In addition to the universities, cathedral schools, located in numerous dioceses, educated students of the nobility for work in the Church. Their history reaches back centuries but, in the eighth and ninth centuries, Charlemagne established numerous schools associated and located at cathedrals and created the momentum for their proliferation. In time, these schools expanded to teach the liberal arts and contributed to the enhancement of education and literacy among at least the upper classes. Several influential saints in this century built upon this foundation of schools and universities and leavened their intellectual pursuits with a strong faith. These were the forerunners of the advancement of Christian intellectual life.

The greatest of Franciscan scholars, **Saint Bonaventure** (1221–1274) was born in Italy five years before Francis's death. In fact, Francis may have cured him of a childhood illness (though whether this is truth or legend is unclear). Bonaventure taught Scripture and theology at Paris, overlapping with Thomas Aquinas, whom he met. His theological and scholarly writings, like Augustine's, emphasize a heartfelt understanding of the love of God. Bonaventure also defended the mendicants from their critics and became the head of the Friars Minor. In that position he worked to resolve disputes and divisions within the Franciscans (an unfortunate but perhaps inevitable development after their founder's death). His "constitutions" helped to heal those divisions and to preserve the Franciscan order. Without Bonaventure's intervention, the Franciscans may not have survived. As his gifts became more known, the popes called upon him for assistance and he was made a cardinal-bishop. He left to posterity a body of philosophical and theological writings, sermons, and the first biography of Saint Francis. He is a Doctor of the Church.

St. Thomas Aquinas (1225–1274), one of the greatest scholars in the history of the Church, first and foremost was a man of extraordinary faith. He was born in Italy and as a youth sought to become a monk. When he decided to become a Dominican, his rich and regal family resisted, believing that an order of "beggars" was beneath their family's dignity. They even imprisoned him for two years, but he escaped to Paris, where providentially he met and learned under St. Albert the Great. His theological writings and their philosophical system, now called *Thomism*, have informed the Church for centuries and remain influential today. Along with Albert, Aquinas fostered the marriage of faith and reason. This was not new — Church Fathers such as Justin Martyr and earlier saints including Anselm also recognized the consistency of faith and reason — but he advanced this seemingly obvious concept. One can accept the doctrines of the Faith as divinely revealed truth and at the same time delve deeply into them to understand them and to teach why they are true.

Aquinas did this especially in his *Summa Theologiae*, his greatest work and his gift to the Church in posterity. Thomas, along with Albert, also initiated the use of the pre-Christian Greek philosopher Aristotle in his theology — highly controversial in his time. Aristotle provided a basis for reason, for the use of the mind to discern truth. He also provided a foundation for ordering thought and examining material things in a way that their true nature could be identified. This, Aquinas discovered, was useful in explaining the truth of Revelation. The *Summa* is set up logically with topical statement, objections to the statement, and then his reply, which was most always a brilliant and thorough exposition on the question. From the existence of God through most of the teachings of the Church, Aquinas laid out a methodical exposition, explanation, and defense of the Christian Faith. The depth and breadth of his insights and analysis is extraordinary. It would seem that he thought of everything — and thought with brilliance, clarity, logic, and the mind of faith.

Aquinas did not finish the *Summa*. Late in life, after creating a massive body of work, he had a vision of God's majesty that convinced him to stop writing. He explained: "All that I have written appears to me to be so much straw after the things that have been revealed to me."[1] To know God as Creator, as Savior, as one who loves us is the true knowledge. That may be his greatest teaching. Aquinas laid the foundation for the future of theology in the Church. His popularity among theologians comes and goes (saying more about subsequent theologians than him) but he provided the tools for future theologians to interpret Scripture, reflect on God and the Church, and address the coming advances in science. Without Aquinas, the Catholic Church would be much more fundamentalistic than it is today. Not only a Doctor of the Church, he is known as the "Angelic Doctor."

St. Albert the Great (1206–1280) was an influential and trailblazing scholar in his own right; but, like Barnabas and Monica before him, he is particularly important for influencing and nurturing a great saint. Without Albert, Thomas Aquinas would not have been all that he is for us. Albert and Thomas studied and taught together at Paris and Cologne for many years. Still, had Aquinas never been born, Albert would have his place as a great saint. He advanced the *Scholastic method* of theological study initiated by Anselm, which applied Aristotle's methods of intellectual inquiry to theology. Aquinas developed it further, and these two are considered the leading proponents of the Scholastics, a school of theology that would last for centuries, and still has a place today as an authentic path to theological truth. Albert became provincial of the Dominican order in 1254 and was a consultant to popes for many years. He also was arguably the leading natural scientist of his day, with vast knowledge of biology, physics, astronomy, and geography. He, too, is a Doctor of the Church.

⑲
MORE MEDIEVAL SAINTS

Although not many saints came out of the Crusades themselves, a number of influential saints left their mark on the Church from back home while the battles of the Crusades raged in the Middle East. We have already met several significant twelfth-century saints who lived during the first four (and most significant) of the Crusades. And we just met some of the greatest saints in the history of the Church, whose lives corresponded with the Crusades of the thirteenth century. Now we turn to several other saints of the thirteenth century whose impact centered upon the westernmost areas of Christendom.

A Renaissance man before the Renaissance, **St. Raymond of Peñafort** (1175–1275) from northeastern Spain, was, in his one hundred years, a Dominican, a scholar, an evangelist, and a strong influence on an array of thirteenth-century Church affairs. Called upon to collect, organize, and make sense of various diocesan and papal documents, his work became a foundation for the development of canon law, the governing regulations for practice and procedure for the entire Catholic Church, directing Church activities toward conformance with her Gospel mission. The canon law of the Catholic Church was the West's first legal system and is the oldest continuing legal code in the Western world. Canon law continues to govern Church matters in the present day. Raymond was also a powerful preacher who helped to "re-Christianize" areas of Spain that had been under Muslim control. He preached to Moors, Jews, and Christians who had been under Moorish control, leading to thousands of conversions and baptisms. He became head of the Dominicans in 1238 and enhanced the order's constitution and training. And Raymond even persuaded Aquinas to write his *Summa Contra Gentiles*, a series of treatises which helped missionaries explain the Catholic Faith, particularly when encountering Muslims and Jews in Raymond's native Spain.

Many Spanish Christians through the end of the fifteenth century had to endure living under Muslim authority. The *Moors*, as they were called, had secured control of most of the Spanish peninsula in the eighth century and built an advanced culture that lasted for several centuries. In addition to Christian subjects, a large population of Jews settled in Moorish Spain. Some historians suggest that this may have been in part because persecution of Jews in Christian Europe made Moorish Spain, while far from ideal, a more livable place. Such persecution, though not at all times and places, did occur, prompting numerous popes to condemn anti-Semitism.

The Moors' central city, Cordoba, was home to many beautiful buildings, including a magnificent mosque built over a former cathedral (which now has been converted back to a cathedral). The Moors held onto large portions of the peninsula until the Spanish throne, under Ferdinand and Isabella, drove them from their last foothold on the peninsula in 1492, just months before Columbus's first voyage to the Americas. (Victory over the Moors allowed the Spanish crown to pivot with greater energy toward exploration of Africa and the Americas in the ensuing years.) The Moors' hold in Spain gradually shrank as Christian armies of the *Reconquista*, with many fits and starts over long stretches of time, pushed the Moors further and further down the peninsula. As Christian forces continued this push, many Moors and Jews came under the control of Christian government. This raised the problem caused by efforts to convert the Muslims and Jews to Christianity. This was not always a noble endeavor: Forced conversions and persecution were common. One of the primary tasks of the Spanish Inquisition, as we shall see, was to address the situation of these "conversions."

Like his namesake from Penafort, **St. Raymond Nonnatus** (1204–1240) was also from Catatonia in northeastern Spain. *Nonnatus* is a title, Latin for "not born." Raymond's mother died in childbirth and he was taken by Caesarian section, and thus was "not born" via the birth canal. Raymond joined the *Mercedarians*, an order whose mission was to ransom Christians slaves from the Moors. A wealthy Frenchman, **St. Peter Nolasco** (1189–1258), founded the Mercedarians in 1218 with the help of his confessor, St. Raymond of Peñafort, and Peter used his wealth to pay ransoms. Raymond Nonnatus succeeded Peter as the leading ransomer and relocated to Algeria to further his work. Raymond offered himself as a hostage to free numerous Christian slaves until his funds were exhausted, all the while evangelizing the Algerian Muslims. Several converted. For this the Algerian governor pronounced a death sentence upon him. Raymond did have enough money to ransom himself out of execution and endured torture before Peter Nolasco rescued him and Raymond was able to return to Spain. The pope appointed him a cardinal but Raymond died shortly after the appointment.

Wars of the *Reconquista*, social upheaval, and the clash of civilizations in the thirteenth century made this an especially challenging time for Christians in Spain. These Spanish saints, along with countless anonymous faithful Catholics, helped to hold together the Faith on this peninsula in the midst of the turmoil of the times. Spain was to play a major role in the Church in centuries to come.

Among the myriad of noteworthy thirteenth century saints were a number of remarkable women. **Saint Hedwig** (1174–1243), daughter of a Bavarian nobleman, was married to the Duke of Silesia in central Europe. She and her husband had seven children. While raising them, she formed the first Cistercian monastery for women in her area, as well as other monasteries and hospitals. Upon her husband's death she entered the women's monastery she had helped to found. A number of miracles are attributed to Hedwig. **St. Juliana of Mt. Cornillon** (1192–1258) was a nun from Flanders. She experienced visions of Jesus, who told her that the Church had no feast honoring the Blessed Sacrament. Juliana spent much of her life, including her years as a convent prioress, advocating for such a feast, suffering regular opposition and occasional banishment from her convent. Six years after her death, Pope Urban IV approved the feast of *Corpus Christi*, largely due to her persistence. **St. Elizabeth of Hungary** (1207–1231), another laywoman, wife, and mother, lived a short but memorable life. She married a nobleman and they had four children. Elizabeth burned with charity and sought to do all she could for those around her. She founded hospitals, including one at the base of the castle where she lived. After her husband died during a Crusade, she devoted the rest of her life to caring for the sick, elderly, and poor.

Of the many extraordinary saints of this remarkable century, **Saint Louis** (1214–1272), one of France's greatest kings, was one of the most prolific. In 1234 he married and became King Louis IX. He and his wife, Margaret, had eleven children. Louis was a deeply devout man for whom his Catholic Faith was at the center of his life. Louis pursued not only personal piety, but also justice and charity throughout his reign. He founded a series of religious and educational institutions across France, including the great Parisian university of the Sorbonne; he protected vassals from ill treatment by their lords; he arbitrated disputes toward fair resolutions; and through his administrative skill and attentiveness, he fostered unprecedented prosperity and peace within his own realm and kept the peace with neighboring realms as well. He handled with success the various inevitable battles with nobles and rivals, securing expanded borders for France, and, in mid-century, led the Seventh and Eighth Crusades to Egypt. These were to become some of his few failures. After failing to achieve his military objectives, he was captured, ransomed, and then spent several years in the Holy Land before returning to his throne in France. Many of the great Gothic cathedrals rose with his approval during his reign. Saint Louis represents the finest of the most noble aspirations of Christendom and demonstrates what Catholic culture, at its very best, can produce. Unfortunately, as a ruler, Saint Louis was one of a kind.

As the thirteenth century gave way to the fourteenth, the Church was at a high water mark in influence, practice, and piety. Christendom was fully established in Europe. However, the times of comparative peace and piety began to fade. The fourteenth century would be one of the Church's most difficult. Corruption and immorality among kings and bishops again began to flourish, prompting the great Italian poet Dante Alighieri (1265–1321) to banish to hell several high clergymen, including a pope, in his *Inferno*, the first part of his monumental classic of Catholic and world poetic literature, the *Divine Comedy*.

20

THE AVIGNON PAPACY AND THE WESTERN SCHISM

One of the darkest periods in Church history began at the dawn of the fourteenth century: the *Avignon Papacy*, also called the "Babylonian Captivity." From 1305 to 1377, seven consecutive popes — all French — did not reign in Rome, but remained in France, in the southeastern city of Avignon.

As popes sought greater authority in secular affairs, they ran into obvious conflict with secular rulers. This included the French crown, which was coming into its own as a power in Europe and sought to wield that power — in both Church and state. This came to a head when Pope Boniface VIII asserted papal authority and was assaulted by henchmen of the French king. At the conclave after Boniface VIII's death in 1305, French authorities influenced the gathered cardinals to elect a Frenchman as pope — a friend of the king. This pope, who took the name Clement V, accepted the urging of the French crown not to conduct his papacy in Rome. He set up his papal court in Avignon instead, and the following six popes were also elected through the influence of the French crown and remained in Avignon.

The popes and the papal court in Avignon still aspired to do Church business and to represent the whole Church, but the separation from Rome challenged the very nature and identity of the "Roman" Catholic Church. Since the days of Saint Peter himself, the Catholic Church had been rooted in the primacy of the Bishop of Rome as universal pastor of the Church. For the pope to be located elsewhere was unthinkable for many. To be under the direct influence of one particular political power challenged the nature of the Church even more.

The Avignon popes took on princely trappings, and local clergy often bought their positions. Although this *simony* was a continuation of the practice of preceding popes in Rome, who in these times were often put in place by powerful Roman families, it was arguably worse under the Avignon popes. The situation lasted until 1377, when St. Catherine of Siena, along with some other strong voices, persuaded Pope Gregory XI to return to Rome. This ended the "exile," but did not remove the political rivalries that had caused the exile in the first place, and the cascading papal crisis grew worse.

After Gregory's death in 1378, the cardinals, despite French sympathies and while under threat of harm from Roman mobs, chose a Roman — Urban VI — to replace Gregory. Urban was not conciliatory and took action to reduce French influence. This prompted the French to try and rescind Urban's election and then to choose a new pope who would reign from Avignon. They did, and elected Clement VI in 1378 and then Benedict XIII in 1394, now known as *antipopes*, and they remained in Avignon. Meanwhile, during the same time as these two antipopes, the Romans and their allies elected a line of Roman popes. This situation of competing popes lasted for nearly forty years, eluding the best efforts of bishops and cardinals to bring clarity and peace to papal succession. One can imagine the confusion and the angst for the Church as for several decades two different popes claimed authority, in an event now known as the *Great Western Schism*.

At one point early in the fifteenth century, a third pope was chosen with the hope of replacing the two rival popes. However, this made matters even worse, since neither of the two preexisting rival popes, the one in Rome and the other in Avignon, abdicated. Thus, for a short time, three men claimed the papacy. Finally, at the Council of Constance in 1417, frantic Church leaders chose a new pope who took the name of Martin V, and finally were successful in removing the other claimants. The matter was resolved: The Schism was over. However, the Schism did enormous damage to the Church and demonstrated the continued negative impact of fierce rivalry between popes and kings. The spiritual state of the Church was dealt a serious blow. She needed saints.

While the leaders of the Church were behaving thus, the Faith of the Church was carried forward by countless ordinary people who took their Faith seriously and lived it accordingly. Even some in royalty lived saintly lives. These people, by their daily witness, kept pressure on their leaders to reform.

One royal saint was from the southwest corner of the continent: **St. Elizabeth of Portugal** (1271–1336). The grandniece of her namesake, St. Elizabeth of Hungary, she married the king of Portugal. While other royalty across Europe were caught in the intrigue of Church-state relations and schism, Queen Elizabeth of Portugal lived an exemplary life of piety, devotion, and charity to the poor. The very fact that she was inspired to sanctity and ministry was a sign that faith in the Church was far from dead. She opened convents and shelters for the poor and, like Saint Hedwig before her, tried to be a peacemaker amidst her family's conflicts. After her husband's death, Elizabeth wanted to enter a convent herself but settled for becoming a third order Franciscan.

Other saints were called to go beyond personal holiness and strike out in action against the failures and sin within the Church. The most remarkable and instrumental saint in leading the Church out of the Avignon wilderness was not a diplomat or bishop, but rather a surprise of the Holy Spirit: a young laywoman from a mercantile family in a mid-sized Tuscan city-state. **St. Catherine of Siena** (1347–1380) was the youngest of twenty-five children and, from a young age, was drawn powerfully to faith, prayer, and fasting. By age six she was experiencing mystical visions. At sixteen, she resisted her parents' hopes that she marry and instead became a third order Dominican and consecrated virgin.

Catherine's intense faith and spiritual gifts attracted the attention of the people of Siena and beyond. She stood out as a radically holy (if eccentric) woman who reflected the divine in unique ways. Numerous physical healings are attributed to her prayer, as well as a series of extraordinary conversions to the Faith. Her reputation as an extraordinary woman of faith grew throughout the region, opening doors for her to interact with leaders in the Church and various city-states, and she often became the go-to person to solve problems and concerns, sacred and profane. This young, illiterate laywoman once even mediated a rift between the papacy and the powerful city-state of Florence. Catherine became a spiritual advisor to many and a tireless evangelist for Christ. Illiterate until late in life, she dictated a vast number of letters to prelates, popes, nobles, war-mongers, and many others, always urging complete repentance and return to God as the solution to the issues and sin surrounding those to whom she wrote. In 1375, she visited the city-state of Pisa, west of Siena, and her visit led to a religious revival in the city.

Catherine was also a woman of great charity. She spent much of her life working in hospitals, throwing herself into tending to the sick with such a fervor that other caregivers marveled at her intensity. At first, she served those stricken with leprosy and cancer, and later, after an outbreak, victims of the Plague.

Her greatest contribution to the history of the Church, however, was her role in bringing the Avignon papacy to an end. As the Avignon papacy droned on with no sign of ending and Rome remained without the pope, this young Spirit-led woman began to dedicate herself to the pope's return to Rome, even making it happen. It is nothing short of astounding that this woman in her late twenties, who held no secular position or power, could be successful. Yet, with the extraordinary gifts necessary for her time, she was. She dictated a series of letters to Pope Gregory XI, urging him to come to Rome. Then, in 1376, Catherine traveled over four hundred miles from Siena to Avignon, succeeded in meeting with Pope Gregory, and persuaded him to move to Rome. It is hard to fathom how remarkable a feat this was. This French pope, set up with his court and all the papal retinue in a French city with the blessing and protection of the French crown, up and left for Rome at the insistence of an unconnected, seemingly powerless woman. Gregory's relocation ended the Avignon papacy, though after Gregory died two years later, things got worse before they got better. But Catherine's determination to persuade the pope to relocate to Rome was the necessary first step in the ultimate resolution of this issue forty years later.

All these ministries, carried out by a woman who died in Rome at age thirty-three, were possible only because of the exceptional way Catherine exhibited the grace of the Holy Spirit. People from all walks of life — from criminals to popes — recognized her to be a person filled with the Holy Spirit, with a prophetic charism of making known the mind of God for her times.

Catherine is one of just four women to be declared a Doctor of the Church, particularly for her powerful mystical writings, called *The Dialogue*. (St. Hildegard of Bingen, St. Teresa of Ávila, and St. Thérèse of Lisieux are the other three.) Dictated as the voice of God the Father speaking to her, *The Dialogue* is a product of prayer and communion with God, and is filled with profound spiritual wisdom and insight. Along with over four hundred of Catherine's personal letters, *The Dialogue* remains available today.

St. Bridget of Sweden (1303–1373) was a contemporary of Catherine. Bridget was born into a wealthy Nordic family, married young, and had eight children. She lived out her early vocations of wife and mother with a deep faith. Like Catherine, early in life she began to experience visions. She, too, was appalled by the Avignon papacy and in 1344 she wrote a letter to Pope Clement VI, telling him that she had received a vision which demanded that he return to Rome. Clement did not leave Avignon, but this added Bridget's voice and intercession toward the goal — which she never abandoned — of an end to the Avignon papacy.

In 1349, Bridget traveled across Europe from Sweden to Rome, no minor undertaking. She impressed the Romans with the depth of her faith and its practice, which included caring for pilgrims and the poor and reforming monasteries. In Rome she kept up her tireless efforts to persuade the Avignon popes to return to the Eternal City. Urban V did return briefly in 1370 at her urging, and he approved the constitution for her group of followers, but he returned to Avignon. Like Catherine, she urged Gregory XI to return, but Bridget died three years before he did. Without a doubt, however, Bridget's efforts were a beneficial prelude to Catherine's mission and the end of the Avignon Papacy.

21

THE BLACK DEATH

One of the most calamitous occurrences in Church history — and all human history — was the emergence of the Plague, often called the Black Death. In the middle of the fourteenth century, this sweeping pandemic turned both the Church and society upside down. There is no good way for us today to fathom the devastation brought by the Plague. Its breadth, scope, and virulence were unprecedented in world history — before or after — as it ravaged society, the Church, and families.

Believed to be a series of infections which were carried by fleas from rats, the Plague arrived first at Italy in 1347, possibly by ship from war and trade zones in the Middle East. In less than three years, about half of the population of Europe was dead. Europe's population in the mid-fourteenth century had been at least eighty million,[1] and historians have assessed that thirty to fifty million people succumbed to the Plague. The population would not recover for several centuries. Towns and cities were devastated. People lived in unimaginable fear. Dead were piled up, buried, burned, dumped in rivers, by the thousands. The disease (actually three separate but similar diseases) was so contagious that the infected often died alone as their family and loved ones feared — correctly — that tending to them would result in their own infection and death.

The Plague arced from southeast to northwest and back, a direct hit on Christian Europe (missing much of the non-Christian world). As it traveled, first via land and sea trade routes, people knew it was coming but had little ability to avoid it. Its relentless spread caused fear and panic when villagers heard that the neighboring villages were hit, and the disease crept closer and closer, until their first victim succumbed. The Plague roared through most major cities, including Florence, Paris, Avignon, and London, killing thousands and driving thousands more into the hills and countryside to try and escape. Then it followed roads into the villages and countryside. After the first wave seemingly burned out, it returned in succeeding waves over many decades (and never entirely disappeared) although nothing matched the devastation of the first wave. The infection was so strong in the first wave that, as one scholar described it, you could be fine at nine o'clock in the morning, feel sick at noon, and be dead by four o'clock.[2]

The impact of the pandemic created a monumental crisis of faith. People looked to their leaders for help and solace, but Church and civil leaders were just as helpless in the face of the Plague. Believers — which was just about everyone — prayed for help, healing, and relief. What was God doing? Where was he? Why was this happening? No good answers came. The clergy died at the same rate as the populace. And most often, it was the best of the clergy who died because they were the ones who had the courage and compassion to tend to the sick, contracting the disease themselves as a result.

Penitential processions sprang up all over Europe. In some places, anti-Semitism reared up and Jews were blamed and persecuted, even killed. Popes tried to hide inside their quarters in Avignon. At one point, local clergy requested that the pope scold the mendicants for interfering with pastoral care in their parishes. The pope angrily replied that it was the mendicants who were doing the most for the people. The entire situation seemed apocalyptic.

The question naturally arose whether the Plague was punishment sent by God for the sins of the people. This question is mostly beyond the scope of this book and better addressed by the best of Catholic theologians. Suffice it to say, however, that it is not sound Catholic theology to say that the Plague was punishment sent by God. For one thing, the sins of the era were no worse than many other times. Also, see Luke 13:1–5, where Jesus specifically teaches that victims of disasters were not singled out by God for punishment. Yet at the same time, events like the Plague can indeed be warnings and calls to repentance. The Plague took the lives of tens of millions, but millions of others throughout history have suffered in smaller numbers as well. We live in a fallen world where pandemics and natural disasters occur and both original and human sin contribute to human suffering. Ultimately, suffering and disasters, on large or small scales, remain a mystery. God sees in eternity, and no doubt holds close to his bosom millions of his children who died in the Plague.

Interestingly, a few cities escaped major outbreak. One was Rome.[3] This raises an interesting question. The Plague occurred in the middle of the Avignon Papacy. While Rome was mostly spared, Avignon was hit hard. A punishment on Avignon? For the reasons discussed above, the answer likely is no. After all, the ordinary citizens of Avignon were not responsible for the location of the papacy. And the citizens of Rome were certainly not holier than those of Avignon. But might there be some underlying reason why Avignon was devastated and Rome was spared while the popes were absent from Rome? Perhaps Rome being spared was a sign, not a punishment. Perhaps God was *inviting* the popes to return to the Church of Saint Peter, not by punishing Avignon, but by sparing Rome. Jesus describes the two disasters in Luke 13:1–5, not as punishments, but signs for us all. Admittedly, this is speculation, but given the magnitude and timing of the Plague as it visited the Body of Christ, it is reasonable for Christians to ponder these matters.

AFTER THE PLAGUE

In time the Plague subsided, but the European world was forever changed. It was smaller. Its economy was altered. The number of priests was shrunken. Confidence was shaken. Survivors picked up the pieces of their daily lives as society was knit back together, as the Church sought a way forward in this new world. By the grace of God, belief was not abandoned. Through it all, most people held onto their faith, devastated and confused as they were. A sense of hope and renewal grabbed a foothold. The human spirit and the Holy Spirit prompted the populace and the Church not to give up, but to rebuild lives and society.

Spiritual renewal movements began to appear and to attract the faithful. A particularly influential movement became known as *devotio moderna*, or "modern devotion." A Dutch deacon, Gerald Groote, began this grassroots movement in the late fourteenth century, during the time of the Western Schism, as an effort toward reform and personal spirituality. It spread throughout Dutch and German areas and from there across Europe. Christ-centered personal piety, devotional reading of the Bible, and communal living were among its most prevalent features. It attracted both laity and clergy. The emphasis on one's personal and devotional relationship with God was in contrast to existing movements, which tended to be scholarly and analytical. Perhaps most influential was the emphasis on meditative prayer. For the ordinary Catholic, prayer was mostly liturgical or formal (e.g., the Lord's Prayer). The popularizing of a devotional, meditative form of prayer not only guided many faithful toward an experience of God, but influenced future saints who advanced prayer of meditation, including Ignatius of Loyola and Teresa of Ávila.

This movement produced a series of mystics and writers who influenced thousands. Most prominent was Thomas á Kempis, whose spiritual classic, *Imitation of Christ*, was written and disseminated in the 1420s. It is second only to the Bible in number of readers over the last six hundred years. This book offers a window to the spiritual perspectives of medieval Christian faith, as well as the timeless wisdom of grace applied to the same issues and challenges in our Christian lives today.

Devotio moderna as a movement faded by the sixteenth century. Its community houses were largely swept away during the Protestant Reformation and its best features were absorbed into the spiritual movements of the Counter-Reformation.

Beyond its renewal movements, the post-Plague era was a time when the Church needed saints. Indeed, God raised up many in the 1400s. They were pastors, scholars, mystics, and preachers, and they strove to steer the survivors toward God as they picked up the pieces of their lives. These saints were also instrumental in laying the groundwork for the Counter-Reformation of the following century. As historian Christopher Dawson has pointed out, the concerted efforts to renew Catholicism in the wake of the Protestant Reformation had their roots in reform efforts in this century, before the Church was split asunder.[4]

Bl. Julian of Norwich (1342–1423) was an English anchoress and mystic. An *anchoress* was a woman who lived a life of consecrated seclusion. Her real name is unknown. She lived in a cell in the Church of Saint Julian in Norwich, England, and in 1373, she received a series of revelations on the Passion of Christ and the Trinity. She spent the next twenty years meditating on her visions. Her reputation for sanctity and her writings on her visions — titled *Revelations of Divine Love*, a key topic for people in the aftermath of the Plague — helped to encourage the faith of believers in England and beyond. Her writings survive and are available today.

Bl. Fra Angelico (1395–1455) was a Dominican Friar with a reputation for sanctity. However, it is for his gift that he is known: He was a master painter in the early Italian Renaissance. Almost all of his works are of Christian themes. Though many of his best-known paintings are various portrayals of the crucifixion, his *Annunciation* is one of the most iconic paintings in all of European art. He prayed as he painted and felt that much of his work was inspired, and reportedly said that one who illustrates the acts of Christ should be *with* Christ. Art with Christian themes — often commissioned by Church officials — was widespread in the Middle Ages and beyond, and played a catechetical role for a society not well literate, illustrating themes of the Faith, especially in churches throughout the Christian world. Fra Angelico provides inspiration to all Christians who seek to use their artistic gifts for the glory of God.

A nearby contemporary of Fra Angelico was **St. Rita of Cascia**, Italy (1381–1457). Rita was forced into an unwanted marriage at age twelve and endured eighteen years of unhappiness until her husband died in a brawl. After his death, she tried to enter an Augustinian convent but was rebuffed several times. Finally, her persistence paid off and she embarked on a remarkable ministry. Her sanctity, austerities, concern for others, and profuse intercessory prayer attracted many lapsed Catholics back to the Faith. She had visions later in life and a number of miracles were attributed to her after her death.

St. John of Kanty (1390–1473), also known as John Cantius, was a priest and town leader in Krakow, Poland. He was a Scripture scholar, powerful preacher, and parish priest with notable concern for the poor of Krakow. The care of souls was his overriding concern. The townspeople looked up to him as a moral and civic leader, and with this reputation, he helped to sustain and nourish the Faith in the strategic eastern European city, later home to Pope John Paul II. The Newbery Medal–winning early twentieth-century young adult novel, *The Trumpeter of Krakow*, well portrays John of Kanty's influence and reputation for leadership and faith in his home city.

In Switzerland, **St. Nicholas of Flüe** (1417–1487) was a happily married husband and father of ten children, a community leader, and a man known for his sanctity. He lived his last nineteen years in prayerful seclusion, like a hermit. From there, he was a consultant to leaders and commoners alike. He was called "Bruder Klaus."

ST. JOAN OF ARC

St. Joan of Arc (1412–1431) is one of the most improbable, controversial, and misunderstood saints in history. A mystic and a warrior, this teenage girl was burned at the stake at age nineteen.

Joan was an uneducated peasant girl from an obscure village in France. This fits the pattern of so many "small" people whom God calls to confound the wise. Hers is a remarkable story of bravery, faith, grace, and providence.

She grew to have a strong faith as a young girl, even leading little prayer meetings among friends in the fields near her home. At about age thirteen, she began to experience supernatural visions and voices. Joan claimed that these voices of saints revealed to her a vocation (akin to Moses going to Pharaoh) to assist the French in their ongoing war against the English. This series of wars, known as the Hundred Years'

War, took a huge toll on society and also enhanced the position of emerging nation-states as an alternative authority to the Church. This teenage girl's claim to be called by God as a military leader seemed preposterous. Yet, a number of her prophecies came true and she displayed inexplicable knowledge of secret facts. This convinced the French authorities that her calling was authentic. As improbable as it may seem, this young girl, at age seventeen, led the French army in an attack on the English army that had laid siege to the French town of Orleans in 1429. Remarkably, after previous attempts had failed, Joan rallied the French to victory, breaking the siege and rescuing the city. With a clear focus on God, Joan led the French to a string of other victories. However, she finally suffered a defeat. Joan was captured and sold to the English.

In 1430, an English-dominated court, out to eliminate this French girl, put her on trial for heresy and witchcraft. Jesus had said that when you are seized and led before governors to give an account of yourself, do not worry about your defense; the Holy Spirit will give you what you are to say (see Mt 10:17–20; Lk 21:12–16). Joan experienced Jesus' words. Her interrogators tried to trap her in speech by asking her a trick question: whether or not she was in the state of grace. Say yes and she commits heresy by presumption, say no and she admits her guilt as not commissioned by God. This uneducated peasant girl's answer: "If I am not, may God put me there; and if I am, may God so keep me."[5] Her interrogators were astounded. With trumped-up or twisted evidence, reminiscent of the trial of Jesus, Joan was found guilty of heresy and burned at the stake. To the end, she remained resolute in her faith in God. A posthumous retrial years later vindicated her.

Joan's legacy is complex but significant. No, she is not a sign that God favored the French over the English. This long and brutal war was a contest for power and territory between two ruling houses who claimed to be Christian. If indeed God raised her up, why as a leader of an army in an unholy war? That is a difficult question. One thought is that Joan offered a change in perspective on war from royal imperialism to one of faith, beyond either the French or the English. In this violent time just decades after the Plague, Joan was an icon of Christ, seeking, along with other saints, mystics, and reformers, to raise people's sights toward God

— beyond themselves and their plans. The improbable rescue of Orleans might well have been a sign that warmongers and power-seekers ought to repent of their sinful designs and turn to God — witness the faith-filled peasant girl and the acts of God working through her. Through her visions, prophecies, victory at Orleans, and stunning wisdom at her trial, Joan of Arc, humble peasant girl, was — and remains — a sign of the hand of God at work in this messy world.

St. Joan of Arc remains a sign of contradiction, a flashpoint in the battle between people of faith and people who deny the Faith. Perhaps this is because she followed and reflected Christ himself: raised up from humble beginnings, calling attention to God, suffering and responding in ways similar to Jesus himself. Secular "experts" have tried mightily to provide natural explanations for her visions (epilepsy, tuberculosis, deception, etc.), not at all considering that they may indeed have been supernatural. Some historians have claimed — without basis — that much of the account of her life is legend rather than fact. There is something about Joan and her life that prompts nonbelievers to fight fiercely against it. Interestingly, one exception was Mark Twain, not at all a devout Christian. Twain was so fascinated with Joan that he wrote a biography of her. Despite being mostly ignored by literary critics, Twain considered this book, titled *Joan of Arc*, to be one of his most important works.[6]

THREE TRAVELING PREACHERS

Three fifteenth-century saints are among the most outstanding traveling preachers in all Church history. First Vincent Ferrer, then Bernardine of Siena, then John of Capistrano traversed the roads of Europe, each inspiring the next, each preaching to thousands. Collectively, their preaching not only led to spiritual revival in their own time, but also helped to plant the seeds of the Catholic Counter-Reformation in the following century.

St. Vincent Ferrer (1350–1419) was a surprising yet exceptional instrument in sustaining the Faith in post-Plague Europe. A Spaniard, he became a scholar in the Dominican order, and taught in universities. He first supported the Avignon popes and spent some time in their service. But after a powerful vision of Christ, he turned to the Dominican charism of preaching. Vincent crisscrossed the roads of Europe, preaching a stirring message of repentance for sin. Wherever he went he attracted enormous crowds, offering an authentic spiritual voice that resonated in the villages of discouraged believers. He traveled throughout numerous countries, leading tens of thousands to deeper faith and conversion. Vincent was also part of the effort to resolve the Great Schism, using his considerable influence to help convince the Avignon antipope to step down. The Schism ended just before his death.

The preaching of Vincent Ferrer was one of the inspirations for **St. Bernardine of Siena** (1380–1444). He was an educated Franciscan who lived a quiet life until he was stirred into action. He, too, embarked on a powerful preaching ministry, traveling throughout Italy on foot, preaching repentance from sin and conversion to God, often using humor to draw the attention of the large crowds he attracted. It was he who introduced and popularized the symbol IHS, an acronym for Jesus, taken from the first three Greek letters of his name. Bernardine also worked tirelessly under terrible conditions in hospitals, tending to Plague victims.

In America, **St. John Capistrano** (1386–1456) is best known for the California mission named after him, where it is said that the swallows miraculously return on Saint Joseph's feast day. Mission San Juan Capistrano was named after this saint for good reason. John was the third powerful mendicant preacher in the line started by Vincent Ferrer. He had been married but received a dispensation to enter the Franciscans, where he became a protégé of St. Bernardine of Siena. John's preaching also had powerful effect, leading thousands to conversion, first in Italy, then in the Bavarian and Saxony areas of present-day Germany, and then in Poland. However, many have questioned his harsh tactics against followers of the reformer Jan Hus (who had been condemned to death at the Council of Constance in 1417). John also collaborated with Bernardine for reform of the Franciscan order.

22

THE MUSLIM THREAT

The Ottoman Turks were bent on expanding their Islamic Empire during the fifteenth century, and John Capistrano, in his later years, recognized their threat to Europe and Christendom. It is hard to appreciate how real that threat was. Europe's future as a Christian continent was at stake. The Turks were the greatest military force in that part of the world — superior to any army of Europe. John Capistrano preached a crusade against the Turks which did not bear much fruit, but he did align himself with the Hungarian army that opposed the Turks' advance. In 1456, he fought in the crucial battle against the Turks at Belgrade, actually leading the army's left wing. The Hungarian Christian army was able to repulse the Turks, stopping — for a time — the momentum of the Turks' advance toward Europe. Some historians maintain that had the Turks won the "Battle of Belgrade," they might have been able to advance into much of Europe, bringing Islam as the new faith of the land. They had already done just that in the Balkans and the areas of the Byzantine Empire.

Even as the Ottomans were repelled at Belgrade, their attempts to press into Europe did not end. In 1480, a large Ottoman force invaded southern Italy. They sieged the town of Otranto, which stubbornly resisted. Eventually the Ottomans took the town, desecrated the cathedral, beheaded the bishop and other clergy, and killed or put to slavery thousands of others. Then they demanded that 813 selected men convert to Islam or be killed. Led by **St. Antonio Primaldo,** a tailor, these men refused to convert, and were put to death. Pope Francis canonized them in 2013. The resistance at Otranto slowed the Ottoman advance and allowed other defensive forces to stop the Ottoman expedition from advancing further through Italy.

These Muslim advances were possible because of what had happened just before, in 1453: the fall of Constantinople to the Ottomans. After several attempts over the centuries, the Ottomans finally captured Constantinople. This was the fall of the Byzantine Empire and a terrible blow to the Eastern Church, whose most significant patriarch was seated at Constantinople. For three days, the invaders sacked this city, one of the jewels of Christian Europe. They ransacked and desecrated the spectacular church of Hagia Sophia, seat of the patriarch, at that time still arguably the most magnificent in the Christian world. Soon after, the Ottomans turned Hagia Sophia into a mosque. It is hard to fathom how catastrophic this was: one of the greatest monuments to the Christian Faith desecrated and now converted to a Muslim place of worship. All Europe was shaken, both for their brother Christians (rivalry aside) and for fear that this fate awaited them as well. Thus the importance to the West of the Battle of Belgrade.

Holding off the Muslim Turks was certainly crucial for Christian Europe, but a much more serious crisis was about to break out in the waning days of "Christendom." The Church was about to be split asunder.

REFORMATION, REFORM, AND RENAISSANCE

AD 1500 to AD 1700

This painting of St. Martin DePorres is in the patriarchal Basilica of San Domenico in Bologna, Italy. Photo by Father Lawrence Lew, OP.

23
A CHURCH CORRUPT

The events of the sixteenth century which led to the breakup of the Church in Europe are among the most devastating in Church history. The Body of Christ was torn asunder. The ability of the Christian peoples to give witness to the Good News of the Incarnation was severely compromised. Jesus foresaw this possibility of division and he had warned of it, telling the apostles that he was praying that it would not happen (see Jn 17:20–23). The multitude of sins — of both Catholics and Protestants — enabled Satan to be active in pulling the Church apart. The door was opened to a future in which belief in God would no longer be the foundation of society. Christendom came to an end.

These events came to pass over time. The Church as a unified body had begun to fade in the decades before the Plague. Wars and disease had weakened the resolve of the people. The growth of the state — as opposed to assorted kingdoms — created competition to the Church as an organizational structure across the continent. And the leadership of the Church grew more secular, and even corrupt as the sons of powerful families filled out the ranks of many bishops, cardinals, and even popes.

Yet, the seeds of future renewal were present in the rocky soil even before the catastrophic events of the Reformation. Many thousands of people with sincere faith carried on in efforts to follow Christ despite the state of Church leadership. The Church of the worldly Renaissance popes was also the Church of the faithful in the villages; of stalwarts such as St. Thomas More of England who stood up to his king because, as More put it, he was "the king's good servant, but God's first"; or the villagers in the fields, stopping their work at the sound of church bells at noon to pray the Angelus, as later depicted by in the nineteenth-century French painter Jean Millet.

By the grace of God, saints were dispersed throughout the Church as the Reformation dawned. Two saints in this period stand out. When **St. Francis of Paola** (1416–1507) was young, his faithful parents sent him to be educated by the Franciscans. They left a lifelong mark on him, and he joined the Franciscan third order. He visited Rome as a teenager and was appalled by its decadence. This led him to remove himself to the countryside, where he moved into a cave and lived as a hermit as had Benedict and Francis of Assisi. Like his namesake, he attracted followers. Francis built a monastery and discerned a new rule for his band of hermits. In 1474 Pope Sixtus II approved his new order, then called the Hermits of St. Francis of Assisi. As his fame for holiness, prophecy, and miracles spread throughout Italy, other monasteries opened. Even the King of France heard of him and requested that Francis visit to pray for a healing. Francis went to the opulent French court, reluctantly, but still shoeless and in poverty. The court took notice of him and was moved. The king's son even funded the founding of monasteries throughout France, Spain, and Germany. The stir that Francis created throughout Europe flowed from his simple life of holiness, poverty, and humility.

St. Catherine of Genoa (1447–1510) also impacted the pre-Reformation world. Born into an aristocratic family, she was married off at age sixteen. Her husband was an unfaithful spendthrift and Catherine endured a decade of misery and eventually even poverty. But, due to her example of faithfulness, he reformed. Together, they took up in earnest her ministry at a hospital, even moving into the building. Catherine was administrator, but, like Catherine of Siena and Mother Teresa, she tended to the sickest of the sick. In 1493, the Plague swept into Genoa and killed over three-fourths of its citizens. Catherine caught the disease while tending to a patient and nearly died. However, she recovered, and is known for the fruits of mystical experiences that she put into writing. Books recounting her experiences circulated throughout the Catholic world in the early years of the sixteenth century.

These and many other saints, known and unknown, helped to anchor the Church in the midst of the turmoil about to unfold, and the seeds they planted blossomed into the movement of renewal known as the Counter-Reformation. But first came the explosion.

As the Church entered the sixteenth century, Martin Luther and other professed reformers had every reason to be aghast at the state of the Church. Simony was prevalent — including the ability to buy one's way to a bishopric. The clergy were infected with many who were corrupt, secular, or sexually delinquent. Church finances were a mess. Pope Julius II (d. 1513) was building the magnificent new Saint Peter's Basilica, pressing in dubious ways for construction money. This included taxes and the offering of indulgences in return for contributions to his building fund. Pope Leo X followed, and simply failed to see the urgent need of reform, even letting the Fifth Lateran Council, called in part to foster needed reform, fizzle out with little to show.

These two popes were among a series of so-called Renaissance popes, who came from elite Italian and Spanish families and were caught up in politics and the cultural flowering in Italy and elsewhere in Europe. Their patronage of the arts, though in a sense noble, preoccupied them at the expense of their pastoral calling. And in this time of rising nationalism, nobles and rulers throughout Europe began to resist papal authority, often seen as "Roman" influence. This was especially true of the German nobles. These local princes resented the "foreign" Church as an obstacle to German strength and unity. Princes, nobles, and regional kings were coming into their own in power and were pushing for independence from forces that would limit them, including the Catholic

Church and the papacy.

Previous efforts at reform had been put down as a threat to the existing order, most dramatically in 1417 when Bohemian reformer Jan Hus, a disciple of the English reformer John Wycliffe, was burned at the stake at the direction of the Council of Constance. Had the Church handled his situation differently, Hus might have been a catalyst for much needed Church reform. The Dutch humanist scholar Desiderius Erasmus pressed for reform in the early sixteenth century, but those benefiting from the entrenched corruption were more intent on holding onto their privileged positions. His writings critical of the state of the Church and society, such as the satirical *Praise of Folly*, were too little heeded to stem the worldly tide.

The Fifth Lateran Council, held from 1512–1517, was the last chance for Church leadership to address the need for reform before the explosion of the Protestant Reformation. Even though a number of reform-minded bishops sought to address the many issues, this council was not poised to be an instrument of reform. Called to counter opponents of Pope Julius II, it was political from the start. Its primary contribution was a rejection of *conciliarism*, the concept, debated throughout the Middle Ages, that councils were more authoritative than the office of pope. One effect was a widening of the gap with the Eastern Orthodox churches, which look to councils as the primary doctrinal authority. Without a commitment from Pope Leo X, this council faded away with little impact.

24

MARTIN LUTHER AND THE PROTESTANT REFORMATION

Martin Luther (1483–1546), a German Augustinian priest and monk, entered the monastery after being thrown from his horse by a bolt of lightning during a fierce thunderstorm. He was an intelligent but scrupulously introspective monk, who developed anxiety over his spiritual life and concluded that he was not able to be good on his own. He became a professor of biblical theology at Wittenberg and a deep reader of Saint Augustine. Luther came to a spiritual crisis as he agonized over his salvation, discovering that efforts to be holy in order to reach certitude of salvation did not work. From his angst, Luther embraced a new doctrine, which he called justification by faith alone (*sola fide*), as he understood it in Saint Paul, especially in the Letter to the Romans. Like the Catholic Church, Luther believed that we are saved by God's grace through the sacrifice of Christ on the cross, not by our own works. However, his understanding of *faith* was narrower and more passive than Catholic doctrine, which teaches that faith is both a gift of grace and a human act, an active and ongoing response of the will to God's grace.[1] At this time in history, Church practices and preoccupations with money and temporal affairs — including the use of indulgences to raise money — had obscured the Catholic doctrine of salvation and overemphasized human actions.

As Luther observed the misuse of indulgences and other external acts that seemed to indicate that one could earn salvation, he began to preach reform. His preaching created controversy by the mid-teens of the sixteenth century. Although his early core insights were mostly correct, he did veer from Catholic doctrine in his claim that man was totally corrupt and without free will. Catholicism teaches that we are weakened and stained by original sin but still have free will to choose the good, to choose God.

Luther saw the horrendous misuse of indulgences surrounding the financing of Saint Peter's Basilica in Rome and the unseemly way the proceeds were collected, and he revolted. He posted his famous *Ninety-Five Theses* in 1517, theological statements mostly directed toward indulgences, and sought to debate Church authorities. Events spun out of control. His Ninety-Five Theses became the talk of Germany, were debated widely, and piqued the German nationalistic spirit. What Luther stirred up could have been the catalyst for a genuine reform, but for the most part Church leaders did not engage him on theological grounds, but opposed him because he threatened the flow of money. Pope Leo X cared little for theology and at first did not take Luther seriously. In time, as Luther continued to preach and spread his views, the papal theologian condemned him, and Luther was excommunicated in 1521. However, Luther was popular in Germany. And while he at first did not intend to leave the Church, Luther dug in his heels to the point of defiance.

His preaching was bolstered by the invention of the printing press in 1450. Luther flooded Germany with pamphlets, and soon took a harsher turn. He rejected papal authority, preached that authority derived from *sola scriptura*, Scripture alone, and even called the pope the Antichrist.

He drifted away from the structure of the Church and its hierarchy and sacraments and toward a "priesthood of all believers." In 1520, he burned the papal bull condemning him and a book of canon law. The Protestant Reformation was born.

Luther's movement spread quickly throughout Germany, forcing people, towns, and civil rulers to take sides. Their decisions were not based on theology — which most did not understand — and much of them were rooted in the regional and national spirit that also was sweeping Germany. Independence from Rome was attractive, and Luther provided a hook for those who cared little for doctrine. Much of the spread of his rebellion against the Catholic Church was due to the support of German princes and nobles. As the princes went, so did the local churches. Some historians indicate that the absence of Holy Roman Emperor Charles V — who was preoccupied with Spanish affairs at the height of the Reformation — created an opening for German princes to decide for themselves whether to stay Catholic or follow Luther. So, for political as well as theological reasons, hundreds of churches broke away from Rome and cast their lot with Luther's movement. Parishes and priests turned Lutheran or remained Catholic with their parishioners having little say, and some of the now "Lutheran" clergy began to marry — as Luther himself eventually did.

The scholar Philip Melanchthon was Luther's closest collaborator. He and Luther complemented each other in style, Luther being the fiery battler, Melanchthon the quiet thinker. It was Melanchthon who was the primary author of the "Augsburg Confession" in 1530, the declaration of Lutheran beliefs that was a turning point in the final break with Rome.

ZWINGLI AND CALVIN

While Lutheranism spread in Germany, Ulrich Zwingli inspired numerous cantons in Switzerland (governmental units like states) to reject the Catholic Church, working to combine faith and civil authority. However, by 1529, it became evident that Luther and Zwingli differed sharply over the Lord's Supper — Luther maintaining a more Catholic understanding — and the two reformers went their own ways. This was the first of many splits among the reformers, and it had a huge impact on future direction of the reform movements.

Shortly after Zwingli began advancing his break with Rome, a Frenchman, John Calvin, also began reform efforts in Switzerland. In time, the followers of Calvin numbered more than those of any other reformer, Luther included. He was most active in the 1530s to the 1550s, mainly in Geneva, Switzerland. Calvin was less a firebrand than Luther or Zwingli. He was more the scholar, but still his passion against Catholicism was strong. Like Luther, Calvin opposed the priestly and hierarchical structure of the Catholic Church. He emphasized the sovereignty of God, to the point that he preached predestination — that some are destined to be saved, while others to go to hell. This determinism, in Calvin's view, limited man's free will.

Calvin opposed images in churches, becoming a leading advocate of iconoclasm among the reformers. In the wake of his iconoclasm, a vast number of Catholic churches across Europe were vandalized, especially their statuary and artwork. Calvin set up a straightforward system of leadership, consisting of pastors, doctors, elders, and deacons. In time his theology and structures did not coincide with Luther's and became an alternative to Lutheranism. Due to his considerable leadership skills and his passion for the faith as he understood it, his form of Protestantism spread through parts of France, where Calvinists were called *Huguenots*; through the Netherlands where they were known as the Dutch Reformed; to central Europe and Bohemia; and via the strong advocacy of John Knox, to Scotland.

ENGLAND

Other countries remained aligned with Rome, led by the sensibilities of their rulers. Henry VIII of England was a staunch defender of Catholicism against Lutheranism. The pope even awarded him the title of "Defender of the Faith." Spain under Charles V, the French crown, most all of Italy, and Hapsburg Austria all remained Catholic.

The Reformation spread to England in the 1530s and had enormous impact. England, however, was a special case. It was situational, not theological, and not driven by a reformer. The catalyst was "Defender of the Faith" King Henry VIII himself.

Years earlier, Henry VIII had been granted a papal dispensation to marry Catherine of Aragon. She had previously been married to Henry's brother, who died shortly after their marriage. Critically, she did not give birth to a surviving male heir to Henry. That, and Henry's attraction to Anne Boleyn, led the king to petition for a marriage annulment so he could marry Boleyn. The pope declined the annulment. Had he done so — whether justified or not — England might have remained Catholic, although the issues with any of Henry's four subsequent marriages might also have caused a break later in time. Henry, conveniently tapping into the long history of kings claiming religious authority in their realms, declared himself to be head of the Church in England and proceeded to divorce Catherine and marry Anne Boleyn. The Church of England remained theologically similar to the Catholic Church in most areas other than authority, but gradually became entrenched and fully independent of Rome. Henry sought to bring all Catholic institutions to heel and was especially violent toward the English monasteries and their perceived wealth. He shut them down and commandeered their holdings for the crown. He even had a number of abbots executed.[2]

Even Henry's former friends were not spared. **St. Thomas More** (1478–1535), a married layman and father of four daughters, along with his fellow Englishman, the bishop **St. John Fisher** (1469–1535), were among the first of many English Catholic martyrs. More is one of the earliest saints of note after the beginning of the Reformation. He lived in the Reformation, and died in it, defending the Catholic Faith. As the battles heated, he engaged in an exchange of fiery, polemical letters with Luther. These letters probably did not affect history, but they do show his passion and full commitment to the Catholic Church. Yet More, a close friend of Erasmus, the Dutch Catholic reformer, was well aware of the many failures within the Church.

More's profound faith and prayer life are a testament that the Church, while struggling with corruption, still had spiritual energy. He was a first-rate scholar and lawyer who advanced through the ranks of the crown, reaching the position of lord chancellor of England in 1529, and was one of King Henry VIII's most trusted advisors. More even wrote a defense of the king when the king first opposed Luther. Things turned sour for

More when Henry decided that he wanted out of his first marriage so he could marry Anne Boleyn. Henry sought More's help, or at least his approval, as he battled the pope and sought to be declared head of the Church in England. Most of the English Church leaders relented and sided with the king. This isolated More — and Cardinal John Fisher as well, who also opposed the king's efforts to seize control of the Church in England. More refused to assent, and, rather than directly challenge the king, he chose to remain silent, reminiscent of Jesus at his trial. Henry had More and Fisher beheaded in 1535. Thomas More's famous last words were "I am the king's good servant, but God's first." His life is portrayed in the play and Oscar-winning movie *A Man for All Seasons*. More's courageous stand for principle, along with his resulting martyrdom at the hands of a supposedly civilized government, remains a compelling example today.

The English church briefly reverted back to Catholicism when Henry's daughter Mary succeeded him, but turned and remained Protestant when his other daughter, Elizabeth I, succeeded Mary. Because the new "state church" structure was royally created, opposition to it was deemed a threat to the power of the crown. It was a bloody time, as both Mary and Elizabeth conducted persecutions, creating both Catholic and Protestant martyrs. The devout Jesuit priest **St. Edmund Campion** (1540–1581) was one of the most prominent of the English Catholic martyrs of the Elizabethan era. He conducted an underground Catholic ministry but was captured by the crown's priest hunters, hanged, and drawn and quartered. England remained Protestant, and the practice of banning the Catholic Church and persecution of Catholics became settled practice in the decades going forward.

WARS OF RELIGION

As the polemics and discord of the Reformation movements spread throughout Europe, it was inevitable that wars and armed conflicts would break out. The "Peasants' Revolt" of 1524–1525 was a series of regional uprisings in Germany led by, among others, preacher Thomas Muntzer. With a somewhat Reformation-oriented philosophy, Muntzer preached revolt against the corrupt authorities who upheld the social, political, and ecclesiastical orders — be they Catholic or Lutheran. He saw in the developments of the day, as did Luther, signs of the Second Coming. He urged peasant farmers to revolt, promising divine protection. They started a violent insurrection which, ironically, was put down by a combination of Catholic and Lutheran forces. More than five thousand peasants were killed, with some estimates much higher.

Chaos continued in 1527. Pope Clement VII, fearful that Catholic Holy Roman Emperor Charles V was seeking to dominate the Church, had formed an alliance against Charles. War followed, but a soldiers' mutiny over not getting paid led the mostly German army to attack and sack Rome itself — an attack not supported by either Charles or Luther. Although not directly a Reformation event, it had wide-ranging consequences. Having now attained the influence over papal policy that the pope had feared, Charles made sure the pope denied Henry VIII's request for an annulment of his marriage to Catherine, Charles's aunt, triggering the English Reformation. Charles also pushed the pope to call for a council, leading to the Council of Trent. The sack also effectively ended the High Renaissance, as Rome's economy and population plummeted.

In 1535, the Anabaptists, another new sect, set up a radical "kingdom" in Munster in northern Germany. It was crushed after a siege led by the former bishop of Munster. France was embroiled in a series of wars and violent conflicts from 1562 to 1598 between Catholics and Huguenots, known today as the Wars of Religion. Thousands lost their lives in violent engagements. Perhaps the most famous event was the Saint Bartholomew's Day Massacre in Paris in 1572. Catholic civil leaders ignited a rampage that led to the killing of three thousand Huguenots. This triggered more violence from each side, as much political as religious.

The Thirty Years' War (1618–1648) was far and away the most destructive war in this era. It began with the "Defenestration of Prague": Calvinists in Prague threw Catholic Hapsburg negotiators out of a window in the imperial palace during a dispute over burned churches. The Hapsburgs responded by sending an army. Like so many European wars, this one started in one place and spread throughout the continent. There were Bohemian, Danish, and Swedish phases, with the brunt of the fighting in German territory. Catholic armies sometimes prevailed, and Protestants at other times. As time went on, the religious motivations gave way to political ones. A poignant example: Late in the war, French Catholic Cardinal Richelieu persuaded the Lutheran king of Sweden to invade northern Germany and attack Hapsburg Catholics — for the political benefit of France. Over seven million people died in the Thirty Years' War, the largest wartime loss of life in European history until the two twentieth-century world wars. It ended with the Peace of Westphalia, which changed the map of an exhausted Europe and provided for a balance between Catholic and Protestant territories. The treaty recognized nation-states along both political and religious lines, reduced the size of the Holy Roman Empire, and created political borders that in many respects resemble the modern era.

25

THE INQUISITION

Infamous both in popular lore and among historians unfriendly to Catholicism, the Inquisition conjures up images of medieval dungeons, torture and cruelty at the hands of sadistic clerics in robes, and forlorn victims such as the man in Edgar Allan Poe's story "The Pit and the Pendulum." The truth, though complicated, is far different. To begin with, the Inquisition was not a monolithic entity, but an array of mostly regional courts scattered about parts of Europe and the Americas over different times, with varying missions and practices, and under a variety of different forms of leadership.

These institutional tribunals had, as their primary goal, the rooting out of heresy. In today's relativistic age, this seems harsh, but in the medieval times of Christendom, truth was supremely valued, and linked to the goal of eternal salvation, which most everyone aspired to. The tribunals were most active in western and southern Europe — areas that were mostly Catholic. The Inquisition courts were usually appointed by a pope and worked in tandem with the civil authorities, as Church and state in Catholic areas remained intertwined. Without the close association of a Catholic civil state, the inquisitional courts would not have been able to function. Franciscans and Dominicans commonly ran these regional Inquisition courts. The most noted Inquisitions were the Spanish, the Portuguese, and the Italian. Each had its own sense of how to proceed.

From the Church's point of view, the salvation of souls was at stake. Church authorities, even with their flaws, genuinely desired that people brought before the tribunals attain salvation and that they not lead others astray by what the Church deemed false teaching. The Church sought to make the legal process of cases brought before her tribunals to be fair, and was remarkably successful, if not perfect — witness the common desire of accused people in civil tribunals, who asked that their cases be transferred to Church tribunals so they might receive better treatment or lighter sentences.[1] From the state's point of view, order in society was paramount, lest the state's existence be threatened, and civil authorities often used the tribunals for that end. This is certainly a less noble justification for inquisitional courts, but it was tempered by the close association with the Church and her more religious motivations.

The punishments imposed by the Inquisition courts were usually tailored to the situation of the convicted man or woman and often included assigned pilgrimages, the wearing of crosses, the duty to say certain prayers, and exile, or in infrequent cases of defiant refusal to adhere to Catholic doctrine, death. Although many courts tried to mete out reasonable sentences for the right reasons, there were abuses and overzealous prosecutions. Popes and bishops often would step in and direct an extreme tribunal to reign in overly harsh practices. Statistics on the number of cases and the number of death sentences is, per most historians, difficult to determine. However, the frequency of torture and the number of death sentences at the hands of the Inquisitions has been often subject to wild exaggeration by opponents of the Catholic Church. The best estimates put Inquisition deaths at several thousand — not millions as some pundits claim — spread over several centuries, though the small number of unjust verdicts of death is not an excuse.

The first Inquisition, or Church court specifically set up to address heresy, is traceable to 1231, in the aftermath of the brutal Crusade against the Albigensians in southern France — for the purpose of creating a more humane and nonviolent way of dealing with them. The Inquisition's primary goal was not so much to punish the Albigensians as to seek their conversion, after Saint Dominic had been called upon first to preach to them with the hope of voluntary reversion to the Catholic Faith. Although abuses did occur, the inquisitional courts were an improvement on the existing system of justice.

The most notorious of the inquisitional courts was the Spanish Inquisition. It was set up in 1481 and controlled by the Spanish crown with Dominicans chosen to be the chief inquisitors. The Spanish authorities used it as much to consolidate civil rule as to root out heresy. In addition, during the *Reconquista*, the bloody era of Catholic recapture of southern Spain from the Muslims that culminated in the late fifteenth century, Jews and Muslims were often forced to convert or felt it expedient to do so. The Inquisition tried many of these "converts" for suspected reversion to their original Faith, and many were executed. This was the Inquisition at its worst.

Most of those brought before a court of Inquisition, however, were Catholics suspected of irregular beliefs or writings. St. Teresa of Ávila and St. Ignatius Loyola each ran into trouble with the Spanish Inquisition and were forced to defend their teachings before suspicious tribunals. Although exact figures are elusive, upwards of three to four thousand people were executed at the hands of the Spanish Inquisition. One of the difficulties in determining the number executed was the Spanish Inquisition's practice of often executing "in effigy" — sparing the convicted person's life, despite a death sentence.

The Spanish and Portuguese Inquisitions established satellite courts in the New World as well, including in Mexico, Colombia, Peru, and Brazil. The accused were tried for idolatry, conversion to Protestantism, and immorality, among other offenses. The fairness and severity of these courts depended upon who was in charge of the local Inquisition. Some Latin American Inquisitions were, at times, too severe and authorities back in Europe would step into temper the local practices. Both European colonists and indigenous peoples faced charges before the tribunals as well as Catholics accused of heresy.

The inquisitional courts throughout the world began to fade after the sixteenth century, and by the nineteenth century, they had run their course. The reasons were several. The Protestant Reformation spawned new denominations and churches, usually under the protection of associated civil authorities, and this removed the near-monopoly of the Catholic Church, putting most "heretics" out of reach of the inquisitional courts. The Enlightenment movement of the eighteenth and nineteenth centuries enhanced the power of the various states at the Church's expense, and reduced both the cooperation between Church and state necessary for the functioning of the inquisitional courts and the pervasiveness in society of Catholic doctrine, rendering trials for heresy effectively obsolete. And the Church experienced her own evolution of thought away from forced belief and toward persuasion, instead.

The Inquisition evolved gradually into what today is the Vatican's Dicastery for the Doctrine of the Faith, which investigates cases of variance from Catholic doctrine. Its typical penalties, directed mostly at theologians, include dictates to rethink questionable theological opinions in light of Church doctrine, or removal of the status of Catholic theologian. This is a far cry from the days when an Inquisitional tribunal might impose torture or a sentence of execution for failure to conform to Church teaching. Times change, and we are products of our times. It is difficult to understand the ways of other times or the foibles of our own. The Catholic Church reached the present state through a long, messy process of reflection and trial and error. We can look back upon the excesses of the Inquisition and rightly abhor as terribly misguided the use of violence to force orthodox belief. And we can relish in today's more advanced understanding of religious liberty. At the same time, it is easy to miss the high value the inquisitional times placed on truth and the mission of the Church to facilitate the salvation of souls through a commitment to the core of God's Revelation in Christ. Steps forward in Church history are often accompanied by steps back. Today, we have come to live in a "believe and let believe" age, in which the emphasis on truth is minimized. This can obscure the Gospel message of salvation, a message that the

Inquisition, with all its evident flaws, sought to protect. And, lest we think that the modern age is more open-minded than in times past, history tends to repeat itself. Witness the rise of modern dictators throughout the world who suppress all dissent, and of "cancel culture" among our institutional elites and so common on social media, in an effort to impose present-day orthodoxies upon all others. If this development continues to grow in strength and into the bureaucratic state in Western societies — not assured but possible — the excesses of the Inquisition will not look so foreign.

It is worth noting that the seeds of respect for religious liberty were sown even before the advent of the Inquisition. Some, including saints, saw outside the box of their own times that imposing belief by force violated the religious liberty of the individual. St. Bernard of Clairvaux, himself a warrior against heresy, observed that faith is a matter of persuasion, not force. This insight foreshadows St. John Paul II's observation centuries later that the Church does not impose, but proposes.

26

CATHOLIC COUNTER-REFORMATION

As we have seen, the Protestant Reformation gained momentum in large part because of the weaknesses in the Church. Too many in the hierarchy were entrenched in a worldly outlook, and a deep spiritual renewal was desperately needed.

At this time of great need, God raised up a number of gifted and devout men and women. Like Francis of Assisi, they reformed the Church not by polemics, but by pointing the way back to God, by fostering profound spiritual renewal. They crisscrossed the Christian world, preaching, teaching, writing, exhorting, giving example, and inspiring thousands around them. And these thousands took the call to follow Christ more to heart and, in turn, influenced countless others to return to, maintain, or grow in their faith. In the parishes, the farm fields, the monasteries, the villages and cities, ordinary people found reasons and inspiration to keep and grow the Faith. These saints ushered in what we call the Catholic Counter-Reformation.

Most of these men and women were influential in their own time, helping to stem the tide of chaos and lead the way back to Jesus, the true Head of the Church. Most also remain influential today. Just as the Reformation has echoed throughout history and has impact today, so too has the Counter-Reformation echoed throughout history and impacted the Church for the last half millennium. Although the Church did not become fully transformed, she made substantial progress toward recapturing her bearings of faith and morality. The Counter-Reformation was primarily a spiritual movement, a movement of grace, more than a human or institutional restoration project. It is significant that most of the saints identified with it were scattered about the world and were not part of the hierarchy.

THE JESUITS

Perhaps the single most influential reformer in the sixteenth-century Church was **St. Ignatius of Loyola** (1491–1556), from Catholic Spain — the other end of Europe from the battles of the Reformation. He fostered, ignited, and spearheaded Catholic reform all across Europe.

Ignatius had been a soldier for a city-state in Spain that was engaged in one of the mini-wars that seemed always to be occurring in Europe. He was wounded and forced into a lengthy convalescence. During this time, he had only religious materials to read. He read a life of Christ and a collection of lives of the saints. (We can thank the authors of these books and those unknown people who made the simple act of placing these books where Ignatius would find them.) The solitude and spiritual reading led to a profound conversion. Upon regaining his health, Ignatius made a pilgrimage and then a long retreat at Manresa, Spain, where he experienced visions. At Manresa, he likely wrote much of his *Spiritual Exercises*, a classic of practical wisdom, conversion, and discernment, still widely used today. According to Christopher Dawson, "almost everyone, cleric or layman, who played an important part in the Catholic Reform" practiced Ignatius's *Spiritual Exercises*. It was "in so many ways the fundamental text of the Catholic revival."[1] This is extraordinary: A book of personal spiritual renewal, prayer, and discernment fostered Catholic reform more than polemics or even theology.

Ignatius traveled to Paris, where, in 1534, he and six like-minded companions founded what came to be known as the Society of Jesus. The seven men were ordained as priests three years later, and in 1540, they traveled to Rome. On the way, Ignatius had a vision that all would turn out well in Rome. Pope Paul III approved their society, which later became known as the *Jesuits*. From these beginnings, the Jesuits traversed all over the world, founding Jesuit houses, retreat centers, schools, colleges, and seminaries. These were like seeds planted in troubled soil that sprouted and grew into a renewal of faith. Ignatius's three goals were Church reform — especially through education and frequent use of the sacraments — missionary activity throughout Europe, and the fight against heresy.

Ignatius and the Jesuits made great headway in all three areas. They nourished an effective movement of spiritual revival that helped to sustain the Catholic Church that was assailed from both corruption and worldliness within and revolt and separation without. By the time of Ignatius's death in 1556, over one thousand Jesuits were ministering in Europe. The order he started grew and became a leaven within the Church for hundreds of years after his death.

An early Jesuit from Holland, **St. Peter Canisius** (1521–1597) was inspired by a retreat and joined the Society of Jesus in 1546. He attended the first two sessions of the Council of Trent and by 1549 was assigned to help revitalize Catholicism in Bavaria. He spent most of the rest of his life ministering in Bavaria, Bohemia — including Prague — and Austria. Peter published an enormously successful Catechism that was translated into fifteen languages. He traveled throughout Germany, preaching, debating Protestants, founding colleges, and fighting to restore the Catholic Faith and to implement the decrees of the Council of Trent. Peter has been called the second apostle to Germany (after Boniface) and is largely credited with the success of the Catholic Counter-Reformation in Bavaria. Bavarian southern Germany has been the most Catholic region in Germany ever since.

REFORM IN ITALY

The Jesuits were not the only Catholic reformers. **St. Angela Merici** (1470–1540) was a third order Franciscan laywoman in northern Italy who developed a ministry to young women. From teaching poor girls, her ministry grew into founding communities for single young women to grow in the

Faith together. This, in turn, led to the founding of the *Ursulines*, an innovative community for women with a vocation outside convent walls to teach mostly poor young women. This community spread throughout Europe and has served the Church through several centuries to the present day.

In Rome, **St. Philip Neri** (1515–1595) worked to re-Christianize the lukewarm and often corrupt people and clergy. He preached and exhibited faithfulness to Christ. That, and only that, would lead to genuine renewal, he realized, since the lack of faithfulness to Christ was the problem that led to the crisis. In this regard, he was a typical Counter-Reformation saint. Rome was not ground zero in the Reformation battles as were France and Germany, but, as the city of the pope and Curia, its spiritual revitalization was critical to the Catholic Church as she sought to regain her footing amidst the battle with the Protestant reformers.

Philip preached on the streets of Rome, was ordained a priest in 1551, and became a famous and powerful confessor. Thousands converted (or reverted) through his ministry and many clergy were attracted to him and became followers and coworkers. He founded what became known as the *Oratorians*, named after gatherings of people for prayer in *oratories*, gathering places set aside for ministry. He became known as the Apostle of Rome and was arguably the most popular person in Rome — a testament to his evangelical zeal. He exhibited numerous gifts of the Holy Spirit, including prophecy, wisdom, miracles, and the ability to look into people's minds. Both the poor and the elite admired him. He even helped to settle a dispute between the pope and France.

CARMELITES

Among the greatest saints of all time, **St. Teresa of Ávila** (1515–1582) was another Spanish saint who did not interact directly with the Reformation but whose ministry helped to renew and strengthen the Church during this time. She entered the Carmelite convent at Ávila at a young age, suffered periodic health problems that forced her to leave and return, and for years was a pious but ordinary nun. Young women often entered convents in those times as a reasonable way to live a pleasant life more than from devotional fire for God. Teresa did have a good measure of early spiritual zeal and was eager to be a nun, but was no great exception. As Teresa began to move forward in her spiritual life, she read widely. This included Saint Augustine's *Confessions*, which helped her to overcome scruples and to have more confidence in God's mercy.

However, God called her to a deep conversion as she approached age forty. She experienced powerful visions, which confused and disturbed her at first, but her confessor and spiritual advisor at the time, the Jesuit St. Francis Borgia, advised her that her visions were authentic and from the Holy Spirit.[2] She became a thoroughly changed person and for the rest of her life she was on fire for God. Her mystical experiences led her to become an authority on prayer, but she never thought of prayer to be an alternative to being in the world. Charity was at the center of the Christian's life, she taught.

She saw the need to form new Carmelite convents for sisters who desired a spirituality deeper than the relaxed style common among the religious. She collaborated with the younger **St. John of the Cross** (1542–1591) and the two of them worked to establish what is called the Discalced (reformed) Carmelites. She founded sixteen convents across Spain, while John founded men's houses, each running into fierce resistance along the way. Their work helped first to strengthen the spiritual vitality in Spain, and from Spain, throughout Europe. Carmelite cloisters formed throughout the continent and drew thousands into the religious life, in their turn leavening the secular communities around them.

Teresa was intelligent, charming, attractive, witty, and often outgoing, yet deeply contemplative. She composed some of the most significant spiritual classics of all time, including *Interior Castle*, her mystical account of a soul prayerfully moving, stage by stage, toward union with God, *The Book of Her Life*, also called her *Autobiography*, which focuses more on contemplative prayer than the facts of her life, and the *Way of Perfection*, written for the spiritual growth of the sisters in the convents she founded. Although her writings on prayer, so informed by her mystical experiences, can seem at first beyond the reach of ordinary Christians, Teresa was ever mindful of the practical, and sought to balance the ultimate goal of communion with God and the ordinary Christian's daily struggle to pray. In *The Book of Her Life*, she observes, "For mental prayer … is nothing else than an intimate sharing between friends; it means taking time frequently to be alone with

Him who we know loves us."[3]

St. John of the Cross also penned influential spiritual classics, including *Dark Night of the Soul*, which offer profound insight into a soul wrestling with obstacles as God guides that soul toward union with him. He also composed some of the best Spanish poetry. These readable yet powerful mystical writings exploring the way to God, on contemplative prayer, and on God's deep love for us, became a significant contribution to the life of the Church as she moved forward in the aftermath of the Reformation.

As they fought their way through reform of the Carmelites in Spain, Teresa and John could not have fathomed the scope of their impact on the history of the Church. They inspired the founding of Carmelite communities throughout the Catholic world in the decades and centuries after their deaths. Their teachings on prayer and devotion to God also inspired thousands of ordinary Catholics beyond the monasteries to grow in a life of prayer and the practice of the Christian life. Building upon earlier spiritual movements such as *devotio moderna*, Teresa, John, Ignatius, and other reformers moved the Church further into the life of mental and contemplative prayer and toward a deeper union with Christ. This was the heart and purpose of what we call the Counter-Reformation.

In light of what Teresa has taught — and continues to teach us — in her writings about prayer, devotion to God, and service to others, she has been declared a Doctor of the Church. And, like all authentic mystics, she stands as a sign that the faith of Christians is more than a mere moral code. It is a proclamation of the existence of God and his accessibility to the human soul and mind.

THE REFORM COUNCIL

After a series of mostly underwhelming popes, God raised up a saintly pope in the midst of the Reformation. **Pope St. Pius V** (1504–1572, r. 1566–1572) is considered the greatest of the reform popes. He was a man of great faith and ascetical practice, and these, coupled with a strong personality, allowed him to set such a standard that the Church has seen no serious moral relapse in any pope since.[4] That, in itself, has left a lasting and extraordinary impact on the Church.

It fell on Pius to implement the reforms of the monumental *Council of*

Trent, called — well later than it should have been — to craft a response to the Reformation from the perspective of the whole Catholic Church. Trent, which Pope Paul III commenced, was held in multiple sessions scattered between 1545 and 1563. The politics in Europe were raw, as many civil rulers either became entrenched as Catholic or Protestant. Several popes reigned in this period and had differing notions on the role of this or any council. This is why Trent was spread out for so long. Ultimately, the council took a strong, conservative approach, refuting the theological claims of Luther, Calvin, and the other reformers. In the judgment of the council fathers, this was not a time for ecumenism. The council reaffirmed the role of both Scripture and Tradition as sources of Divine Revelation (countering the Protestant teaching of *sola scriptura*). It also affirmed that there were seven sacraments, denied Luther's assertion that man was totally corrupted by original sin, stated that charitable works as well as faith were part of the economy of salvation, and reaffirmed that the priesthood was divinely instituted. The council reaffirmed papal supremacy and declared that the Mass was a true sacrifice, making present the sacrifice of Christ on the cross, and that it was the legitimate form of Christian worship.

Pius became pope just three years after the end of Trent, and vigorously set out to implement its reforms and decrees. He promulgated the *Catechism of the Council of Trent,* which served the Church as the authoritative statement of doctrine for over four hundred years, revised the *Missal* of official church liturgical prayers, and put in place the liturgical reforms which gave rise to the Tridentine Mass, the approved Roman liturgy for four hundred years. Pius also worked to reform the priesthood and seminary instruction, enhancing the level of intellectual training and reemphasizing the spiritual and moral character necessary for the ordained priests of the Church. This may well have been his most significant achievement.

Pius fostered aid to the poor, visited the sick, and revitalized the status of Thomas Aquinas and his theology. He worked to clean up the Curia (the governing body of the Church) and its practice of selling offices to the highest bidder. Such reforms were huge challenges, given the entrenched forces of the status quo and the cauldron of Reformation polemics assailing the Church. His relentless determination, fueled by a life of prayer and faith, gave him the strength to move forward and help to steer the Church in a spiritual direction. The Church desperately needed a saint to be working not only in the trenches, but also from the top.

Pius was also instrumental in holding off the Ottoman Turks, who remained a persistent threat to Christian Europe. The Ottomans, fierce and effective fighters, remained relentless in their efforts to move west into Christian Europe. They had succeeded in capturing much of the Balkans, and were only temporarily slowed down by their loss to the Hungarians at Belgrade in 1456. Europe feared them — with good reason. In 1571, the Ottomans unleashed an enormous naval force in the Mediterranean that created a serious military threat to Europe. Pius organized a Christian "Holy League" to oppose them. Battle was joined on October 7, 1571, at Lepanto, on the western coast of Greece. This was the biggest and most significant naval battle of the era, involving hundreds of ships and thousands of combatants (including Cervantes, Spanish author-to-be of the classic, *Don Quixote*). The Christian forces were drawn from several countries, commanded by Don Juan of Austria. He led his charges in prayer and fasting, including the Rosary, before battle. The Christian forces won an unexpected and complete victory. The Ottoman naval threat was ended. Back in Rome, Pope St. Pius V experienced what many believe was a prophetic sense from the Holy Spirit that the prayers were answered and victory was achieved. Days before receiving word of the battle's outcome, he stopped his activities to give thanks to God for victory.

In commemoration of this answer to prayer, October 7 was designated as the feast of Our Lady of Victory. This feast is now called the feast of Our Lady of the Rosary, in recognition of Mary's intercession, as thousands of combatants and Catholic supporters prayed the Rosary before and during this battle for help against this extraordinary threat to the Christian world. This is also a testament to the Catholic devotion to Mary, the Mother of God and of the Church. The Protestant Reformation did not weaken Catholic devotion to Mary but, if anything, increased it. The Rosary remains among the most pervasive Catholic prayers throughout the Catholic Church to this day.

㉗
THE COUNTER-REFORMATION ADVANCES

During the seventeenth century, a number of pivotal saints continued to push forward ministries of the Counter-Reformation. Few of these ministries were organized or directed from Rome and none of these saints fathomed that their work was part of any movement. The term *Counter-Reformation* came later. They simply sought to follow the Holy Spirit's call in their circumstances and served. Yet, taken as a whole, these saints wove a remarkable thread of renewal in the seventeenth-century Church.

Saint Ignatius's successor as head of the Jesuits, **St. Francis Borgia**, (1510–1572) has been called the order's "second founder." He is the one saint from the notorious Borgias, a wealthy Spanish family that produced two morally challenged Renaissance popes. Francis married, raised eight children with his wife, and served for years at the highest levels of the Spanish ruling class, as was his family's role. After his wife's death, however, he entered the Jesuits and became a priest. He was an effective preacher, reformer, and spiritual advisor. As we have seen, Francis played a decisive role in the life of Teresa of Ávila by counselling her that her visions were of divine origin. In 1565, Francis was chosen as father general of the Jesuits. In his seven years as head, he enhanced the order's rule of life, fostered growth in Poland and Germany, and launched missionary activity in Florida, Mexico, and South America. Organizations often diminish after an illustrious founder dies, but Francis took the baton from Ignatius and skillfully carried on the order's crucial Counter-Reformation ministries.

One of the most influential Church leaders during the early Counter-Reformation era, the brilliant scholar **St. Charles Borromeo** (1538–1584), was an important force at the Council of Trent, guiding the bishops through potential pitfalls, and working with his uncle, Pope St. Pius V, to implement council reforms. Charles was the primary author of the Catechism of the Council of Trent. As Cardinal of Milan, Charles fostered major reform in his diocese that became a model for reform in the Church at large. He improved the spiritual state of the priesthood, worked to establish the seminaries that Trent had called for, fostered religious education, and, as is so typical for great saints with ecclesiastical ministries, he worked hard in charity to meet the needs of the poor. He also marshalled resources to tend to victims of an outbreak of the Plague in the late 1570s. His preaching was effective in countering Protestantism and in inspiring many to return to the Faith.

A violinist and writer of poetry, **St. Robert Bellarmine** (1542–1621) was yet another Counter-Reformation Jesuit. Ordained in 1570, he, too, was a brilliant scholar who wrote and taught in defense of Catholic theology that the reformers had attacked. His seminal work was *Disputations on the Controversies of the Christian Faith*, which drew from Scripture and the Fathers to explain the Catholic Faith. Robert was named a cardinal in 1598, and despite his rise through the ranks, he was devoted to helping the poor. He put charity first, even in his theological writings. He never engaged in personal attacks on Protestant theologians but instead prayed for them. Interestingly, the controversy surrounding the astronomer Galileo occurred in his time, and Robert expressed sympathy for him as the Church tried to discern how to respond to advances in science. Robert has been declared a Doctor of the Church.

St. Francis de Sales (1567–1622) was a reformer in the later stages of the Counter-Reformation, which stretched into the seventeenth century. A Frenchman, he left a career in law to become a priest. Francis reached out to the poor and entered into a highly effective preaching ministry from which he gathered local fame. He ministered in the Chablais area, which bordered France and Switzerland, and there he worked to draw Calvinists back into the Catholic Church. He had to contend with mobs and even assassins who violently opposed his efforts. Despite the obstacles, thousands of Calvinists returned or converted to the Catholic Church. In 1602 he was made bishop of Geneva — the heartland of Calvinism — where he ministered effectively and with charity. He was known to use the time-honored phrase, "You catch more flies with honey than vinegar." He is also known for writing the spiritual classic *Introduction to the Devout Life*, which stressed that it is possible — including for lay people — to attain sanctity in everyday life. For its great wisdom, it remains heavily read and consulted to this day.

St. Jane Frances de Chantal (1572–1641) was a protégé of Francis de Sales. They collaborated in various ministries, especially in her life's work of forming and fostering an order of nuns, which became the Visitation order. Jane had been married and was a mother. Her work in the Church took shape after her husband died. Following the advice of Francis, who had become her spiritual director, she continued to be mother to her children and began to serve the poor and sick. In time, she became a nun and, despite difficulties, drew others into a community. With guidance from Francis de Sales, she served as superior to her order, and the Visitation order grew to eighty-six convents in less than thirty years. It maintained a strong Christian presence, especially in France, for centuries.

St. Vincent de Paul (1581–1660) also knew Jane and called her one of the holiest people he had met. Vincent, too, lived a life of strong faith. He was born into a peasant family and became a priest at age nineteen.

However, it was years later that Vincent's faith caught fire, and he spent the rest of his life ministering to the poor. He worked to extricate both himself and other priests from the worldly perks of priesthood, founding a society of parish priests who lived simply and served in peasant villages. And like Charles Borromeo, he also established seminaries. Building upon the vision of his acquaintances Francis de Sales and Jane Frances de Chantal, he founded a society of women religious who would work "outside the walls" in charity. This society grew rapidly, and became well known for its work among the poor, especially in hospitals, orphanages, elder homes, and prisons. With Paris as his base, Vincent worked in many directions, seeking to meet the physical and spiritual needs of the poor and peasants. In addition to his associations of priests and nuns, he and his associates preached missions. These missions grew to be highly popular. Vincent's renown grew throughout France even in his lifetime, as people of all walks of life admired his devotion and zeal and saw or experienced his many outreaches. He even sent missionaries to other parts of Europe. The charitable Society of St. Vincent de Paul, which serves globally today, is one echo of Vincent's extraordinary commitment to the poor.

St. Margaret Mary Alacoque (1647–1690) had a much different vocation, although as a Visitation nun, her ministry was fruit of the order's founders, Francis de Sales and Jane Frances de Chantal. In the 1670s, she experienced a series of visions of Christ, revealing to her — and through her to the Church at large — the tremendous love and mercy of Jesus. She appeared on the historical scene just as the ultra-scrupulous Jansenist movement, which we will discuss shortly, was sweeping through France. Despite initial opposition to her claims of these visions, Church leaders eventually concluded that they were authentic. Out of these visions arose the image of and devotion to the Sacred Heart of Jesus and the First Friday practice of prayer and reparation for sins.

The feast and devotion of the Sacred Heart and the First Friday devotion, each still vibrant today, are the fruit of Margaret Mary's faith. From her ministry, millions of Catholics over hundreds of years have offered millions of prayers via the Sacred Heart devotions. Although it is impossible to quantify the impact and to identify specific fruits of so much prayer, such massive prayer for conversion and reparation and for the gates of mercy to be opened has made a powerful difference in the world. Her plea for prayer in reparation for sin foreshadowed later apparitions, as the world turned further from the Christian Faith.

Many of these reforming saints were from France. Some of this is due to the influence of the French Church, but it is also an indication of the central place that France occupied in these early-modern centuries. France grew to become the most powerful nation in Europe, and numerous movements that challenged faith arose in France. France was often the main battlefield between the forces of Catholic Faith and those opposing faith. It is not surprising that the Holy Spirit inspired the vocations of so many great saints in France.

RENEWAL AMONG THE EASTERN CATHOLICS

While the efforts of Counter-Reformation saints and their thousands of allies and followers worked for renewal among the Catholics in the wake of the Protestant Reformation, others gave witness to the Faith in the East, away from the polemics with Protestants and in the midst of lands dominated by the Eastern Orthodox churches. One such saint was **St. Josaphat Kuntsevych** (1580–1623), a monk, a bishop, and a martyr.

In 1618, this monk, with a wide reputation for holiness and successful at attracting many to the monastic life, was named *archeparch* (archbishop) of Polotsk, near Vilnius, in the Polish-Lithuanian Commonwealth, which, at that time, included modern-day Ukraine and Belarus. Josaphat's primary task was to implement the controversial Union of Brest of 1596, which recognized the Ruthenian Uniate Church's union with the Catholic Church. The Ruthenian Church, also known as the Ukrainian Greek Catholic Church, was centered in Kyiv. (*Ruthenian* referred then to the Belarussian and Ukrainian peoples, and *uniate* is the term denoting churches in that region which were in union with Rome and not with the Orthodox.) The creation of this Eastern Catholic Church was highly contentious — opposed vigorously by the Orthodox, and not popular with the lay Christians. Josaphat worked with skill and charity to guide his flock into acceptance of this uniate church, strengthened the clergy, restored churches, affirmed the eastern liturgy within the Church, and called synods to resolve the many issues with moving the Church forward in union with Rome. All the while, he remained a devout monk and was committed to charity. The force of his personality and his holiness was crucial to the survival of the fledging uniate Catholic Church. His efforts cost him his life. In 1623, an Orthodox mob lynched Josaphat in the town of Vitebsk.

The Ukrainian Greek Catholic Church of today views Saint Josaphat as a hero and one of the key founders of the Church which, despite repeated efforts to quash it, survives to this day, both in Ukraine (especially in western Ukraine, around Lviv) and among a diaspora around the world.

28
THE NEW WORLD

As the Reformation raged on and split Europe, and as the Catholic Church sought to regain her spiritual footing, two other monumental developments also occurred in the sixteenth and seventeenth centuries: the Renaissance and the contact with the "New World." When Christopher Columbus, an Italian Catholic sailing under Spanish patronage, crossed the Atlantic in 1492 and made contact with the Americas, everything changed. Until this point, the history of the Catholic Church had been centered in Europe. From this point on, that would less and less be true.

Other explorers followed, and the Americas, Africa, and Pacific Asia became connected to Europe. The French, Dutch, Spanish, Portuguese, and English invested heavily in these territories — both as places for settlements and for new economic opportunities. The technologically and militarily superior Europeans often did not treat the indigenous peoples well, and the advent of colonialism and slavery (not always, but significantly opposed by Christians) were real occurrences. These issues are under heavy scrutiny and debate today.

For the Christian churches — both Catholic and Protestant — this meant looking west, south, and east for missionary activity, to spread the Gospel to new peoples and vastly different cultures and civilizations. Nonbelievers consider efforts to bring the Gospel to these new continents to be an indelible part of colonialism, but for the believer, an essential communication of the universal Good News of God's love, the Incarnation, and the promise of eternal salvation. Jesus did say go and teach *all* nations. How to do that, however, was and remains a challenge. The European Christians who flowed to these continents with missionary zeal — Catholic and Protestant — did not have a good template on how to evangelize in a culture alien to them, and among people to whom they were alien. The situation was unique in Christian history. Today's 20/20 hindsight does not do justice to this difficulty. The fact is a zeal to spread the Faith swept through European Christians, and missionaries sailed the seas and went to work in the Americas, Africa, and Asia.

Among Catholics, the Jesuits, Dominicans, and Franciscans were the most prominent missionaries and acquitted themselves well, though not perfectly, in their efforts at charity and respect for indigenous peoples. Numerous saints partook in evangelizing these newly contacted cultures. They worked with great courage to preach this message of good news, to look for ways to bridge cultures, to fight for proper treatment of all peoples, and to temper the often exploitative and cruel treatment of indigenous peoples by military and political leaders who had different agendas. Other saints were indigenous converts who were lights in their communities.

As the Reformation raged back in Europe, **St. Juan Diego** (1474–1548), an indigenous peasant in central Mexico, helped to change the course of Church history in the new world. The army of Hernán Cortés, the powerful Spanish conquistador, had overcome the Aztecs and Mayans in central Mexico, beginning in 1521. As the Spaniards consolidated their conquests and began a process of wealth-seeking and colonization, missionaries followed with the goal of bringing the Gospel to the native peoples. Twelve Franciscans were active in the area near present-day Mexico City, and through them Juan Diego and his wife became Catholic Christians and were baptized. Juan had genuine faith and piety. This prepared him for what was to happen.

In December 1531, on a hill called Tepeyac, near present-day Mexico City, and later named Guadalupe, the Virgin Mary appeared to Juan Diego. Four times he saw her. Mary asked him to go tell the local bishop, Juan de Zamarraga, to build a chapel. Juan obeyed. The bishop asked for a sign. On Juan's next visit to the bishop, an image of the Virgin inexplicably appeared on his garment or *tilma*. This image of the Virgin — of Our Lady of Guadalupe — remains today at the Basilica of Our Lady of Guadalupe in Mexico City. No credible natural explanation for this image and its endurance over centuries emerged either at that time or since, despite several scientific analyses. It has a genuine claim to be miraculous, as do the apparitions. Word of this sign at Guadalupe spread throughout the land and led to the conversion of millions of indigenous peoples in short order and to the spread of the Faith throughout Spanish-held lands. No other event or missionary activity came close to matching the dramatic effectiveness that the Guadalupe miracle had on the spread of Christianity in the New World.

Mary's apparition at Guadalupe to Juan Diego and the resulting conversions to Christianity were possible because of the missionary zeal of those Franciscans, the faith and obedience of Juan Diego, and the bishop's eventual but genuine acceptance of Juan Diego's assertion that Mary had appeared to him. Had these people not been faithful to God, the great wave of conversions in Mexico may not have taken place.

The Jesuits were prolific in their travels and missionary zeal, first in post-Reformation Europe, then around the globe. **St. Francis Xavier** (1506–1551), one of the seven original Jesuits, traveled to the other side of the world. Many consider Francis Xavier to be the greatest missionary after Saint Paul. Sailing to Pacific Asia, Xavier organized a number of Christian communities in and around Goa, India, tending to the poor and baptizing thousands, and by 1549 he was planting the seeds of Christianity in Japan. It is hard to appreciate what a feat this was — a country so far away and with a culture, alien to Europeans, that harbored deep reservations toward outsiders. Yet, through persistence, prayer, and an example of holiness that transcended language barriers, Xavier attracted thousands of Japanese to this new Faith. Through his efforts, the city of Nagasaki in southern Japan became a center for Japanese Christians. Despite setbacks, Xavier inspired hundreds of thousands of Asians to become Christian. He died while on the way to China.

In time, Japanese rulers, concerned that this foreign religion would threaten their culture, severely persecuted the fledgling Catholic communities in Japan in a mostly successful effort to eradicate this new religion from their land. A Japanese convert who became a Jesuit, **St. Paul Miki** (1562–1597), suffered crucifixion near Nagasaki, along with twenty-five companions. They were among thirty-five thousand Christians who were put to death by Japanese authorities. Although the Catholic presence in Japan today is small, Nagasaki has always been the site of a constant, often underground Catholic community, surviving centuries of persecution and even an atomic bomb.

Venerable Matteo Ricci (1552–1610), an Italian Jesuit, began the missions to China. He spent nearly thirty years in China, learning the language and culture and creatively explaining the Gospel to the Chinese. He attracted both imperial court officials and peasants to the Faith and even became an advisor to the imperial court. Ricci sought to make Christianity intelligible and attractive to the Chinese by emphasizing links and similarities to Chinese culture and Confucianism. This caused Church leaders in Rome to question, and, years after his death, put a stop to this strategy. Whether Ricci or Church leaders were correct in their understanding of how to mix or not to mix Christian teaching with local culture is beyond the reach of this book. However, Catholic missionary efforts in China were essentially suspended for three hundred years after Ricci's methods were disallowed. The early twentieth century saw renewed efforts take effect, but when the Communists came to power in the 1940s, Christian missions — Catholic and Protestant — were forced to a halt. Christianity in China now is either underground or under government supervision and is subject to constant persecution. Ricci's cause for canonization has resumed after a long pause, and Pope Francis declared him Venerable in December 2022. It will be interesting to see how the Chinese government, often hostile to the Catholic faith, reacts to the advancement toward sainthood of the foremost Catholic evangelist to China.

The Jesuits were also active in North America, working among the indigenous peoples and creating a Catholic presence. Among the Jesuits active in the north was Fr. Jacques Marquette (1631–1675). Marquette traveled extensively in Michigan and across the Midwest, founding missions and churches, especially in the Mackinac area in the 1600s. Along with Louis Joliet, he also explored and mapped the upper Mississippi River. Marquette University in Milwaukee is named after him. He is buried in Saint Ignace, Michigan, a city he founded and named after St. Ignatius Loyola.

As with all missionaries, evangelization was mixed with nationalism, as the Spanish and French missionaries moved with the advancement of their country's military and territorial ambitions. By and large, they maintained independence from secular authorities and kept focus on their evangelism. The missionaries from these European Catholic countries also planted seeds for the Faith to grow among settlers as well.

St. Isaac Jogues (1607–1646) was one of a number of French Jesuits, whom the indigenous often called "Black Robes," who worked among the Hurons east of Lake Huron, in what is now Ontario, setting up a faith presence in many of their villages. Jogues even took up residence in the Hurons' longhouses inside their villages. Amid inter-tribe contention, Isaac was tortured by the Iroquois, enemies of the Hurons, and was forced to return to France to recover from his wounds. Amazingly, Isaac chose to return. Once again the Iroquois captured him, and this time he was tortured to death. His fellow French Jesuit, **St. John de Brebeuf** (1593–1649), who like many Jesuits learned the local languages, suffered the same fate three years later. Evangelization of the Hurons and other eastern indigenous nations had limited success, however. Although many Hurons became Christian, disease and fierce attacks by the Iroquois virtually wiped out the tribe.

The Jesuit priests and lay brothers worked to respect the humanity of the indigenous peoples. Understanding their nature and how they should be treated was a contested issue among all the missionaries, settlers, and soldiers from Europe — Catholic and Protestant. Given the striking cultural differences and evident technological superiority of the arriving Europeans, this was not as obvious as it is to us today. Just who these "primitive" peoples were was much-debated. The differences among the various indigenous peoples themselves and their sometimes barbaric practices — such as child sacrifice — further complicated this issue. The Christian missionaries, though far from perfect in their treatment of the native populations, led the way in advocating for their humanity and for treating them with dignity and respecting their welfare and property. As the more powerful Europeans poured into the New World in the sixteenth century, the advocacy of the missionaries on behalf of the local populations was not well followed. Furthermore, diseases from the Old World, for which the indigenous had no immunity, ravaged the populations more than violence and exploitation.

The Spanish in particular wrestled with the issue of proper treatment and understanding of the indigenous people, perhaps none more so than Dominican Bishop Bartolomé de las Casas in the sixteenth century, who served in the Caribbean in the midst of Spanish colonization and slave trading. He came to realize the immorality of slavery, first of the local indigenous people, and later of African slaves brought to the area. He railed against slavery to hostile Spanish colonizers and to a more sympathetic Spanish crown, and advocated proper treatment and respect for the indigenous and Africans. In a real way, de las Casas was a man ahead of his time.

In addition to the overseas missionaries, a number of local inhabitants — some indigenous people, some European residents, some of mixed race — also planted the seeds of faith. One was **St. Kateri Tekakwitha** (1656–1680), a native Algonquin, who enriched the faith of many in French Canada with a simple yet unwavering faith despite obstacles of health and unaccepting family members. Numerous shrines honor her memory today.

In South America, the Faith — and martyrdom — spread through Spanish and Portuguese Jesuit missionaries. The 1980s movie *The Mission* is a stirring dramatization. In time, the Church planted roots on the South American continent and a structure emerged. One of the most outstanding early leaders and bishops of this early era was **St. Turibius of Mogrovejo** (1538–1606). He was a lawyer in Spain and chief judge of the Spanish Inquisition at Granada until he was chosen to be bishop of Lima, Peru in 1581. He protested that he was not a priest, which the Church answered by ordaining him. Turibius served as bishop of Lima for the remaining twenty-five years of his life. He was especially devoted to charity and serving the poor. He built churches, schools, hospitals, and the first seminary in the New World, learned the languages of the indigenous people, was an effective preacher, and traveled extensively to meet and minister to the people in his far-flung diocese. Turibius was relentless in defending the indigenous peoples, often clashing with the secular authorities who mistreated them, a frequent occurrence in missionary-government relations.

St. Peter Claver (1580–1654) was a Spanish Jesuit priest who served in Colombia for forty years. He tended to the thousands of slaves who were shipped from West Africa into the port of Cartagena. Peter could not stop the slave trade, but he gave all he had to assist slaves upon arrival and in the slave yards where they were held under horrendous conditions. He sought to provide food and medicine, to give them a sense of dignity, and to advocate for improved treatment. Many slaves were sent to plantations and Peter would visit them, staying in their decrepit quarters. He is credited with leading over three hundred thousand slaves to conversion and baptism into the Catholic Faith — an amazing accomplishment considering the behavior the slaves were seeing from their "Christian" slave traders and owners. Peter preached in the city center and gained a reputation for holiness and even for miracles. Peter contracted the Plague in 1650 and died alone and nearly forgotten in his own room, but he left an enduring legacy in Colombia.

The two most well-known saints of South America were not celebrated bishops or missionaries but humble, ordinary people. **St. Rose of Lima** (1586–1617) was the beautiful daughter of Spanish parents residing in Lima, now capital of Peru. She refused marriage and became a third order Dominican, taking on significant austerities which she offered for the remission of sins, and lived alone in a garden, where she began to have visions. Church authorities deemed them to be authentic.

Her reputation for holiness spread and her garden became a spiritual center, drawing local people hungry for faith. She died young, having performed no great feats in the eyes of the world — but her life inspired thousands in South America. **St. Martin de Porres** (1579–1639), also from Lima, was a close friend of Rose. Martin was born from a liaison between a Spanish knight and a freed African slave. He became a Dominican lay brother and threw himself into tending to the sick and the poor, at times exercising a gift of healing. He was a man of prayer, who, like Rose, took on many penances, and attained a deserved reputation for holiness. His also ministered to the African slaves who were being transported to the New World. For years he worked to improve their lot.

Turibius, Peter, Rose, and Martin were at the forefront among the thousands of faithful Catholics in South America who built the Church across the continent. Through their ministry, thousands of indigenous converts and European Catholic settlers — mostly from Spain and Portugal — built the Catholic Church into the predominant Faith on the continent for centuries.

㉙
SCIENCE AND THE RENAISSANCE

Along with the Protestant and Counter-Reformations and contact with the New World, the third major occurrance of the sixteenth century was the Renaissance, the cultural, scientific, and artistic awakening prompted by the rediscovery of classical Greek and Roman civilization. It originated in Florence and spread outward, first through Italy and eventually through much of Europe, and flourished from the late fifteenth through the late sixteenth centuries. Reasons for the Renaissance include the following:

- enhanced economies and social structures that facilitated art and science
- exposure to the arts and Greek philosophy from earlier scholars and writers such as Dante
- an influx of cultured refugees from Constantinople after its

fall to the Ottomans
- a remarkable confluence of artistic and scientific geniuses

Art, architecture, and science soared and advanced. This was the age of Leonardo DaVinci, Michelangelo, and Raphael; of Shakespeare, of the construction of Saint Peter's, and of the rediscovery of the classical culture and philosophy of Greece and Rome. A series of popes associated with the leading families of Florence, Spain, and Rome, including the Medici and Borgia families, were strong patrons of the arts in this era. This was a mixed blessing. Much of the greatest art and architecture in world history — including much religious art — was commissioned, preserved, and made widely available, but often the price was distraction of Church leaders from their fundamental mission of advancing the Gospel.

Copernicus and Galileo were among the first wave of modern scientists, and their discoveries caused consternation for the Church. Copernicus came to the then-novel conclusion that the earth rotated around the sun, and Galileo later affirmed him. This forced the Church to wrestle with the question of faith and science, and it particularly forced the Church to rethink how Scripture is interpreted. Until scientific discoveries began to come to the fore, there was little reason to doubt the literal accuracy of historical narratives in the Bible. Some of the Church Fathers and theologians had always maintained that Scripture was not intended to be scientifically literal, but many others disagreed. It had not been necessary to test this proposition until the Renaissance. When science began to establish things such as heliocentrism, the theory that the earth revolves around the sun, Scripture scholars had to take a closer look. The first reaction was defensive. Although many within the Church were open to the discoveries of these new scientists, others were not.

Nicolaus Copernicus (1473–1543), a multi-gifted scholar, scientist, and a believing Catholic, developed his theory of heliocentrism in the early 1500s. In order to avoid controversy, he did not publish his findings. That, and being from the Polish-Prussian area near the Baltic Sea — far from Rome — kept him out of the limelight. His findings were published shortly before his death. Galileo Galilei (1564–1642) traversed a different path. Though Catholic, he was much more assertive, an Italian near the headquarters of the Church, and harbored some misgivings on certain doctrines. He did publish his heliocentrism theory, but failed to convince Church authorities, who remained steeped in the traditional understanding of millennia that the earth, home to God's creatures made in his image, was the universe's center. Galileo was tried by the Roman Inquisition in 1633 and found "vehemently suspect of heresy," but, interestingly, short of actual heresy. He was placed under house arrest for the rest of his life — a testament to the civil power that the Church still wielded.

It was over a hundred years later before the Catholic Church withdrew her opposition to these and similar scientific discoveries and found a way of mutual benefit between science and faith. The judgment against Galileo was lifted. But this controversy over heliocentrism did open the door to new and deeper ways to look at Scripture. Catholic theologians began to see that passages that seem to conflict with scientific discoveries need not be read as literal truth, yet still hold deep theological truth. Aquinas had proposed this and Galileo himself had so suggested.[1] This allowed for a deeper understanding of the "literal and spiritual senses" of Scripture as well as debates on how scientific techniques, such as historical criticism, are to be applied to biblical studies. That debate carried on into the twentieth century. Meanwhile, most Protestants at the time, including Luther and Calvin, stuck to a fully literal interpretation of the Bible and rejected the accuracy of these scientific discoveries. This opened the door for modern-day Fundamentalism.

The Counter-Reformation period of the sixteenth through the eighteenth centuries also saw the rise of countless magnificent churches and cathedrals across Europe and even Spanish South America. In contrast to most Protestants of the day, Counter-Reformation Catholics built soaring and exquisitely decorated churches, particularly in the Baroque period, often adorned with gold. Their purpose was to use splendor and beauty to lift the mind of the worshipper to the transcendent God, the source of all beauty. Baroque art and architecture

— sculpture, paintings, and resplendent churches — were purposeful and powerful fruits of the Catholic Counter-Reformation, particularly in the seventeenth and eighteenth centuries. Many Baroque artists — including the great masters Bernini and Rubens — were active, praying Catholics.

These magnificent churches and much of the great art of the period demonstrate the mutually supportive relationship between the Counter-Reformation Catholic Church and the Renaissance. Great Renaissance and Baroque artists and architects provided beauty to the Catholic world, and in turn, were able to practice their art due to the support and patronage of the Church. (The decorative and energetic Baroque period of the late sixteenth and seventeenth centuries developed after and out of the Renaissance.) An example is the religious art of the Italian Baroque painter Caravaggio. He painted numerous masterworks of scenes from Scripture, including *The Conversion of St. Paul*, *The Crucifixion of St. Peter*, and *The Call of St. Matthew*. The Church commissioned a number of his paintings for the spiritual benefit of pilgrims traveling to Rome during the Holy Year of 1600, at the height of the Counter-Reformation efforts. Bernini's magnificent sculpture, *The Ecstasy of St. Teresa*, one of the greatest sculptures of all time, adorns a Roman church. And the Vatican is home to an extraordinary array of priceless art, including the Renaissance paintings of Raphael and Michelangelo's paintings in the Sistine Chapel. These and countless other art works both lift the hearts of Christians to this day toward the heavens and are also considered among the greatest masterpieces in all of Western art.

The invention of the printing press in the fifteenth century, as the Renaissance was dawning, opened the door for the proliferation of the written word and of music. Books spread throughout the continent, including lives of saints (such as those which inspired Saint Ignatius), Scripture, including the Douay-Rheims English translation from Saint Jerome's Vulgate in the late sixteenth and early seventeenth century, catechetical materials, and great literature, including wider circulation of Dante's magnificent *Divine Comedy* and the plays of Shakespeare (who some historians speculate was a secret Catholic). Though less is known of Renaissance music, the development of musical notation, along with printing, fostered the growth of beautiful music with the objective of lifting the soul to God. The Council of Trent encouraged sacred music and, in the years following, many composers stepped forward. Among them was the Italian Giovanni Palestrina (1525–1594), who, building on the development of polyphony in the previous two centuries, composed over one hundred Mass settings and other sacred music. He and other Renaissance musical composers paved the way for the many great classical musicians of the ensuing centuries and their many beautiful compositions.

30

THE OTTOMAN THREAT AND THE SIEGE OF VIENNA

The seventeenth century closed with a history-changing event not associated with the Reformation. The ever-powerful and ever-feared Ottoman Turks had continued to threaten Christian Europe with invasion and the spread of Islam. This came to a head at the siege and Battle of Vienna in 1683.

The threat was real. For centuries the Ottoman Empire, centered in modern-day Turkey, had sent powerful armies into Europe, seizing much of eastern Europe, even taking Constantinople. This brought the Byzantine Empire to a crashing end. In the seventeenth century, the Ottoman army remained the strongest and most feared force on the continent. Still in control of the Balkans and still seeking to expand west and north, the Ottomans had for some time set their sights on the city of Vienna, in central Europe on the Danube River which flowed from the heart of Europe. Vienna was the capital of the vast Catholic Hapsburg empire, which encompassed Austria, Spain, the Netherlands, and much of Germany — a major strategic target. And, wherever the Ottomans conquered, they sought to instill Islam as the faith of the land. This is what Christian Europe faced in the summer of 1683.

For the Ottomans, the time was right. Europe was more vulnerable than it had been for a long time. The continent was religiously divided. At best, Protestant countries left the defense of Europe to the Catholic countries which were closer to the threat. At worst, they considered the enemy of their Catholic enemy to be their friend. And Catholic but mercurial France had become a trading partner with the Ottomans and a fierce opponent of the Hapsburgs, and thus had no interest in helping to defend the Hapsburg's capital of Vienna. The Thirty Years' War, which had ended just three decades earlier, had devastated Europe and left the continent exhausted and short on military resources. Seeing this, the Ottomans pounced. Take Vienna, and the paths to central Europe and likely beyond, and to Rome, would have been open to them. It is little exaggeration to say, as do many historians, that the future of Christian Europe was at stake as the vast Ottoman army gathered in the fields outside the walls of Vienna.

The Ottomans planned their assault on Vienna for the summer of 1683. The massive Ottoman army wound its way that summer through the Balkans toward the Danube. However, they were slowed by heavy rains. Arriving at last in midsummer, they placed Vienna under siege. Despite a huge military advantage over the Viennese defenders, for weeks the Ottoman army was unable to breach the city walls. The reason was that the heavy rains and mud-filled roads on the way had forced them to leave behind much of their heavy artillery.[1] The one thing the Ottomans lacked was enough firepower to pound the walls. This proved to be crucial. They finally did break through the defenses in September and were poised to take the city. However, a relief army with cavalry from various European nations, led by Polish king John Sobieski, arrived just in time. Sobieski, having entrusted his forces to Our Lady of Częstochowa, the patroness of Poland, also known as the Black Madonna, led the largest cavalry charge in history down from a height and onto the Ottomans in the plain below. His "Winged Hussars," coordinating with the beleaguered defense forces already in place, surprised the much larger Ottoman force before it could storm the city, and routed them. Vienna — and likely Europe as well — was saved. It may well have been God's providence that the rains forced the Ottomans to leave behind their artillery, allowing the city to hold out until Sobieski and his Hussars arrived.

This was the turning point. After the battle of Vienna, never again were the Ottomans able to threaten Europe. In fact, the Hapsburgs were able to push back and recapture formerly Christian territory that the Ottomans had conquered, including Hungary and parts of the Balkans. Europe remained Christian — for a while.

The Catholic Church was in a much different place in 1700 than she had been in 1516. Though severely wounded, she had survived her greatest crisis. The Christendom of the Middle Ages had come to an end. Upwards of half the continent was now Protestant. But by the dawn of the eighteenth century, the Church had stabilized. Both Western civilization and the Christian Faith began to reach into the New World, Asia, and Africa. Christianity would no longer be so centered in Europe. The rise of industry was in full swing, transforming the economies and increasing the pace of life, and nation-states had grown larger and continued to battle each other, now more for political than religious reasons.

These severe tests — the Reformation, social upheaval, and the advance of science — had actually made the Catholic Church stronger and more committed to her mission. Without the Protestant Reformation, there would likely not have been such a vigorous Counter-Reformation and the renewal of faith and structure that it brought. Without the challenge of science, the Church would not have been able to address the nature of faith and Scripture as the modern world dawned. Without the discoveries of new worlds, missionaries would not have been able to spread the Gospel of Jesus Christ beyond the continent of Europe — to the ends of the earth.

ENLIGHTENMENT AND MODERNISM

AD 1700 to AD 1920

St. John Vianney. AdobeStock

31

ENLIGHTENMENT PHILOSOPHERS

Ideas matter. Powerful ideas can change the course of human history. This is how Christianity took hold and captured the imagination of a continent for more than a millennium. In the eighteenth century, radically new ideas rose up and changed the world. For centuries, the Catholic Church — both the institution and the millions of ordinary believers — had pride of place in Christian Europe. Through times good and bad, the Church was the most significant part of most people's lives. Nearly everyone was a believer, even if many did not live out their faith well. The Reformation, however, had split the Christian faithful, and the Catholic Church no longer enjoyed a monopoly among believers in Europe. Explorers had opened up contact with the Americas, Africa, and Asia. The Industrial Revolution was gaining steam. Travel, printing, and methods of production were advancing. Nation-states were coalescing and gaining in power and size; France, England, Spain, and Hapsburg

Austria were developing a clearer self-identity beyond their religious heritage. The many wars in the sixteenth and seventeenth centuries had taken a toll on European psyche. All these changes led to more pluralism in thought. Faith was weakened. European society had encountered a paradigm shift.

In this context of massive societal change, a new set of ideas that was to be one of the greatest threats to Christian faith in history took hold in the eighteenth century — what we now call the *Enlightenment*. With Christian philosophy and theology divided, and in many eyes discredited, new thinkers rose up to fill the void. They were not beholden to Christianity, and for the first time since the days of the Roman Empire, belief in the God of the Christians was questioned on a major scale. A host of new philosophers began to speak and write. They were to have enormous influence — both in their own times and into our own day.

Among the most influential were René Descartes, David Hume, Voltaire, John Locke, and Immanuel Kant. At first, they asserted that "reason" was the key to knowledge — apart from faith. Aquinas and other Christian theologians had previously recognized the role of reason in discerning truth, but not apart from Divine Revelation. These new philosophers began to reject Revelation as a legitimate source of truth, and their ideas began to spread. *Rationalism*, as an allegedly more mature, "enlightened" way of discerning reality, began to fill the void. This led to skepticism — a deep questioning of long-held truths — a serious challenge to Christian pursuit of truth. The skeptics began to question the Christian claims of God, the Incarnation, and the inspiration of Scripture. From this came the theory of the autonomy of the individual as the primary arbiter of truth and knowledge. Anything from outside the individual mind — such as Revelation — was subject to skepticism, and without rational proof, could be rejected. Immanuel Kant was a leader in fostering this way of thinking. This philosophy grew and became influential, to some degree even within the Church herself.

The culmination of this first stage of the Enlightenment was the French Revolution at the end of the eighteenth century. A cauldron of numerous forces turned French society upside down: resentment of the king and the ruling class which were identified with the Catholic Church, rationalism, poverty among the masses, and hostile leaders who were not afraid to use violence. Anti-clericalism led to severe suppression and persecution of the Church, sending a large number of priests, nuns, and faithful Christians into hiding or to the guillotine. The renowned Cathedral of Notre Dame in Paris was for a time in the 1790s turned into a pagan "Temple of Reason" as the revolutionaries sought to replace France's millennium of Catholicism with a rational Deism. The rest of Europe was not as dramatically affected as France, but Enlightenment thought did spread across Europe and created a gradual separation of Church and state and a lessening of the influence of Christianity. Still, the Faith persisted, especially in the countryside.

These forces impacted the Church internally as well. A new wave of "-isms" encroached upon the core Faith. The leaders of a mostly French movement called *Gallicanism* advocated national autonomy from Rome in church affairs. Many priests embraced this movement, nearly causing a schism.

Jansenism swept through France in the seventeenth century. Influenced by the teachings of a French bishop, Cornelius Jansen (d. 1638),[1] the Jansenists preached that human nature was radically corrupted and, without grace, humans were unable to escape wickedness and depravity. And grace was given only to those predestined. Strict austerities and a hyper-scrupulous spirituality were necessary to push back against this depraved human nature. A significant number of French clergy embraced Jansenism in the seventeenth century. It became an influential movement within the Church in France and caused debates and division. In time, however, Jansenism gave way to the Church's traditional understanding of grace, freedom, and original sin.

The brilliant French philosopher Blaise Pascal was a Jansenist, but he was also a sincere believer who opposed the rationalists. His classic work, *Pensées*, is a formidable defense of Christianity, even if from the Jansenist perspective. Pascal developed a proposition known as "Pascal's wager": Without proof, it is more logical to live as if God existed than if he did not.

The Jesuits in the eighteenth century became a casualty of the Enlightenment spirit that spawned Jansenism and Gallicanism. Vital to the

Catholic Counter-Reformation movement in Europe and at the vanguard of missionary activity in the Americas and around the world, the Jesuits ran into opposition from these new movements and also a number of monarchies, including the French. The Jesuits were considered too traditional by some and too international and loyal to the pope by others. Under pressure, Pope Clement XIV disbanded the Jesuits in 1773. This was a blow to missionary and other spiritual activities supported by the Jesuits. The order was reinstated in 1814, but much damage had already been done. The Jesuits never regained the stature and missionary zeal they enjoyed in the sixteenth and seventeenth centuries.

Many Enlightenment-influenced Scripture scholars turned to new scientific ways of discerning the meaning and interpretation of Scripture. This was beneficial in part, but without a foundation in faith that Scripture was the Word of God, it often drifted into a purely rationalistic method that questioned the truth of the Bible. "Historical Jesus" scholarship developed. This was an effort to determine who Jesus was as an historical figure only, using only secular historical methods, and usually with a preexisting premise that Jesus was no more than a man, and with the aim of explaining away the divine or miracles. Some have observed that, as scholars look for the "historical Jesus," they inevitably end up finding a Jesus who looks just like themselves. Deism, which influenced a number of the American founders — Franklin and Jefferson included — acknowledged a vague concept of the divine, but rejected the Christian proposition of a personal God and the Incarnation.

As these ideas began to affect society, they gave birth to further ideas, including *scientism* (sometimes called *positivism*), the idea that only scientific inquiry can produce authentic knowledge; *materialism*, the idea that only exterior forces, not spiritual ones, control humanity; and eventually *modernism*, a bundle of ideas that encompassed much of Enlightenment thought, particularly including the idea that reason without faith must control in scholarship — even Scripture scholarship, and even to the point of questioning the nature of God. These concepts are deeply ingrained in today's world and contribute mightily to the demise of the Christian perspective. This second generation of Enlightenment thinkers — who inhabited the nineteenth and early twentieth centuries — included Marx, Freud, Darwin, and Nietzsche. Nietzsche popularized the notion that "God is dead," and predicted that without a belief in God, the "will to power" would prevail in human society. From this sense came the further concept of *nihilism*, the idea that life lacks any real meaning. Jean Paul Sartre and Albert Camus were twentieth-century proponents of nihilism. Most of these ideas remain entrenched into today's Western societies.

The Enlightenment movements created huge and unprecedented challenges for the Christian churches — both Catholic and Protestant. For the first time since the days of the early Church in the Roman Empire, pagan philosophies were at the forefront in the public square. And for the first time in all of Christian history, a growing atheism began to challenge Christianity's very reason to exist in society. Enlightenment thought has embedded itself deep into the societal psyche of former Christendom and its influence and challenge to Christian belief has grown to become arguably the greatest challenge facing the Church from the eighteenth century up to the present day.

Christian responses, many and varied, did rise up. Fundamentalism, an exclusively literal interpretation of the Bible in the face of growing scientific and historical methods, had its origins during the Reformation, coalesced in the late nineteenth century, and grew to be a significant response to the Enlightenment in many Protestant churches. From the Catholic perspective, Fundamentalism was an overcorrection, but despite its shortcomings, it sought to preserve the "fundamentals" of the Christian Faith in the midst of rationalism and nonbelief. Catholics today have more in common with Fundamentalists than with modernists, who reject much of Revelation.

Powerful Protestant preachers such as John Wesley of England (1703–1791) inspired strong Christian revival movements in England and America, called "great awakenings." Wesley once said, "Give me one hundred men who love no one but Christ, hate nothing but sin, and preach nothing but Christ Jesus and Him crucified, and I will convert the world."

32

EUROPEAN SAINTS IN ENLIGHTENMENT TIMES

The witness of the saints to the challenges of the Enlightenment was that the grace of God is a more powerful tool than well-meaning human effort on its own, and an increase in faith is more effective than head-to-head debate.

St. Alphonsus Liguori (1696–1787) was tucked down in southern Italy and away from much of the philosophical currents of the day, but he rallied people to follow the path of faith in Jesus. He left a law practice to become a priest, and was ordained in 1726. Alphonsus toiled away at serving the poor and grew to be a powerful preacher in the Naples area. He founded an order of priests with a preaching ministry — which became known as the *Redemptorists* — and struggled against numerous attacks on his order. The Redemptorists still serve today throughout the

Catholic world, including America.

Liguori became a bishop and set out on a program of reform and service to the poor in his diocese. He was an influential writer as well, particularly on moral theology — an area of which he was perhaps the foremost expert in the Church during his time. In his moral teaching, he advocated a balance between rigor and leniency, and this enabled him to become a key opponent of the hyper-strict Jansenists. He also harbored a deep devotion to the Virgin Mary and wrote devotional works in honor of her. Liguori endured a dark night of the soul late in life but endured through it to a time of peace, during which he had visions and spoke prophecies that were fulfilled. Liguori had significant influence in fostering the Faith in southern Italy, and his legacy remains alive today. He has been declared a Doctor of the Church.

St. Clement Hofbauer (1751–1820), born in Bohemia, worked as a baker in a hermitage when Austrian Hapsburg Emperor Joseph II abolished monasteries as part of an Enlightenment program to limit the reaches of the Church and to impose state controls. This policy, called *Josephism*, was limited to Hapsburg areas, and was unusual because Joseph (son of the sincere Catholic empress Maria-Theresa and older brother of Marie Antoinette) remained Catholic and the Hapsburgs were generally faithful Catholics. Clement became a Redemptorist (the order that Liguori had just founded) and tried to set up a Redemptorist foundation in Vienna, but was stymied by the dictates of Josephism. He moved on to Warsaw, Poland where for many years he worked with the poor and conducted successful missionary work among Poles, Germans, Jews, and Protestants. But Napoleon Bonaparte — the French general-emperor whose conquests wreaked havoc in Europe in the early nineteenth century and who sometimes persecuted, sometimes tolerated the Catholic Church — shut his work down and imprisoned him. After his release, he eventually returned to Vienna where his sermons, holiness, and wisdom made him popular. He was instrumental in revitalizing the Faith in German-speaking areas and in fighting off a movement to create a German national church. He fiercely opposed the final stages of Josephism, and would have been expelled from Vienna had not Joseph II died first. Mercifully, Joseph's successor turned away from Joseph's Enlightenment-influenced anti-Church policies.

The Enlightenment was firmly rooted in France and spawned the French Revolution in the 1790s, with its waves of violence and severe persecution of the Church. Several French saints were caught up in the strife and gave witness which, in time, helped to lessen the persecution. **St. Julie Billiart** (1751–1816) suffered paralysis at a young age but still maintained a vibrant faith, tended to the poor, and even helped to hide fugitive priests who were in hiding from the revolutionary authorities. This forced her into hiding herself. Later she joined with others to offer catechetical classes to villagers in the town of Bettencourt and from there she helped found an orphanage and educated religious teachers and young girls. One day, at the end of a novena, a priest ordered Julie to stand up. She was miraculously healed from her paralysis.

St. Elizabeth Bichier (1773–1838) fought against the oppressive directives of the Revolution's French National Assembly, moved to the town of Bethines where she fought against atheism and government priests, and then focused on care of the sick and needy. She founded a congregation, the Daughters of the Cross, which cared for the sick and elderly. This congregation grew to include over sixty convents across France — remarkable at a time when the Church was under attack from French authorities.

Those attacks took aim at a large number of priests, nuns, and active lay Catholics who were put to death during the 1790s Reign of Terror. The **Martyrs of Laval**, a group of nineteen Catholics — a laywoman, three sisters, and fifteen priests — were guillotined at various times early in 1794 in western France by the leaders of the French Revolution. The laywoman, **Bl. Françoise Mézière,** was caught and condemned for daring to nurse wounded soldiers. All have been beatified.

During the final rampage of the Reign of Terror, convents and monasteries were ordered closed; nuns and monks were turned out and ordered to pledge support to the government. In July of 1794, sixteen Carmelite nuns were sent to the guillotine in Paris. These **Martyrs of Compiègne** declined to renounce their religious commitments and continued to live in community. They were condemned as counter-revolutionaries in a show trial. On the march to the guillotine, they prayed, sang hymns, and renewed their vows. The beheading of these nuns — many of whom were elderly — prompted a backlash from the public and their deaths are credited with bringing an end to the killings. All sixteen, including their prioress, **Bl. Teresa of Saint Augustine,** have been beatified.

St. Rose Philippine Duchesne (1769–1852), who became a Visitation nun — the order founded by St. Jane Frances de Chantal and St. Francis de Sales — was forced to return home when the Revolution's Reign of Terror in 1791 drove the Visitation order out of France. There, she tended to the sick and visited imprisoned priests. Napoleon eased the direct attacks on the Church soon after coming to power, but Rose, having then joined the Society of the Sacred Heart, was sent to America. She founded a number of convents near Saint Louis and along the Mississippi and a school for Native Americans, planting seeds for the Faith to spread in America. She was among the first of the Catholic missionaries into the American heartland.

One of the most influential saints of the Enlightenment era, a man who met the rationalism of his time head on, intellect for intellect, faith for unbelief, was the English convert **St. John Henry Newman** (1801–1890). Newman was a brilliant Anglican scholar whose influence in the Church of England grew as his academic career progressed. While a scholar in residence at Oxford University, he led what is now called the *Oxford Movement*, a concerted effort of Anglican scholars at Oxford to reform the Church of England. They sought to inspire deeper faith and to reintroduce more traditional liturgical and theological elements into church practice. This movement enjoyed considerable success, along with a good measure of controversy as these reform elements steered the movement closer to its Roman Catholic roots.

In 1845, Newman became Catholic, arguably the most famous convert to Catholicism in the nineteenth century. He once said — bluntly, but with the intention of showing how the Catholic Church is rooted in history — "To be deep in history is to cease to be Protestant."[1] As a Catholic, Newman continued his career as a scholar and writer of theology. His theological insights helped the Church adapt its theological perspective while remaining fully orthodox. He was the century's foremost opponent of Enlightenment thought — which he and others called *liberalism* — both within society and within the Catholic and Anglican churches. One of his more important treatises was *An Essay on the Development of Christian Doctrine*, his explanation of how truth can be understood more deeply over time, yet remain the same orthodox truth. Both before and after his conversion, Newman was an insightful preacher, as evidenced by his *Parochial and Plain Sermons*, given during the time of the Oxford Movement. Newman founded the Catholic University of Ireland (an ultimately unsuccessful endeavor) and wrote essays on the mission of a Catholic university, now gathered into *The Idea of a University* and worthy of reflection today.

One of his biographers, Louis Bouyer — himself an intellectual giant — said, "What Saint Augustine was for the ancient world, that St. Thomas Aquinas was for the Middle Ages, and that Newman must be held to be in relation to the world of today."[2] Newman's exceptional work on behalf of the Catholic Faith in Britain during the nineteenth century was so instrumental that Pope Leo XIII named him a cardinal. Though a priest, Newman offered great insights into the value and proper role of the laity. Newman's teachings on the laity, the papacy, and the development of doctrine impacted both the First and Second Vatican Councils. Due to his great gift of explaining the meaning and significance of Catholic doctrine and his great personal sanctity, it is likely that this newly canonized saint will one day be named a Doctor of the Church.

33
SAINTS IN AMERICA, ASIA, AND AFRICA

While the heart of Christianity remained in Europe, the Faith had obtained a foothold in all parts of the New World, led by waves of missionaries. After the Jesuits were shut down by civil and Church authorities, the Spanish Franciscans began missionary activities up the Pacific coast of northern Mexico and present-day California. These Franciscans worked among the local indigenous peoples and founded a vast series of missions. These missions also served as anchors for the Catholic Faith as it grew among the ensuing generations of settlers. The state of California today is dotted with cities with the prefix "San" and "Santa"; they all began as Franciscan missions.

Most prominent among the Franciscan missionaries was **St. Junípero Serra** (1713–1784), a priest and a brilliant scholar. After receiving training in Mexico City, Serra and other Franciscans traveled to their assignments on the Pacific coast. All but Father Junípero accepted a horse for the arduous journey. Serra declined a horse, saying that, if his father, St. Francis of Assisi, journeyed by foot, then so would he. During the long journey, he developed a leg condition that caused him serious pain and difficulty walking for the rest of his life.

Serra founded a series of missions along the California coast, seeking to evangelize the local indigenous peoples. He founded Mission San Diego in 1769 — the first of eight which he directly founded — and made it all the way to Monterrey the following year, naming the new mission there after St. Charles Borromeo. Among others that he personally founded were San Juan Capistrano and San Francisco. He also introduced agricultural techniques to the indigenous who were mostly hunters. His method was to build a mission compound, invite in those who became Christians, then teach them the Faith and farming. Serra continually clashed with the local Spanish military authorities who exploited, bullied, or even did violence to the indigenous people. This was one of the reasons that Serra sought to keep them within his compound after they had joined the mission society. He saw them as God's people, for whom baptism would lead them to eternal life. In this sense, he was ahead of his own time. Not all Europeans had this attitude of respect for the humanity of the indigenous peoples.

Fra Junípero has long been recognized for his advocacy on behalf of the indigenous, his holiness of life, his founding of missions which grew to become major cities, and for his part in the founding of the state of California. However, he has come under fire in modern times for his alleged methods. In 2020, several statues of Father Junípero in California and elsewhere were torn down and his reputation attacked. That criticism is mostly unfair and uninformed. It is more a reflection of misguided modern sensibilities than a true assessment of the saint's life and work. One observer in his time complained that Serra cared more for the indigenous than he did for his fellow Spaniards. With a broad brush, one can associate Serra and the missionaries with the Spanish colonizers, but their objectives were not the same — as evidenced in the regular conflict between Serra and the political or military authorities. Once, Father Serra even journeyed from California to Mexico City, walking much of the route on his injured leg, to obtain from the viceroy a declaration of legal protection from the Spanish authorities in California for the indigenous people.[1]

Overall, he and the Franciscans founded twenty-one missions up and down the California coast. These missions created a solid Catholic presence in California.

However, Mexican civil authorities took over and secularized the missions in the 1830s, driving out the Franciscans. This ended the mission era. Much of the persecution of the indigenous in California occurred in the decades after the Franciscans were forced to leave.

Many of California's major cities, including Los Angeles and San Francisco, grew from the mission sites. Serra's contribution not only to the Faith in California but to its early growth as a state has been so recognized that a statue of Serra, one of two representing California, stands in the US Capitol rotunda (although modern revisionists have challenged its presence). Serra is even credited with planting the first vineyard in California.

St. Elizabeth Ann Seton (1774–1821) was the first American to be canonized a saint. She was born near the beginning of the Revolutionary War into a prominent Episcopal family in New York. After a challenging youth, she married a wealthy businessman. They had five children. She and her relatives were active in the Episcopal Church and they tended to many of the poor in the city. But when her husband contracted tuberculosis, they traveled to Italy with the hope that the warm climate would help. It did not — he died in 1803. As providence would have it, her husband's Italian business associates and their family members introduced Elizabeth to Catholicism. She experienced a powerful draw to the Catholic Faith, returned to New York, and two years later became Catholic — at a time when anti-Catholic feelings were high. The American colonists, before and for decades after the Revolutionary War, were almost exclusively Protestant, and had arrived in the two centuries after the Protestant Reformation and the ongoing turmoil it had unleashed. Consequently, feelings of anti-Catholicism, particularly in elite society, ran deep. After her conversion, Elizabeth was ostracized by her Episcopal family and friends and the high society that she had been part of. The doors back to her old life closed.

This forced Elizabeth to reinvent herself. Seeking a source of income for her family and, with the influence of providence, Elizabeth moved to Maryland. There she founded a Catholic girls' school in Emmitsburg, Maryland and a small congregation of nuns to run it. Other schools followed, including in New York and Saint Louis. Mother Seton, as she became known, can rightly be considered the one who launched the vast American Catholic parochial school system.

From the women who gathered around her, she also founded the first American society of women religious: the Sisters of Charity of Saint Joseph. This order grew to twenty communities by her death, serving across the eastern half of the United States.

St. John Neumann (1811–1860) was a contemporary of his namesake across the Atlantic, English Cardinal John Newman, but they are separate men. Neumann was an immigrant from Bohemia who became bishop of Philadelphia, and the other significant pioneer of the Catholic school system in America. Interestingly, he came to America due to a surplus of priests in Bohemia. A Redemptorist, he worked at first as a missionary mostly to German-speaking Catholic immigrants in New York and other eastern states. As bishop, he turned to education, adding to the work of building Catholic schools that Mother Seton had begun, launching over one hundred Catholic schools. In addition to his work in education, he was renowned for his holiness, preaching, and works of charity.

It is not an exaggeration to recognize that **St. Frances Xavier Cabrini** (1850–1917), also known as Mother Cabrini, was one of the great missionaries in Catholic Church history. She exemplified the extraordinary work of American nuns in the nineteenth and twentieth centuries. The nuns' stories are not well known outside of their ubiquitous staffing of Catholic parochial schools during the twentieth century. Yet quietly, these women religious, in their strange-looking habits and in the face of persistent anti-Catholicism, stepped into inner cities and the countryside, tending to immigrants, the poor, and disease victims, where few others would tread. They taught the Gospel, and founded hospitals, schools, orphanages, and whatever was needed. They practiced nursing, teaching, fundraising, and problem-solving. They tangled with bureaucracies to get approval for their ministries, using dedication, intelligence, and negotiating skills — whatever it took, with the love of Christ — to care for people in need. In a real sense, these remarkable women were the first, and perhaps the most authentic, feminists.

Mother Cabrini, who had founded an order of sisters in her native northern Italy, pined to be a missionary to Asia. In her late thirties, at the invitation of the archbishop of New York and the urging of Pope Leo XIII, she instead voyaged to New York City in 1889 to work with dirt-poor Italian immigrants. Over the next twenty-eight years she worked extensively throughout the United States, Central and South America, and Europe — including New York, Chicago, Denver, Seattle, Los Angeles, New Orleans, Buenos Aires, and Paris, traversing the Atlantic dozens of times. She overcame numerous obstacles to evangelize and catechize poorly churched immigrants, and founded hospitals, orphanages, schools, and convents of her order, the Missionary Sisters of the Sacred Heart. Despite nagging health problems, Mother Cabrini's ministry was so fruitful first and foremost because of her constant prayer and trust in God, but also due to her personal magnetism and uncanny ability to get things done. She died in Chicago, having started over sixty houses of sisters and countless hospitals, schools, and orphanages in eight countries. One of many places named for her was the massive, now torn down "Cabrini Green" housing project in inner-city Chicago.

Mother Cabrini's work among immigrants — along with the work of so many other religious and lay people, well-known or not — was crucial. The nineteenth and early twentieth centuries saw a massive flow of immigrants from Europe to the Americas, especially to the United States. This changed the face of Catholicism in the world. Millions of Catholics emigrated from Italy, Ireland, Germany, Poland, and other Slavic countries to find a new life. Unlike in most of Latin America and the Philippines, where indigenous or mixed ethnic majorities became Catholic, most American immigrants huddled together in cities, not mixing for the first generations. Language barriers, grinding poverty, limited religious resources, and anti-Catholic prejudice exerted a huge toll on the

Catholic immigrants, endangering their faith. That is why Pope Leo sent Mother Cabrini to New York rather than to Asia. The work of these saints and their uncanonized coworkers to marshal resources and establish ethnic parishes and schools went a long way to save the faith of millions and plant Catholicism firmly in the United States and other English-speaking countries.

The Church spread in Asia as well, including into the Philippines, Vietnam, India, and Korea. The seed of this faith was the blood of martyrs, including **St. Andrew Kim Taegon** in 1846, as Korean authorities perceived Christians as a threat. Andrew Kim was the first Korean-born priest. After ordination in China, he returned to his homeland to preach and evangelize. The leaders of Korea's Confucian culture, suspicious of Christianity, began a persecution in the late 1830s. Kim was tortured and beheaded near Seoul, one of thousands of Korean martyrs from 1839 to 1846. The Christian Faith — both Catholic and Protestant — remains significant in Korean society today.

A similar scenario unfolded in the southeast Asian country of Vietnam. **St. Andrew Dũng-Lạc** (1795–1839), a priest, was beheaded during a wave of persecution against Christians. The Catholic minority in Vietnam has held on stubbornly to the present day despite various persecutions and upheavals.

European missionaries began to work in sub-Saharan Africa as several nation-states in Europe opened up contact with this vast continent. Colonialism took hold — especially by the nineteenth century — and led to a severe exploitation of the African peoples. As this was unfolding, the Faith began to spread in Africa. The missionaries, as in other parts of the world, interacted with the indigenous peoples with greater respect and concern than did their civil counterparts. From the seeds of the early African missionaries, the Faith is spreading faster in Africa today than anywhere else in the world. As the Faith in the West declines, Africa may be the future of the Church.

As this age of conflict between Church and state played out, inevitably there were martyrs. Among African martyrs were the **Ugandan Martyrs** (1885–1887). Both Catholic and Anglican, they were put to death for their adherence to the Faith, at the hands of King Mwanga. This king was a power-crazed ruler who used that power to sexually abuse members of his court who caught his eye. Those who resisted or spoke out against his advances were put to death. Among the forty-five victims were sincere Catholics **St. Charles Lwanga** and **St. Joseph Mkasa**.

St. Damien of Molokai (1840–1889) was a missionary from Belgium whose ministry to lepers in Hawaii became his life's work. He was raised on a farm, aspired to be a priest, fought through a deficit in education to reach ordination in 1864, and that same year arrived in Hawaii. He volunteered for an assignment to the leper colony on the island of Molokai and began his ministry in 1866. Father Damien immersed himself in the community of lepers, assisting them in developing infrastructure and leadership. He founded a parish for Catholics and tended to the medical needs of the entire population. In 1884 he caught leprosy himself but continued to serve until his death in 1889. Even in his lifetime his efforts were considered heroic charity in the name of Christ. He was well loved by the community and appreciated by the Hawaiian authorities who honored him with the medal of knight commander of Kalakaua, presented by the crown princess.

Some have criticized his ministry, either due to denominational rivalry or by associating him with European colonialism. However, his total commitment to a life of charity cannot be easily negated, and much of the criticisms reflect more upon the agenda of his critics than on Father Damien. Among Damien's defenders was the author of *Treasure Island*, the Protestant Scottish writer Robert Louis Stevenson. He visited Molokai shortly after Father Damien's death, interviewed the local residents, and wrote a stirring defense of Father Damien's commitment to the Molokai lepers.[2] At the behest of the Hawaiian state government, Father Damien's statue stands in the US Capitol rotunda in Washington, D.C.

34

THE BATTLE AGAINST MODERNISM: FROM VATICAN I TO PIUS X

The momentum of the Enlightenment carried over into the nineteenth century. This was the first century since the beginning of the Church in which a secularist mindset pervaded among the intellectuals and elites of the Western world. The Christian churches were on the defensive as more and more scholars claimed that rapidly developing science offered more rational explanations for the nature of things. And this mindset began to work its way into the Church as well. *Modernism* is the term associated with the rationalism and scientism that found a footing within the Church. Despite some valid contributions to the thought and practice of the Church as she moved into modern times, many aspects of modernist thinking among theologians and biblical exegetes challenged Church doctrine. It also minimized the central place of Revelation and faith in the theology of the Church. The momentum toward "demythologizing" Scripture and Church doctrines grew. This intellectual movement brought new scientific techniques to the interpretation of Scripture, fostered a movement to reform the liturgy, and generally infused theology with a sense of skepticism and relativism.

Popes Pius IX and Leo XIII were at the forefront in the Church's struggles against the rising secular threats to the Church and society, and their inroads into the Church itself. Pius IX presided over the *First Vatican Council*, held 1869–1870, the first ecumenical council since Trent three hundred years earlier. Vatican I, as it is often called, doubled down against Enlightenment influences, particularly rationalism, materialism, and *liberalism*, the growing movement toward building a secular new world order via the materialistic notions of freedom and "progress." The council also delved into the nature of the Church and recognized papal infallibility, defining its scope and limits. The infallibility doctrine of Vatican I stands as the council's most noteworthy and also its most controversial decree. This council was a shot over the bow, asserting that the Church stood for timeless truths to a world that increasingly denied them. Pope Pius IX's authoritative role at the council and beyond contributed to strengthening the role of the papacy.

In 1870, the Italian patriot Giuseppe Garibaldi was in the midst of his fight to unify the Italian peninsula into the modern nation of Italy. His armies swept away the Papal States — territory in central Italy that had been under the rule of the popes since the eighth century. The loss of the Papal States ended the temporal power of the popes, forcing the popes to focus strictly on their global *spiritual* mission. The temporal authority of the popes retreated to the tiny area within Rome we now call Vatican City.

Pope Leo XIII (r. 1878–1903) is often considered the first modern pope. He was the first pope to live into the twentieth century and to serve in the Vatican after the loss of the Papal States. He continued the fight against modernism with diplomacy, and with an eye toward fostering coexistence with science. He wrote extensively. His two most noteworthy encyclicals were *Proventissimus Deus*, which urged deeper study of Scripture — a breakthrough given the Church's retrenchments after the Reformation — and *Rerum Novarum*, in which he tackled the urgent modern issues of labor and capital, and preached justice for workers. This opened the door for development of the Church's social doctrines. Out of a constant commitment to world missions, he authorized missionary activity in Africa, laying the foundation of the massive growth of the Catholic Church in Africa throughout the twentieth century and beyond. And remarkably, in or near the year 1887, Leo had personal meetings with three saints and directed them toward their missionary and spiritual missions: St. Francis Cabrini, St. Katharine Drexel, and St. Thérèse of Lisieux. Deeply spiritual, he claimed that he had seen a vision of God and Satan and the future of the Church. In response, he composed and put into Church practice a prayer to the archangel Saint Michael. The Prayer to Saint Michael widely used in the Church today is derived from Pope Leo's prayer.

Two humble saints gave outstanding witness to love and faith during the pontificates of Pius IX and Leo XIII. **St. John Bosco** (1815–1888) labored on behalf of children in northern Italy for much of his life. His primary ministry as a priest was with young, poor boys. He founded dozens of shelters (*oratories*) for boys, taking care of hundreds with the help of other priests, workers, and even his mother, teaching them the Catholic Faith and providing love and shelter. In time, he also ministered to young girls. In order to secure assistance in his ministries, he founded an order which became known as the *Salesians* — after St. Francis de Sales — an order that has spread throughout Europe and the Americas. John Bosco did not change the world. He did not slow down the spread of Enlightenment thought. Yet his ministries helped to shore up the teetering faith of many in Italy.

St. Maria Goretti (1890–1902) gave her life resisting the sexual advances of a family friend. She was a devout girl from a poor farm family. As she was attacked, not only did Maria resist, but she even protested that her assailant's sexual advances were sinful. She died in a hospital of multiple stab wounds, but not before forgiving her assailant, Alexander Serenelli. He was sent to prison but later had a vision of Maria. Serenelli reformed, and was, according to some sources, present at her canonization in 1950.[1] We live in the age of the sexual revolution — which we will discuss later — and its message of "liberation" from constraints on fulfillment of most any sexual desire. Maria stands as an icon of chastity and purity and a sign of contradiction and holiness to this age of sexual license.

Pope St. Pius X (1835–1914, r. 1903–1914), the first entirely twentieth-century pope, sought to meet head-on the continuing challenges of modernism and the Enlightenment. He served as pope until the eve of World War I. Pius wrote encyclicals condemning modernism and even required priests to take an oath against it. Some say Pius overreacted, but he was on the front lines of a powerful movement that could have overturned the Church's one-thousand-nine-hundred year understanding of divine truth. One could argue that a strong pope was necessary at this time in Church history to stand up to modernism when much of the world was incorporating it. Regardless of whether he was too rigid on every issue, his stance helped to stabilize the Church as a beacon of revealed faith in a world increasingly dominated by modernism.

The Great War of 1914–1918, now known as World War I, devastated Europe and shook its faith to the core. These forces challenged the Church's relevance in the modern world and blunted her voice. A Church influenced by modernism would have little to say to the world. Pius correctly saw that accommodation to the world or even compromise would hasten the Church's irrelevance and take away her central message of salvation through Jesus Christ.

Pius X was also a reformer. He implemented a Code of Canon Law and he encouraged frequent reception of Communion, all while living a life of personal sanctity and charity. He strove to make the papacy strong enough to escape the influences of European monarchies and secular forces — despite the fact that he had been elected pope only after Hapsburg Austria had first vetoed the leading candidate.[2]

35

COUNTER-ENLIGHTENMENT

As the forces of Enlightenment and modernism assailed the Church, two nineteenth-century French saints, St. John Vianney and St. Thérèse of Lisieux, stood as icons of Christ in the midst of the battle for truth and life's purpose. They are linked together in time, place, and the purpose of their mission, and were even canonized two weeks apart. At first, few noticed them. But in their quiet openness to the Holy Spirit, they became spiritual lions. They did so mostly by holiness of life and extraordinary love of God, evident to those around them and to posterity. Unlike the message of the Enlightenment, these two Christian warriors, meek as they seemed to be, showed believers and the world that the meaning of life is found in relationship with God. They did so by their radical humility, love of neighbor, and passionate focus on God. Their humble love rallied countless Catholics from weakness, disillusionment, apostasy, and confusion to deeper faith.

St. Jean-Marie (John) Vianney (1786–1859) is often called the patron of parish priests. Jean-Marie grew up as a shepherd on his father's farm in southern France. Graced with a strong love of God from his earliest days, he pined to become a priest, but, an uneducated farm boy, he struggled with Latin and other academic subjects needed for seminary classes. As Jean-Marie labored through protracted difficulties with academics and admission bureaucracy, his mentor and advocate, Abbe Balley, persuaded the diocesan authorities to make an exception for him due to his evident holiness. At last, in 1815, he was ordained. In 1818, he was assigned as curé (parish priest) of the tiny town of Ars, with the thought that this supposedly unintelligent, simple-minded man could do little harm at such a small, out of the way place. John spent the rest of his life there — over forty years. It was a remarkable forty years.

With tremendous humility, dogged determination, and courageous preaching, Jean-Marie set out to address the lax attitude of his parishioners. In time, his relentless pastoral zeal and example of unassuming holiness and personal poverty moved most of the rough-edged townspeople to conversion. He was so extraordinary that he could not easily be ignored. He preached a total moral commitment, resistance to evil, and an intense love of God, a love he exuded. The depth and directness of his prayer-inspired sermons — God-focused, and unapologetically cutting to the quick — stirred the people of his parish. The credibility of his preaching was enhanced by the way Jean-Marie lived what he preached. He hated sin and loved God resolutely. He practiced fasting and mortifications. As his ministry grew, he spent upwards of sixteen hours a day hearing confessions.

His reputation as an extraordinary priest grew, and thousands of Catholics from other parts of post-Revolution France flocked to Ars to go to confession to this holy man. He had a gift — reminiscent of Jesus and the Samaritan woman in the Gospel of John, chapter 4 — of seeing into the heart of penitents and confronting them with the reality of their sinfulness and the need to repent. As with the Samaritan woman, penitents went back home and told others of their experience with this holy priest. The train station in Lyon had to add a ticket office just for the rail line to Ars to accommodate the flow of pilgrims.

Though visitors flocked to Ars, it was his own parish community that he embraced as his primary mission field. Jean-Marie did not seek glory that could have been his as a celebrity priest. His love and commitment to the people of Ars was absolute. His dedication was total, to the point of exhaustion. He had an extended life of prayer before the Blessed Sacrament and a deep devotion to the Virgin Mary. For decades, he struggled with tangible attacks from Satan, particularly in bed at night. Despite his extraordinary impact on thousands of people, his diocesan superiors were never sure what to make of him. But this humble priest fostered spiritual renewal in southeastern France in the years after the French Revolution and Napoleon, and became the most famous priest in France in his day. Jean-Marie Vianney's witness still inspires thousands and he is considered a model for priests.

The simple yet extraordinary life of **St. Thérèse of Lisieux** (1873–1897), the beloved "Little Flower," also reflects the paradox of God's grace. Unlike John Vianney, at her death at age twenty-four, Thérèse was unknown to the world. Yet today she is considered one of the greatest saints of all time. Why? She was not well educated. Although it was her desire, she didn't traverse the world for souls. She didn't found a congregation. Her extraordinary sanctity was so well hidden that it was not always recognized even within her convent in northern France. As with John Vianney, it was her unreserved devotion to Christ, and her exceptional holiness that struck a blow of faith against the spirit of the Enlightenment.

Thérèse was the youngest of nine children in a deeply devout family. Her parents, **Sts. Louis and Zélie Martin,** are canonized as saints in their own right for their holiness and extraordinary accomplishment of raising passionately Catholic children in a society that was increasingly hostile to the Faith. Thérèse noted that, given her headstrong nature, who knows how she might have turned out if it had not been for the faith and love of her parents.

In the local schooling she had, Thérèse was smart but so gentle that she was bullied. From an early age she was drawn to the Lord but had to work hard to overcome scruples. The death of her mother when she was only four was a tremendous blow to her. She never left Normandy, except for a family pilgrimage to Rome and Italy. While on this excursion, Thérèse was exposed to the human weaknesses of priests and the vanity of elites. This helped her grow in wisdom and overcome provincial naivete. Her reaction: "I realized that real nobility is in the soul, not in a name."[1] Thérèse was much more grounded and aware of the world's foibles than her humility might indicate. She even met Pope Leo XIII in 1887, brashly asking him to approve her entry into the convent. He demurred to her superiors but added that, if it was God's will, she would be admitted. That gave her hope. Two months later she was admitted.

The world might not have known of Thérèse at all had the story of her life not been published after her death — *The Story of a Soul*. She wrote reluctantly at the direction of her superiors in her convent, some of whom were her older sisters. They had begun to fathom Thérèse's extraordinary spiritual gifts and sensed the need for them to come to light.

Thérèse desired to follow two of her sisters as a Carmelite nun. After her second request for admission, she entered the Carmelite convent at Lisieux in northern France and spent seven quiet years as a sister. Toward the end of her life, she suffered greatly from tuberculosis, which eventually took her life. She bore her illness nobly, offering her suffering for the conversion of souls — her deep passion. Thérèse was a powerful prayer warrior — which is a reason why, never having left the convent, she is a patroness of missions — and she was a kind, dedicated sister who sought to be neighborly with everyone, no matter how insufferable. Some of the other sisters in the convent did indeed stretch Thérèse's patience, and she wrote of her struggles to love them. Her effort to do so, and the dedication to pleasing Jesus by loving others in ordinary, recognizable circumstances, is a major part of her inspiration to the world.

Thérèse came to practice what she called the *little way*. Her "little way" is not a program or an organized discipline like Saint Ignatius's *Spiritual Exercises*, but a disposition, a focus of the will toward God. Look to do your best in each moment, she said, and offer that moment to God as a gift of love; seek to take one initial step toward God in virtue; trust that God, in his infinite mercy and love for us, will take us the rest of the way and bring us to heaven; aim for virtue in little things, not so much on things too great for us; entrust ourselves to the care of God, mindful of our weakness; have no concern for the past or future, but live in the present moment. These simple yet profound acts of commitment and devotion, this perspective of trust in God's mercy are what her little way is about.

Through this little way, she came to know her limits to achieving sanctity by herself, and to let Jesus carry her. She loved the metaphor of an elevator. Jesus would lift her up to him. She would carry out humble acts of charity and let Jesus do the rest. She learned and taught that one loves not by great deeds so much as by small deeds done well in a spirit of love of Jesus — "scattering flowers," as she called it. Thérèse understood her acts of love as extensions of her relationship with Jesus and as efforts to please him. "I want Jesus to draw me into the flames of His love … that He may live and act in me."[2] This profound love of Jesus, fostered by grace, is what is most significant about Thérèse.

Few reach this level of sanctity, but Thérèse's embrace of the living Person of Jesus has become an invitation to all who are inspired by her love of Jesus. Thérèse was gifted with a powerful wisdom and insight into life's true purpose: to develop an abiding relationship of love with Jesus. This "ordinary" young girl is now one of only four women Doctors of the Church. In a powerful way, Thérèse was filled with the Holy Spirit. In her humility she reflected the light of Christ. She sought simply to love and follow Jesus, one step in front of the next. This is likely why her legacy reverberates through to the present day. She has affected, inspired, and changed innumerable lives, including many saints, Mother Teresa and Fulton Sheen among them. Her legacy is not merely a memory but a work of the Holy Spirit that has greatly nourished the Church to this day.

John Vianney and Thérèse of Lisieux pointed to the reality of divine truth in a dark time of supposed "enlightenment," in direct contradiction to the godless ways of the luminaries of their time. God is real. He is powerful and worthy of love, obedience, and worship. John Vianney and Thérèse of Lisieux gave witness to these realities as profoundly as anyone in their time. And they did so with humility and simplicity, and a powerful commitment to God that flowed from deep within them.

It is significant that each of them was drawn to God at an early age — so early that one can easily perceive the call of divine grace. It is also significant that they are both from France, as were many other saints of this era. France was the vanguard in Enlightenment philosophy, in persecuting the Church, and in secularizing society. Where the need was greatest, where the battle was most fierce, is where the grace of the Holy Spirit flowed in abundance. Neither Jean-Marie nor Thérèse stopped the tide of modernism, but their lives and legacies have strengthened and enriched the Church as she sought to maintain a powerful witness against it.

36

TWO MARIAN APPARITIONS

A s Enlightenment forces fought fiercely against Christianity, the Virgin Mary herself played a role in bolstering the beleaguered Church. Numerous times in Catholic history, reports of apparitions of Mary have come to light. These private revelations are not required for belief, but the Church does investigate them with a critical eye and has given a nonbinding "worthy of belief" endorsement to several. These apparitions are miraculous divine interventions into our human world, providing a supernatural message important for the Christian people. When God speaks through Mary, it is vital that the Church listens.

Two Marian apparitions in the aftermath of the Enlightenment have had major and enduring impact: Lourdes and Fátima. The Church, after full investigations, has approved each as worthy of belief. Assuming the Church is correct, these apparitions carry enormous significance for the Church and the world. It is providential that miraculous appearances from heaven would occur in an era when belief was under severe attack, when much of the world had taken its eyes off God. The apparitions of Mary at Lourdes and Fátima could arguably be associated with the rising up of key saints such as John Vianney and Thérèse — God opening the door for his people to turn away from the darkness of the times and return to him.

Those who saw Mary at Lourdes in southern France and Fátima in central Portugal were young children from poor rural areas. This is typical of apparitions — Mary appearing to the humble, not to the well-to-do. And after the apparitions in each of these cases, the seers lived a life of sanctity. They were obedient to Mary's directions and overcame fear of ridicule and of aggressive authorities. This faithfulness was vital for the dissemination of the divine messages. They are canonized as saints or are on their way to canonization.

St. Bernadette Soubirous (1844–1879) was a dirt-poor young girl from the small town of Lourdes in the south of France — a country still reeling from the turmoil and persecution of the Enlightenment, the French Revolution, and Napoleon. Bernadette reported that she had visions of a woman, later identified as Mary, on several occasions in 1858. (This was just a year before the death of John Vianney, not far away in Ars.) Her persistent reports of seeing this "Lady" caused a stir among the townspeople and local authorities. Many were curious and came to witness her apparition at a grotto near town. The authorities, however, were alarmed, and they interrogated and harassed the girl. Mary asked Bernadette to communicate to the Church an urgent call to pray for the conversion of sinners. Bernadette dutifully reported the messages from Mary and followed her instructions, even to the point of humbling herself by digging dirt in the ground near the grotto. From her digging came a stream of water, a spring. This water has become a source of miraculous healings, and continues flowing to this day — a sign of the reality of the divine and of God's mercy. Today many of the walls in the churches within the shrine at Lourdes are covered with inscriptions reading *merci* — "thanks" to God for healings received.

Mary, whom Bernadette initially did not recognize as the mother of Jesus, identified herself as the Immaculate Conception — a title little known in rural France, and certainly not to Bernadette. Just four years earlier the pope had proclaimed the doctrine of the Immaculate Conception — that Mary herself, though human, was the one person in human history other than Jesus to be conceived without original sin. Clearly, these apparitions provide an affirmation of this doctrine.

Bernadette's faithfulness to Mary's instructions, steady conviction of what she had been told when interrogated by the authorities, and her subsequent life of holiness as a nun, gave crucial support toward acceptance of the Immaculate Conception doctrine. The shrine at Lourdes draws millions of pilgrims each year who come seeking healing and to pray and intercede for conversion. Bernadette remains today as a witness to the supernatural, God's mercy, and the call to holiness and conversion.

Just under sixty years later, in 1917, Mary appeared again, this time to three shepherd children in rural Portugal, just twenty years after the death of Thérèse. Her message was similar to Lourdes — in a real sense, a follow-up — but with much more urgency. World War I, until then the most destructive war in history, was raging over much of Europe when these three young shepherds in Fátima reported that Mary appeared to them monthly from May to October. The children, Francisco, Jacinta, and Lúcia, reported an imperative call from Mary to pray for conversion of sinners. They reported her warning that great tribulations, including an even greater war, would befall the world unless the world repented of its sin. That greater war — World War II, the most destructive in history — burst upon the world twenty-two years later.

They reported Mary's prophecy that Russia would cause wars, annihilation of many nations, and persecutions of the Church, and urged prayer for the conversion of Russia. This was a seemingly odd, out-of-the-blue message, because Russia at that time was far from a major factor on the world stage. The seers knew next to nothing of this faraway country. But Vladimir Lenin and his cohorts were leading the Russian Revolution which succeeded in the Communist takeover of the country — in the very month of the last apparition. Russia was transformed from an Orthodox Christian nation into an atheistic communist state, the Soviet Union, which began to grow in power and world influence, something these children could not have foreseen.

As much of the world continued to drift away from God, the apparitions at Fátima also were a sign that indeed God exists. The miracle of the sun at the last apparition on October 13, 1917 is an indication that God, in his mercy, was seeking to remind his people that indeed he exists, in all his power and glory. Over seventy thousand people, including many nonbelievers, witnessed in wonder as the sun appeared to fall from the sky toward them and the ground, soaked by rain, instantly dried. Even the main Lisbon newspaper — not at all Christian — reported the incident with no rational explanation for it.

These children, like Bernadette, were unwavering in obedience to Mary's instructions, and sought to live a life of sanctity. Two of them, now **Saint Francisco** and **Saint Jacinta,** died within three years of the apparitions from complications of the flu during the great pandemic of 1918. The third, **Sister Lúcia,** lived to age ninety-seven. She died in 2005 after a life in a cloistered convent. The cause for her canonization is in progress.

But for the obedience and witness of faith of these children, the supernatural intervention of Mary would not have circulated. Yet they did obey, and the messages and shrines of Lourdes and Fátima stand as signs of the supernatural, in direct opposition today to the materialistic, non-believing secular world. Millions of Catholics have been inspired and strengthened by the apparitions at Lourdes and Fátima, and have taken up the call to intercede for peace and conversion in the world.

These apparitions are more fully understood in light of this explosive rise of communism, which emerged in the nineteenth century out of the Enlightenment. It is important to note that the Lourdes apparitions were contemporaneous with Marx and the Fátima apparitions were contemporaneous with Lenin. Communism grew to be a monumental threat to Christianity, as governments throughout the world in the nineteenth and twentieth centuries fell under its spell. It originated with Karl Marx (1818–1883) and grew into a powerful movement whose tenets include virulent atheism and an economic theory of class struggle between the working class and the industrial, or moneyed class, with the goal of the workers seizing the "means of production" and overpowering the capitalists and the rich oppressors. It has led to totalitarian governments around the world that suppress economic and religious freedoms. Marx published his seminal work, the *Communist Manifesto*, with its infamous battle cry, "Workers of the world, unite!" in 1848 — ten years before Mary's apparitions at Lourdes.

In 1917, the year of Fátima, the Bolsheviks in Russia prevailed in a civil war and, under Lenin, established an atheistic communist government that severely repressed the Russian Orthodox Church (which to this day has not recovered). Lenin famously proclaimed that "religion is the opiate of the masses." Building on the Russian propensity toward nationalism and even imperialism, Communist Russia seized numerous neighboring states, creating the Soviet Union, an empire bent on spreading its totalitarian version of communism, and, after World War II, seized control of a number of central and eastern European countries, Poland and part of Germany among them. The abject misery the Soviet Union caused Europe, the world, and the Church for the next seventy years is an evident fulfillment of Mary's prophecy and a divine warning of the dire necessity of prayer, conversion, and repentance. This is what Mary warned about at Fátima.

Through the Fátima children, Mary exhorted the pope to consecrate Russia to her Immaculate Heart as a condition of Russia's conversion. Pope John Paul II's consecration in 1984 was the culmination of several papal consecrations. The Communist Soviet Union, which held Russia in an atheist grip for more than a half century, collapsed seven years later in 1991. The countries it had controlled, including Pope St. John Paul II's Poland, broke free as well. Many hailed the fall of the Soviet Union as a providential response to the pope's consecration and the countless prayers of Catholics around the world for Russia's conversion, as Mary had urged. To be sure, this is likely true.

However, God's providence is not so easily discerned. In the early decades of the twenty-first century, Russia has gradually reverted to totalitarianism and is once again seeking to overpower other countries — as the present-day Russian invasion of Ukraine so tragically demonstrates. It appears that the world's Catholics have more work to do in interceding for Russia's conversion. To that end, in 2022, Pope Francis has completed a new consecration of Russia and the world to Mary. One other key may be relations between the Russian Orthodox Church, which supports

Russia's war efforts, and the Catholic Church. Perhaps bridging this division, and a mutual recommitment to Gospel preaching, will lead to Russia's ultimate conversion.

The battle between the rising secularism inspired by the Enlightenment and the faith in God of Christianity underscores a vital reality. The saints are not just a collection of inspirational people who have found God; they are people filled with grace for a purpose beyond themselves. The Enlightenment saints — like saints in all eras — were soldiers in a war against darkness. Their ministries and especially their holiness pushed back against these modernist forces, not always reversing them but stemming their advance. Without the powerful ministry of these many people of God, the Church could have collapsed under the weight of modernism.

THE CHURCH IN MODERN TIMES

AD 1920 to the Present Day

37

A DIVINE MESSAGE OF HOPE AND MERCY

Technological marvels in this last century have transformed daily life in ways that could not have been imagined in the 1800s. Skyscrapers, jet travel, organ transplants, computers, cell phones, the internet, men on the moon, worldwide commerce — at first glance we seem to see the triumph of science, the vindication of the Enlightenment, human civilization at the pinnacle of technical achievement.

Yet we also see nuclear weapons, wars, mass shootings, genocide, jihad, internet porn, abortion, a sexual revolution that has birthed a rise in sexual assault and plunging birth rates, dictators, the persistence of poverty, and the rise of depression and suicide. This is a brave new world where the Christian message is needed more now than ever before, even as that message is being increasingly marginalized. One of the great divine ironies is that, as man-made marvels transform daily life, we seem beholden to them and are less confident in the future than before their advent. The first world has become the post-Christian world.

In tangible ways, we are living the fruit of the Enlightenment: science as the only path to knowledge, the fierce defense of the autonomous individual's right to be "free" to do whatever he wishes, "the tyranny of relativism," as Pope Benedict XVI called it, and a dark, nihilistic sense that life lacks meaning. Replacing what used to be the Christian worldview of faith in God are elite "experts" who claim knowledge of how we should live — a modern-day form of Gnosticism. And as the Church struggles to craft a message of hope and salvation, it is itself wracked by division, scandal, anemic belief, and shrinking numbers. This is our world in the twenty-first century. Many scholars have come to label this era as *post-modernism*.

But these are not the first challenging times. As in every era of crisis, the renewing power of the Holy Spirit is alive, and he has been raising up modern saints to rearm his Church, do his bidding, and light the way into the future.

Between the devastation of the two world wars, during the rise of Soviet communism and Nazi fascism, and as the illusory "Roaring Twenties" evaporated into the worldwide Great Depression, a young woman from Poland stepped unseen onto the twentieth-century stage with a powerful message. She was a prophet for the modern world, God's chosen instrument to bring a word of hope and mercy to the world. The Holy Spirit's work through this woman was a microcosm of how God has done the unexpected to strengthen his people in these difficult modern times.

St. Faustina Kowalska (1905–1938) was a mystic who experienced visions of Jesus throughout her life. In these visions, or "conversations," Jesus spoke to her a profound message for the Church and people of these modern times: the reality of the love and mercy of God for his people in such a time of spiritual need. This message may well be a finishing touch to the Fátima messages, given when Faustina was twelve. In a real sense, God's message of mercy to Faustina brings to a completion the message of repentance at Fátima.

Faustina had to fight to become a nun. She traveled to Warsaw with nothing, and literally knocked on convent doors until one took her in. In the 1930s — just a few years before the Germans invaded Poland in 1939 — this Polish nun received and delivered a series of divine messages through which God assured us that he is real; he is a God of love; that Jesus, God the Father's eternal Son and Redeemer of the human race, also is real and alive; and that he desires to shower us with *divine mercy*, as he calls believers to respond to him in faith.

It is providential that this messenger of God's mercy came from a country that was about to be torn apart by World War II, the site of massive human atrocities and suffering, and subject first to brutal Nazi, then Soviet occupation for over four decades after this war. As human suffering, rooted in the proliferation of human sin, spread throughout the world, God communicated a compelling reminder through Faustina that his mercy would triumph in the end, and that a deeper commitment to him is what would sustain each believer.

The heart of her message — like Saint Thérèse's — was complete trust in God. That message sustained many during the war and its aftermath and continues to resonate throughout the Church today. Faustina kept a diary of her conversations with Jesus. It has been published in many languages and is available worldwide. The signature prayer from these messages, the *Chaplet of Divine Mercy*, has been prayed millions of times by millions of Catholics in the decades since, raising up to God a powerful incense of prayer and intercession for his mercy and grace, for consolation and conversion, and for the ultimate triumph of the mercy of God in the midst of today's challenging world. To underestimate the impact of Saint Faustina's message is to misread the action of the Holy Spirit in the world. Pope St. John Paul II declared the Sunday after Easter to be Divine Mercy Sunday, in order to take this message to the heart of the Church and to perpetuate surrender to Jesus' divine mercy for a world in desperate need of it.

38
MARTYRS IN WAR

The witness of martyrs has been prevalent in the last hundred years, in two phases — through World War II, and in the most recent generation. The 1920s saw an unusual and bloody conflict between Church and state in a heavily Catholic country. This persecution was a harbinger of things to come throughout the world.

Mexico had been a predominantly Catholic country since the apparitions of Mary at Guadalupe in the sixteenth century. However, its government has often been hostile to the Faith, at times even fiercely anti-Christian. This was particularly so in the 1920s. Seeing the Catholic Faith — and particular its clergy and leadership — as competitors for the loyalty of the people, the secular Mexican government imposed severe restrictions on the clergy, and, when met with resistance, undertook a fierce persecution. This evolved into the Cristero War in the late 1920s. The government persecuted priests, closed churches, and banned many religious celebrations. Catholic peasants rose up, but the government's main target was priests. If priests could be scared away, controlled, or eliminated, then the Catholic Church of the masses might be brought to heel — so the leaders thought. Hundreds of priests were killed during the Cristero War, including **St. Cristobal Jara**, **Bl. Miguel Pro**, and the **Mexican priest-martyrs** (d. 1927–1928). Father Jara was killed in 1927 while on his way to offer Mass. Jesuit Father Pro was arrested on a false pretext and summarily executed at the direction of Mexico's president. Graham Greene's novel *The Power and the Glory* portrays the anguish of this war.

The blood of these martyrs eventually forced an end of the persecution and restored the ability of the Mexican people to practice their Faith. However, damage was done, and the number of priests in Mexico had been drastically reduced. The government only gradually and begrudgingly eased the restrictions. Despite periodic reversions to attacks on the Church among Mexican leaders in decades since, and despite poverty and the frailties of the Church herself, Mexico remains a mostly Catholic country. The courage and witness of those who kept the Faith under persecution — especially these martyrs — was instrumental in defeating the efforts to suppress the Church in Mexico.

A decade later, World War II tore Europe and Asia apart — even more so than had World War I. Tens of millions died. Cities were bombed into ruin. The continents were overwhelmed with carnage and death, hatred and evil. The Holocaust, the Nazi effort to eradicate all European Jews, took the lives of six million Jews — two-thirds of the Jewish population. Many Christian heroes sought to protect, rescue, and hide Jews — including Pope Pius XII, who, contrary to the claims of modern-day revisionists set upon impugning his reputation, worked quietly but diligently on behalf of Jews.[1] The Stalin-led exterminations of Jews, Ukrainian Christians, and other perceived enemies of the Soviet leadership rivaled or even exceeded the Holocaust in sheer numbers of killings.

The devastation of these two world wars, fought primarily in Europe, dealt a monumental blow to the Christian faith of the people of Europe. The inevitable mindset became: "How could a loving God let this happen? He must not exist, or not care." As the twentieth century dawned, most Europeans were Christian. As the twenty-first century dawned, practicing Christians were a distinct and shrinking minority on much of the continent. War and communism had taken a terrible toll.

Amidst the darkness of war, two martyrs stood out as compelling witnesses to faith. **St. Maximilian Kolbe** (1894–1941) was a Polish Franciscan priest and intellectual who had a strong devotion to Mary. In the twenties and thirties, he coordinated a vast media evangelization ministry in Poland, via publications and the new invention of the radio. He also spent several years in the 1930s as a missionary in Asia, with most of his success in Japan, where he founded a monastery outside Nagasaki. The monastery would later survive the atomic bomb. After the Germans occupied Poland, Kolbe remained at the monastery he founded outside Warsaw and even continued his media work. His monastery also housed and hid refugees, including over two thousand Jews.

The Germans eventually shut it down and imprisoned Kolbe in Auschwitz, where he ministered as a priest despite severe harassment and beatings. When the Nazis chose ten prisoners to die of starvation to deter escape attempts, Kolbe volunteered to take the place of a condemned husband and father. He prayed with and ministered to the others in the starvation bunker, as one by one, they died, until only he remained alive. The Nazis, impatient for his death, administered a lethal injection before starvation took him as well. Today, Saint Maximilian is honored for his Christ-like sacrifice. The man whose place he took in the death bunker was liberated from Auschwitz and was present at his canonization in 1982.

Another martyr, **St. Teresa Benedicta of the Cross** (1891–1942) was a Jewish woman born in Silesia, then a German territory, now mostly part of Poland. Given a brilliant mind, Edith Stein — her name before entering religious life — pursued an academic career and became a professor of philosophy before the war, teaching at various German universities. By the 1920s she had become an atheist. In 1921, however, her academic studies led her to the writings of St. Teresa of Ávila. She was so moved, principally by Teresa's *Autobiography*, that she began a spiritual journey which led to her conversion to Catholicism in 1922. After the Nazis came to power in the 1930s, she lost her university position because she was not Aryan. Providentially, this led her to join a Carmelite convent. Edith Stein, Jewish Catholic scholar, became a nun in 1934, taking the name Sr. Teresa Benedicta of the Cross.

By 1938 it was not safe for her, a Jew by birth, to remain in Germany, so her Carmelite order moved her to a convent in the Netherlands. She remained there even after the Nazis occupied the Netherlands in 1940, but she soberly realized that she was not likely to survive. She remained out of harm's way until 1942, when the Dutch bishops courageously issued a statement condemning Nazi racism and anti-Semitism. In reprisal, the Nazis rounded up 243 Jews who had converted to Catholicism, including Sister Teresa Benedicta, and deported them to concentration camps. This kind of persecution persuaded Pope Pius XII to be measured in speaking out against the Nazis, lest it lead to more reprisal killings. Instead, he worked quietly to save Jews behind the scenes. Advocates for the safety of Jews even pleaded with him not to speak out for this very reason.

During her imprisonment, this scholarly nun impressed a Dutch official with her calm faith and turned down an opportunity to escape. Teresa Benedicta of the Cross, along with hundreds of others, died in the gas chamber at Auschwitz in August 1942. Some raise the question whether she is truly a martyr or whether she was killed because she was a Jew. No doubt being Jewish is what motivated the Nazis to kill her, but it is evident that her deep Christian faith led her to the circumstances of her death, including her refusal to escape. She remains a poignant witness to the power and love of God. Her writings are in circulation among Christians today.

Although the Nazis sought to exterminate the entire Jewish race, thousands of others — including Christians — were sent to concentration camps as well, and met the same fate. Many priests ended up in the camps and lost their lives, as well as thousands of courageous lay people. One prominent victim was the Lutheran minister and scholar, Dietrich Bonhoeffer, a fierce opponent of the Nazis, who was executed at the Flossenburg concentration camp just weeks before the end of the war. His book *The Cost of Discipleship* is a spiritual classic. Often these "political prisoners" were sent to Dachau, outside Munich — one of the very few concentration camps inside Germany. Numerous Catholic priests were put to death at Dachau.

Martyrs are, in the real sense of the word, witnesses. These witnesses did not stop the war, but were a sign to the Christians who remained, who were struggling to make sense out of the violence and evil around them. Their deaths proclaimed that, mysteriously, God is still there — so real that he is worth dying for. Their impact is impossible to measure, but in ways known to God, they provided a strength and a lifeline to faith in a world gone mad. The seeds of their deaths helped to sustain the Church.

39

A BRIDGE TO THE PRESENT DAY — MID-TWENTIETH-CENTURY SAINTS

A number of significant saints lived their adult lives and served in the middle third of the century. These saints, though saints of their own times, helped to sustain and bolster faith within the Church as she approached the turbulence of postmodernism.

St. Josephine Bakhita (1869–1947) is a gift to the Church from Africa which may well be one of the areas that holds the future of the Church. The West is rich and tired, and the Church is struggling against secularism and her own weaknesses, partially rooted in prosperity. Throughout history, the Church has usually done best in poorer areas, reflecting the Gospel message from Jesus that the poor and meek shall inherit the earth.

The first Christians populated the African shores of the Mediterranean, but the Muslim conquests in the seventh century virtually wiped out these vibrant Christian communities. Only in Egypt did Christianity survive in any meaningful way. It was not until the sixteenth century, when European explorers opened the door for what turned out to be exploitative colonization, that the Faith was introduced to sub-Saharan Africa. And interestingly, it wasn't until the mid-twentieth century, after the colonial occupiers withdrew, that Christianity began to flourish. There has been an explosion of Christianity in Africa in recent decades — Catholic and Protestant — along with parallel growth of the Muslim population.

Bakhita was a slave girl in Sudan. Arab slavers kidnapped her and she was sold several times. For many years, she suffered cruelties. Her name means "fortunate," as does Faustina's. Eventually, an Italian businessman purchased Bakhita, brought her to his home near Venice, and put her to work as a nanny. On the occasion of a business trip — ironically, to Africa — he boarded Bakhita in a convent. Providentially, it was there that she was introduced to Catholicism. When he returned, Bakhita did not want to leave the convent. She won a battle of wills, obtained freedom for the first time since she was a young girl, converted to the Catholic Faith, and became a nun, taking the name Josephine.

Although she never left Italy, she had a missionary spirit and helped to train other nuns for work in Africa. Bakhita was charming, strong-willed, and exuded sanctity. Her eyes were always on God, and her heart was in Africa, an observer noted. When asked how she felt about her slavers, she said that she would kiss them: But for them, she observed, she would never have become Christian. She lived an exemplary life throughout the first half of the twentieth century, dying just after World War II. After her beatification in 1993, Pope John Paul traveled to Khartoum, Sudan and declared: "*Rejoice, all of Africa!* Bakhita has come back to you."[1]

At the same time across the Atlantic, **St. Katharine Drexel** (1858–1955) continued into mid-century the extraordinary work of the nuns serving in America. Like Elizabeth Seton, she was born into a wealthy East Coast family. As she grew up, she saw in her extended family examples of charity to those in need, and from reading she came to know of the great injustices to Native Americans. Both of these affected her.

Her wealth and position opened the door for an audience with Pope Leo XIII in 1887, who encouraged her to become a missionary. Spurning marriage, she became a nun in 1889 (the same year that Frances Cabrini came to America), and over the next half century, Katharine served as a missionary to the poor and to Native Americans over much of the United States. Katharine was instrumental in founding 145 missions, fifty schools for African-Americans, and twelve schools for Native Americans. She also was a major figure in the founding of Xavier University in New Orleans in the 1920s, the only Catholic college for African-Americans in the country. She used her wealth as seed money and her savvy to secure the necessary land for a proper campus. Like Mother Cabrini, she was bright, indefatigable, of deep faith, and left a legacy of charity throughout America.

Whereas Bakhita brought inspiration and Katharine served the poor, **St. Pio of Pietrelcina** (1887–1968) lived as a witness to the supernatural reality of God. Padre Pio's connection to the supernatural stands as a sign of contradiction in this age of increasing secularism. Padre Pio was an Italian friar of the Capuchin order, a branch of the Franciscans. He came from a deeply religious family who supported him as he sought a vocation in the Capuchin community — once again, a saint is supported by family and people around him. Throughout his life he experienced visions, and he carried out a ministry of healing, both by serving in a hospital and through a gift of miraculous healing. He lived a life of great sanctity and attracted many converts — including some fascists in the time of Mussolini. Pio had an advanced prayer life and taught the importance of prayer, meditation, daily Communion, and examination of conscience. One of his most quoted sayings is "pray, hope, and don't worry." This was an especially pertinent message during the grim years of war in Italy during the 1940s, during which Padre Pio lived and ministered.

Padre Pio became a cult figure, drawing large numbers of people either out of curiosity or out of a genuine search for God. This put him into conflict with Church officials who were not as impressed as the masses. Eventually, Church officials came to appreciate, or at least to tolerate, this eccentric man who was drawing people to God. Like St. John Vianney, Padre Pio had a history of physical attacks from the Devil. This too created controversy, but it also pointed to the reality of the Evil One. Padre Pio may be best known for receiving the stigmata, the miraculous physical manifestation of the wounds of Christ on his hands. He bore the stigmata over the last fifty years of his life. A number of saints, including St. Francis of Assisi, have also exhibited the stigmata, a sign to the world of the reality of Christ's passion.

Padre Pio is one of the most popular modern saints. Books on his life are widespread. Padre Pio prayer groups abound throughout the world. His life has inspired Catholics worldwide to seek a deeper life of prayer and holiness. In this age when the sense of the sacred is fading, the key to his popularity was not only his personal sanctity, but the aura of the supernatural that has always surrounded him. He is an icon of the supernatural reality of the divine, drawing interest in those searching for meaning and the presence of God in a secular world. Despite his celebrity status, his personal humility points his admirers toward God, the true supernatural One. This gives hope for seekers in this modern age.

The next two beloved saints, whose lives and ministries resembled Padre Pio's, did not shake the world, but their humble service and quiet miracles touched many lives. Their legacy, like Saint Joseph's, now reverberates more widely in the Church, drawing many to deeper commitment.

Bl. Solanus Casey (1870–1957) was beatified in 2017. Like his contemporary, Padre Pio, he was a Capuchin friar who struck a chord with ordinary people. Solanus demonstrated that it is the simple, humble people who are the bedrocks of the Faith. Like Padre Pio and Thérèse of Lisieux, Solanus was a counterweight to the proud, secular world. He was born in Wisconsin, the sixth of sixteen children in a devout Irish Catholic immigrant family. Along with several siblings, he was drawn to the religious life. Much credit goes to his parents for their commitment to the Faith and for raising their children in a manner that facilitated their decision to follow Christ. Upon witnessing a brutal murder in Superior, Wisconsin, he sensed a call to the priesthood, and heard an inner voice calling him to Detroit. After a long, arduous effort to become a priest, set back because of his difficulty with languages — he was, in fact, an intelligent man — he was ordained a *simplex* priest in the Capuchin order, meaning that he could not preach or hear confessions.

These restrictions didn't matter. Solanus lived a life of remarkable ministry as the doorkeeper at friaries in Detroit and New York, inspiring people with his piety, his extraordinary advice, and prayer for people who expressed needs of healing. Many were healed through his prayer, though not all. Solanus often seemed to know if someone would not be healed, and he offered compassionate counsel to them that God's plan was still for the person's good. He gave food to the poor who came to his door, noting, "As long as there is one hungry person, this food does not belong to us,"[2] and he started a soup kitchen in Detroit that is still open today. An "inspirational" saint, Solanus's life and legacy has helped to preserve or strengthen the faith of many, and he remains popular today.

Similarly, **St. André Bessette** (1845–1937), known as "Brother André," conducted a quiet ministry of healing and counsel in Canada. André helped build the Saint Joseph Oratory in Montreal, where he spent much of his time in humble service, and where he is buried. Upon his death, a million people viewed his coffin — a testament to the impact of his ministry.

St. Gianna Beretta Molla (1922–1962) was a different kind of martyr, a sign of contradiction in the modern, scientific world. A wife, mother, and doctor from Italy, she stands as a modern witness to the sanctity of life in this day of "abortion rights" and the mantra of "choice." She grew up an active Catholic, became a pediatrician, and married in 1955. She had four children. It is the story of the pregnancy and birth of her fourth child that led her to become a sign of faith to these modern times. While pregnant, she was diagnosed with uterine cancer. Since treatment for her cancer would be harmful or fatal to her baby, her doctor advised Gianna to procure an abortion in order to save her own life. She declined. Gianna wanted to give her child the opportunity to live even if she were to lose her own life. Her daughter, Gianna Emmanuela, was born in 1962. As expected, Gianna died of her untreated cancer days later, having sacrificed her life for her child. Her daughter is now also a doctor and an active Catholic. Appreciative of her mother's sacrifice, she has traveled around the world to tell her and her mother's story. Among the things she shares is a letter her mother wrote at the beginning of marriage, in which Gianna speaks of marriage as a vocation of love, and of the Christian call to serve God in a saintly way. This she did — in life and in death.

One of a number of lay Catholic spiritual organizations to spring up in mid-century was Opus Dei, founded in 1928 by Spanish priest, **St. Josemaría Escrivá** (1902–1975). Opus Dei, meaning "Work of God," is a Church-approved prelature with the goal of leading mostly lay people to personal sanctity and recognition of the spiritual value of ordinary work and the activities of daily life. (Opus Dei has been unfairly and inaccurately portrayed as a cultish underground sect in the book and movie *The DaVinci Code*.) It has grown to claim adherents and chapters throughout the world. Saint Josemaría's little book, *The Way*, a collection of insightful maxims on daily sanctification, is read widely today.

The twentieth century saw the explosion of mass worldwide media, first via radio, then television, and at century's end, the internet. This has created a revolution in communication within modern societies, placing access to information at one's fingertips and opening opportunities to convey real-time messages to millions. As with most of technology, the evolution of mass media has been a mixed benefit. It has linked us together, but has been fraught with terrible misuse and the spread of banality and evil. The sheer power of the media to influence the minds of millions is staggering and, coupled with secularism and relativism, has become a serious threat to the message of the Gospel. It would seem likely in God's providence that the Holy Spirit would raise up saints who would use modern mass communication for spreading the Good News of the Catholic and Christian Faith.

One such saint is **Ven. Fulton Sheen** (1895–1979), whose cause is still moving through the canonization process. Fulton Sheen, born in Illinois, became a priest and eventually a bishop, serving in New York. He was brilliant and a powerful theologian. He also had an extraordinary gift of communication. He was a great writer and teacher, but above all, Sheen was a dynamic preacher who understood the impact of radio and television. From 1930 to 1950 Sheen hosted a widely popular radio program called *The Catholic Hour*. Then, from 1951 to 1957, he hosted a weekly television program, *Life is Worth Living*, which grew to a viewership of over thirty million people. He became one of the most watched personalities — by Catholics and non-Catholics alike — in the early days of American television.

Sheen preached the realities of God's love, of our redemption in Christ, and of our calling to live a life of love. He skillfully applied these theological principles to the issues and demands of daily life and the weaknesses of the human person. He inspired millions in their faith and attracted countless others to embrace the Catholic Faith. Some of society's most well-known elites converted due to his preaching and ministry, including Clare Boothe Luce, Henry Ford II, the famed violinist Fritz Kreisler, and numerous communists.

Fulton Sheen lived during the Cold War, which pitted America against the Soviet Union in a battle for world supremacy. The world lived in constant concern that this economic and political battle would escalate into nuclear war. It almost did in 1962 during the Cuban missile crisis. Consistent with Mary's warning at Fátima, Sheen believed that communism was one of the most profound threats in his time — both to Christianity and to Western civilization — and he preached against it with passion and persistence. In 1953 he even called out Soviet leader Joseph Stalin, attesting that he would have a day of judgment before the Lord. Within days, Stalin suffered a stroke and died.

Like so many saints with preaching ministries, Sheen cared for the poor as well. The Gospel is incomplete if it does not embrace the call to love. For many years he headed the Society for the Propagation of the Faith, an organization devoted to spreading the Faith and addressing the needs of the poor.

Fulton Sheen has been called the first televangelist — an apt title. Perhaps only the great Evangelical preacher Billy Graham could rival him. Sheen's legacy lives on in his books and television shows which are still replayed. And his trailblazing in media is bearing fruit in the Church today. Catholic radio is growing exponentially — in America, from the Vatican, and around the world. Catholic television networks, streaming services, podcasts, print publishing, and preaching ministries reach millions. As modern media continues its tremendous influence on culture today, the Christian media efforts to compete for minds and hearts can trace their beginnings to Fulton Sheen.

40

MODERN-DAY MARTYRS

The twentieth and twenty-first centuries have witnessed the largest number of Christian martyrs in history. Former and present Communist regimes around the world — in Vietnam, North Korea, China, and the Soviet Union — through the twentieth century and beyond have persecuted and put to death thousands of Christians, particularly under Soviet dictator Joseph Stalin in the mid-twentieth century. In the Middle East, thousands of Christians have been killed simply for being Christian — especially in Egypt, Iran, Syria, and Iraq. This has been mostly at the hands of extremist Muslims, including beheadings at the hands of ISIS, an early twenty-first-century radical Muslim organization. No area of the world is without martyrs, as the forces of other religions and non-believing regimes have taken their toll. The Church has canonized many devout and courageous martyrs of recent times.

One of these martyrs was **St. Oscar Romero** (1917–1980), a bishop from El Salvador, who was canonized in October 2018. He was ordained a priest in Rome in 1942 as World War II raged, but returned home, delayed by arrest and internment in Cuba for several months. He served as a priest in his home country for over twenty years. In 1970, he was ordained a bishop. Seven years later he was installed as the archbishop of El Salvador, just as government paramilitary forces began to create violent havoc throughout the country. Romero preached against the violence and injustice and on behalf of the poor, and he became popular among the people, for whom his broadcasted sermons were the one available voice of truth. He was a champion of the poor while devoutly adhering to Catholic social teaching. However, his cries for justice on behalf of the poor made him an enemy to the government. Romero was assassinated on March 24, 1980, while saying Mass at a church hospital.

Although some theologians have claimed that Romero was a supporter of liberation theology, in truth he was not. Liberation theology was an activist gospel perspective developed and practiced mostly in Central and South America during the middle and later decades of the twentieth century. Its tenets include vindication of the poor as a class of people aggrieved by ruling classes, and a particular focus on eradicating unjust systems. Popes John Paul II and Benedict XVI criticized liberation theology for its Marxist perspective and for an overemphasis on solving this world's injustices while minimizing the full Gospel message of eternal salvation in Christ. One of the most significant sources of Romero's spiritual strength and outlook, in fact, was Opus Dei, the organization founded by St. Josemaría Escrivá. Opus Dei is fully faithful to Catholic teaching and vastly different in perspective from liberation theology. Romero remains a hero and a source of hope and inspiration in his beleaguered, still heavily Catholic country.

In recent years, the clashes between Christianity and Islam, which date back to the seventh-century Muslim conquests and have flared up numerous times over the centuries, have returned. Since the defeat of the Ottomans at Vienna in 1683 and the receding military and cultural influence which resulted from that defeat, Muslim nations had not been a major threat to Christianity. However, times have changed. These two religions are the largest in the world and their worldviews are vastly different. Even the common enemies of postmodernism and atheism have not drawn them together. In the last century, Muslim nations have joined the world stage and have rediscovered confidence and an expansionist mentality. This has led to increasing persecution of Christians in the Middle East and Africa, particularly by the radical branches of Islam, and it has produced a host of martyrs in Africa.

In 1996, seven **French Trappist Martyrs** were put to death in Algeria. These monks were the subjects of an award-winning French movie, *Of Gods and Men*. They had lived in harmony with the mostly Muslim population for many years but their faith caught the attention of militants. They were abducted and beheaded. A militant Islamic group claimed responsibility. The monks were beatified as Christian martyrs in 2018.

In Africa, attacks by militant Muslims have led to numerous kidnappings and killings of Christians, particularly in Nigeria, a populous nation split between Christians and Muslims. The radical Islamic group Boko Haram and its spin-offs have on numerous occasions kidnapped young girls from schools, raped them, attempted to force conversions, and married them to Muslim men. In 2014 they kidnapped 276 mostly Christian girls, subjecting them to this fate. Some escaped; others were later released. The story captured the attention of even the secular Western world. Kidnappings and murders of priests and religious continue today in several parts of Nigeria.

Bl. Leonella Sgorbati (1940–2006), an Italian nun who served as a nurse in Kenya and Somalia for three decades. Muslim extremists killed her in Somalia in reaction against Pope Benedict XVI's scholarly, measured, but misunderstood "Regensburg Address" on Christian-Muslim relations.

In 2015, militant Muslims from ISIS abducted twenty **Egyptian Coptic Christians** from a worksite in Libya. When they refused to renounce their faith, they were taken to the beach and, one by one, beheaded. A non-Christian man from Ghana was taken with them and asserted that their faith would be his as well. He, too, was beheaded. Their killers filmed the beheadings and disseminated the video. The Coptic Orthodox Church has canonized these martyrs.

These recent, heroic martyrs have offered a potent witness to the Christian Faith. Where the confrontations between Christians and Muslims will go in the years ahead is unknown. They may well be merely a prelude to more serious persecution of Christians at the hands of forces in the secular world.

41

THE CHALLENGE FOR SAINTS TODAY

Four saints — three popes and a nun (see next two chapters) — stand out in the history of the last sixty years. Each has had worldwide impact, manifesting Christ to the world and standing as a sign of contradiction to prevailing perspectives of the day. To understand the significance of these saints, we will first examine the context of their times, and the extraordinary challenges in the world and Church they have faced and that future saints will also face.

Many historians point to the 1960s as the transition period from the era of *modernism* in the nineteenth century to the era often called *postmodernism* in our present time. Though rooted in currents and movements of the decades preceding, a fundamental change in the nature of society occurred in the West during the 1960s, both in secular and Church worlds. After World War II, technological advances accelerated and the Western world experienced an unprecedented level of prosperity. The resulting growth in freedom and opportunity spawned a number of transformational cultural forces in the West and especially in America, forces which spread throughout the world. With an advanced media linking people together as never before, a "youth culture" came into being, and generational clashes over lifestyles became common. Drug use and rock music proliferated, especially among the young. The women's rights or feminist movement burst onto the scene, inspired by Betty Friedan's 1963 book, *The Feminine Mystique*. Advocacy for equal rights, especially in the areas of sexuality and economics, came to the fore, and women began to enter the work force and institutions of higher education in vast numbers. The most noble of the 1960s movements was the civil rights movement, which confronted the evils of discrimination against Blacks and fostered a national awakening on race relations, especially in America.

The most potent and enduring movement in the 1960s, however, was the sexual revolution. It turned upside down the sexual mores of prior centuries and brought into the mainstream the practice of unrestricted sex outside of marriage. The sexual revolution, with its focus on personal pleasure, has seriously undermined marriage and the family, has led to abortion, gay rights, and other sexual freedom movements, and has separated sexuality from procreation. This has triggered a precipitous drop in the birth rate throughout most of the world in the decades hence, often below the population replacement rate. Behind these developments was a fierce focus on individual or group rights, the natural consequence of the Enlightenment emphasis on the autonomy of the individual.

All the while, the Church, particularly in the Western world, was caught up in the midst of these cultural movements, particularly since her members were also members of society at large. Through mid-century, faith was woven deep within family and parish life, and parishes in North America were still heavily ethnic. As ethnic enclaves faded amidst societal intermingling, and as family structure began to erode in the face of the relentless advance of mass media, the erstwhile tranquil, obedient times gave way to an era of questioning why things were the way they were. Dissent from doctrine, efforts to modify liturgy, and desire for freedom from many rules became common. By decade's end, thousands of priests and nuns had left their vocations. Mass attendance also began to drop. These trends began earlier in Europe and were more pronounced, but by the end of the 1960s, they were in full swing on the North American continent as well.

The 1960s did not fade away. The forces unleashed continued to reverberate through to the twenty-first century. Christians of the last sixty years — and the saints among them — have been and are still living and serving amidst a fierce and rising secularism, rooted in the Enlightenment, which is fast marginalizing Christianity. Many of the 1960s movements sowed seeds for even more virulent trends in the twenty-first century, such as radical gender theories which seek to redefine nature itself. These trends, though seated primarily in the wealthy West, have spread to all parts of the world.

Outside the West, totalitarian regimes have suppressed Christianity and assailed the freedom and well-being of millions. This is true in China, the world's most populous country, and in Africa, the continent where Christianity is growing the fastest. It is ironic that these trends have accelerated since the fall of Soviet communism in the decade before the twenty-first century. Some historians rejoiced over a supposed "end of history" after the fall of communism, but the lesson of history, seen with the eyes of faith, is that mankind does not have the capacity to make a utopian world. This idea of "progress" — the promise of the Enlightenment — lingers today, despite signs that human civilization is fraught with so much unexpected unhappiness, the confounding persistence of war and poverty, and fear for the future.

Despite these travails, the Holy Spirit is indeed working throughout the world. A solid core of dedicated Christians fights on in the West, with many vibrant ministries. As the West continues to lose its soul, it is possible that a new hearing of the "Good News" will reach empty hearts as it did in the Roman Empire eighteen centuries ago. The growth of the Church in Asia and especially Africa is accelerating. Christians on these continents have grown into the hundreds of millions and have contributed large numbers of vocations to the priesthood. Yet even in these places of encouraging growth, challenges abound — particularly from poverty, syncretism, corrupt government, and aggressive and often violent Islam.

As these threats mount, the Catholic Church remains divided from her Orthodox and Protestant brethren. This disunity has diminished the strength of the Christian witness. Efforts to reach unity have been sincere and real, but the breakthrough to genuine Christian unity remains elusive. As one voice rang out: "Mourn and weep, for the Body of my Son is broken."[1]

As the twenty-first century dawned, a worldwide clergy sex abuse crisis burst into the open with revelations of sexual abuse of minors by clergy, mostly over the last half of the twentieth century. These sins severely wounded the victims, caused an understandable furor in and out of the Church, and weakened the morale and reputations of the vast majority of priests who were not involved in abuse. This was not the only time in Church history that clergy sexual abuse came to light — witness St. Peter Damian's rebuke of this same sin a thousand years ago — but it has impaired the Church's standing in this troubled world which desperately needs to hear the Gospel witness. The scandal also uncovered a bureaucratic "protect the institution" mindset among many bishops. Ironically, these efforts have instead worsened the Church's reputation. It does appear, however, that more and more bishops are grasping these problems and addressing them with more prudence and courage. Efforts to improve priestly formation in seminaries are ongoing. This may make the Church — and her clergy — stronger in the long run.

The twenty-first century has also witnessed an alarming decline in Church membership throughout much of the Western world, particularly among the young. Increasing percentages deny association with any religious institution, and have become known as *nones*. Even in traditionally Catholic Latin America, the Catholic Faith is hemorrhaging members, as millions of Catholics have left for vibrant and growing Pentecostal and Evangelical Protestant churches. Vocations to the priesthood and religious life have also dropped severely in the West.

Despite these challenges, the Church, still the Body of Christ, has, as always, continued to survive and minister to the world. Indeed, these modern crises are not the first the Church has faced. As in times past, millions of deeply devout Catholics live their faith each day by the grace of the Holy Spirit. These believers are praying for the Church, faithful priests offer the Mass thousands of times a day, and millions serve and witness, unleashing the power of the Eucharist. Though wounded, the Church has continued to carry the Gospel forward in these modern times.

We can also expect that from among these praying faithful, some will rise up as great saints and leaders to show the way forward into the future, toward God and out of the wilderness of these present crises. Some powerful saints have already begun the work among the leadership in the Church, and they are likely the vanguard of more to follow. Since canonization is a process that often takes many years, most saints of the present day are not yet identified. But some are.

This brings us to the three popes and a nun who have begun to show the way forward and have stood as a sign of hope against the challenges of the times.

42

TWO POPES AND A COUNCIL

The first of these popes, **Pope St. John XXIII** (1881–1963, r. 1958–1963), led the Church into the 1960s. He was chosen at age seventy-seven as a "caretaker" pope, expected to do little. After the devout but formal Pius XII, who had been burdened by the enormous weight of World War II, the beginning of the Cold War, and a divided Europe, Pope John brought a sorely needed spirit of joy. He was optimistic and vibrant and seemed to have a ministry to show the love and merciful heart of God for the people of the Church and beyond, as the world segued from the catastrophes of mid-twentieth century to the postwar era. He was devout, deeply interested in fostering peace and caring for the poor, and a veteran of the Church's ministry to help save Jews during the war. John also harbored a prophetic sense that the world was on the brink of change and thus was in dire need of God. It was from this sense that his legacy emerged.

"Caretaker" John stunned the Church with his decision to call for an ecumenical council. It was the first such council since Vatican I nearly a century earlier, and only the second in four hundred years. Unlike most other councils, this *Second Vatican Council*, or Vatican II, did not have as its purpose to address heresies or doctrinal issues, but to discern how the Church ought to relate to the modern world, so changed from times past. Vatican II, in session from 1962 to 1965, became a turning point in the nature and practice of the Church. It took on a life far beyond, and perhaps much different than, what Pope John intended or envisioned.

Pope John had a vision of God seeking to guide his Church through the stormy waters of the modern era and he wanted the Church's bishops to gather and listen for that divine guidance. He prayed for a fresh outpouring of the Holy Spirit upon the Church: "Renew your wonders in this our day, as by a new Pentecost."[1] In a real sense, Pope John walked the Church into the modern world. He knew that the Church was in need of new pastoral strategies, new outlooks on engaging the world with the Gospel, and new strength for contending with the modern atheism born of the Enlightenment. He knew that the Church needed to turn to God and invite his power and love, if these things were to happen. The council, he discerned, was the way to get there.

Vatican II, and especially its aftermath, shook the Church to its core. It unleashed unexpected forces of reform: some radical, some moderate. With conflicting voices seeking to pull the Church in various directions in the name of the council or in its alleged "spirit," the half century since the council ended has been marked by turbulence and uncertainty. Without doubt, Vatican II has been one of the most significant developments in the Catholic Church of the twentieth century and beyond. Pope John's calling from the Lord got it started, even if these released forces moved beyond his own vision. He died soon after the council began, leaving for his successors the task of finishing and implementing the Second Vatican Council. Pope John can be considered the first saint of the modern world.

Pope St. Paul VI (1897–1978; r. 1963–1978) was a dedicated footsoldier, doggedly pushing through the crushing issues confronting him, all the while enduring criticism from left and right. Lacking his predecessor's charm, he was never much beloved. Perhaps misunderstood, per-

haps daunted by the weight of modern times, certainly under the micro-
scope as a modern pope subject to modern media coverage, Pope Paul
was to some a surprising saint when he was canonized in October 2018.
However, he was a man of great personal sanctity, discipline, and intelligence who served well for decades under enormous pressures.

Pope Paul inherited the Second Vatican Council. He became pope
after the first session and before the great debates on the nature and con-
tent of its final decrees. Some wondered if he would even continue the
council at all. He did, even if it was not his own vision, and he worked
hard to steer a middle course in order to keep the council faithful to
Church teaching yet open to necessary changes in light of the state of
the modern world. He did as well as anyone could have in light of the
unwieldy currents and crosscurrents and battles between liberals and
conservatives. Under his shepherding, Vatican II concluded in 1965 with
sixteen pastoral decrees designed to position the Church for the future.

The council's four most significant decrees addressed the nature
of the Church and her mission. *Lumen Gentium* acknowledged that the
Church was the invisible Body of Christ as well as the visible and institutional People of God. *Dei Verbum* affirmed the truth of Scripture and
Revelation as God's communication with his people, and that the Church
is the custodian of Revelation. *Sacrosanctum Concilium* reasserted the sa-
credness and significance of the liturgy and the Eucharist as the "source
and summit" of Church life, while providing for modifications. *Gaudium
et Spes* reflected how the Church can best engage the modern world with
the truth of the Gospel.

These decrees can at first glance seem straightforward and uncon-
troversial, but the council unleashed an extraordinary reaction among
the faithful that continues to this day. An energy for change and modern-
izing grew, even as many became alarmed at the apparent abandonment
of long-held traditions. Clashes raged between liberal and conservative
— especially at the level of the leading theologians — as each sought to
reach the heart of the Church. It is difficult to gauge how much the energy for change was rooted in the council itself as opposed to preexisting
forces and the powerful movement of the 1960s. Regardless, forces for
change seemed to predominate in the first two decades after the council

and the Church took on a new look. Liturgy was modernized, with introduction of the use of vernacular languages and new rites. A greater emphasis was put on social justice causes and care for the poor. Religious instruction was reoriented away from traditional preconciliar methods. Music, architecture, and the roles and positions of the clergy and laity were altered. Dissent and debate on doctrine and the interpretation of Scripture increased, and many prominent priests and theologians came forward to express new ideas and challenge traditional doctrines. All the while, millions of Catholics moved on with their lives, attending Mass and Catholic schools, living out their faith. It would be years, if at all, before the Church would find her bearings.

Amidst the turmoil, an unexpected wave of renewal movements sprang up around the world. Many have conjectured that they were fruit of the movement of the Holy Spirit. St. Josemaría Escrivá's Opus Dei quietly spread throughout the world and touched the lives of thousands. In Europe, Focolare was one of many movements which gave thousands the opportunity to grow in faith. In 1967, the Catholic Charismatic Renewal was born out of the turn of the century Pentecostal movement in the Protestant churches. This charismatic movement, which emphasized the presence and gifts of the Holy Spirit, spawned thousands of prayer groups and communities, conferences and books, lively praise and worship music, and reached millions around the world, especially in America. The Marriage Encounter and Cursillo movements rose up to assist the spiritual growth of couples and individuals. The ecumenical movement took shape and both theological dialogue among theologians and collaboration among ordinary Christians brought hope that Catholics, Orthodox, and Protestants might one day be reunited.

One of the most significant movements of spiritual renewal since the council has been the growth of the place of Scripture in the heart of the Church and her faithful. Before the Reformation, access to the Bible was limited because of the lack of copies and illiteracy. By the time of the Reformation, Gutenberg's printing press made possible the dissemination of vast numbers of copies of the Bible. Luther and other reformers took full advantage. The Catholic response was to guard the general reading of Scripture lest it be misinterpreted, since the reformers taught that each individual could interpret Scripture on his own. Thus personal reading of Scripture in the fashion of Protestants was not encouraged, and for centuries, the Church sought to hold onto her tradition of careful interpretation of Scripture through the wisdom of the Church. In the decades preceding Vatican II, Popes Leo XIII and Pius XII encouraged theologians and the faithful to devote more attention to Scripture. They also sought to steer the new scholarly approaches to Scripture study (such as form criticism) into the heart of the Church, but with a firm understanding that the Bible is the divine Word of God and must be read and interpreted with the eyes of faith. Vatican II emphasized this in *Dei Verbum*. After the council, the curtain was pulled back and Bible reading was encouraged. The times since the council have seen new translations of the Bible, more Scripture in the liturgy, the growth of Bible study groups and resources, biblical scholarship accessible to the faithful, and widespread individual reading of the Bible — all to the spiritual benefit of the faithful.

The many renewal movements, along with the increased emphasis on the Bible among the faithful, brought a spiritual energy that has resonated throughout the Church. Was this fruit of Vatican II? Were they signs of the "new Pentecost" that Pope John had prayed for? Very possibly. No doubt that, as the controversies and changes flowed through the Catholic Church and the world, the Holy Spirit was moving as well.

All these things were swirling around the Church as the quiet, reserved, often anxious Pope Paul VI sought to steer the Church forward. Not many popes had so much to contend with. He tried to nudge the Church in the right direction, with no consensus on what that direction was. The fact that he held the Church together is a testament to his faithfulness and the power of God.

Beyond what was happening around him, three achievements defined the pontificate of Pope Paul VI. First, the implementation of the council. He had less control over this than one would think; too many powerful forces sprang into action and did not look for the pope for oversight. Yet he did work to moderate abusive trends and foster necessary modernizations. He was, in his quiet way, without the adulation of followers, the man whom the Holy Spirit entrusted to be at the rudder.

His quiet, humble spirit steered the Church through the brawling voices, and kept it Catholic. Changes, even mistakes were made, yet doctrine and practice remained in place. This was no small achievement.

Second, he oversaw the revisions of the Roman Rite, which to this day remain a controversy. He replaced the Tridentine Mass of the previous several hundred years with the *Novus Ordo*, with the goal of making Catholic liturgical worship more accessible to the people. The "new Mass," the product of decades of reflection on liturgical reform, fostered vernacular language, more Scripture, modified liturgical prayers, and more active participation by those in attendance. Change is hard for many, and the Novus Ordo to this day draws criticism. Part of the problem is that the new liturgy seemed to have caused a loss of the sense of sacred and opened the door for abuses. But we need to ask, what would have happened had he declined to reform the liturgy? Would modern Catholics have continued to embrace a passive role in the Tridentine Mass and its prayers in the Latin they did not speak? Many criticisms of the Novus Ordo are well worth considering, but it preserved the Eucharist and the core meaning of liturgy: making present the sacrifice of Christ. The Church can always address perceived shortcomings.

The third, and perhaps the most memorable aspect of Pope Paul's pontificate was his 1968 encyclical, *Humanae Vitae*, which reaffirmed Catholic teaching in opposition to artificial contraception. This pronouncement — given in the teeth of the liberalizing trends of the sexual revolution — created a firestorm of protest throughout the Church and world and wore down the pope's morale in his later years. He saw a Church beginning to be split apart on both sexual and liturgical issues, which grieved him deeply. Many today take note of his tremendous courage in standing up against the sexual revolution. And many today — despite significant division remaining on the issue — see him as a prophet. He predicted that a contraceptive mentality would lead away from seeing sex as a God-given gift to be given in love, and instead would lead toward seeing sex selfishly, primarily for personal pleasure. *Humanae Vitae* is not long, is easily available online, and is worth a prayerful reading. It offers insights into human nature and civilization and the Church's role as a voice of the sacred, even if that voice contradicts the prevailing opinions of the times.

As Pope Paul agonized over what he knew would be a controversial document, he first consulted with many bishops and theologians, including Karol Wojtyła, the future Pope John Paul II. In *Humanae Vitae*, he elaborated on the twofold Catholic vision of human sexuality: the unity of husband and wife in love, and openness to life. This was a powerful, courageous, and prophetic word to a Church and world that was drifting away from the foundational meaning of creation, life, and human sexuality.

Although Pope St. Paul VI will likely never be popular, a closer look at his legacy justifies his role as an instrument of the Holy Spirit. A man of lesser sanctity could have fallen on his face amidst the pressures of his time. Pope Paul was a man of prayer who wanted nothing other than to serve Christ and the Church as best he could. Faithfulness, more than elusive success, is God's calling to us. Pope Paul was faithful. Because of his faithfulness, the real possibility of disaster was averted. The Church lived on through the turbulence of the postconciliar era, muddied and weakened, but most importantly, still intact. Those who came after him were positioned to move the Church further forward.

43

MOTHER TERESA AND POPE JOHN PAUL II

The Catholic Church has always recognized that she has a special mission to the poor. Throughout her history, she has sought to carry this out in various ways, and numerous saints have shown the way. In modern times, the gulf between the rich and the poor has widened and the promise that technology would eradicate poverty has not come to pass. As the world has become a global village linked by media, many modern efforts on behalf of the poor have taken on a more political nature, such as liberation theology in Latin America. But efforts to eradicate poverty by changing political or power systems have not succeeded. They often dilute the core Gospel message of eternal salvation and of loving the person who is our neighbor. Yet we cannot simply point to the promise of eternal life in heaven — true as it is — amidst the grinding poverty on this earth. The call to love, as many saints have shown, compels us to take care of our neighbor. Jesus said so.

One profound answer on how best to do this is simply to imitate Christ. One small, humble woman sought to do just that and has become one of the most visible icons of Jesus in the history of the Church. **St. Teresa of Calcutta** (1910–1997), known to the world as Mother Teresa, has become one of the most admired and beloved saints in modern times. This young Albanian woman became a nun and was an ordinary teacher of well-to-do girls in India until she felt the call to give her life to serving the "poorest of the poor." That is what she did for the rest of her life. Into the most wretched sections of cities — especially in Calcutta, a large city in southeastern India now known as Kolkata — she went to assist the destitute and dying, one by one, recognizing the dignity of and seeing Jesus in each person. She battled bureaucracies and fought for what she needed, but her focus was not on changing political systems, but reaching out and touching individual persons, as Jesus had done.

Her radical commitment attracted others and her order, the *Missionaries of Charity*, was born, and thrives throughout the world today. Like St. Francis of Assisi, she demonstrated by her total commitment that giving our lives to God and trusting in him, not ourselves, is indeed possible. She exuded a profound wisdom, a wisdom rooted in grace, in an intimate relationship with her Creator, the fount of Wisdom. She could "see" with God's eyes more than most others. When asked if she was discouraged at her inability to reach all the poor, her famous reply was "God calls me to be faithful, not successful." Mother Teresa became a celebrity and was sought after as a speaker by those in the Church and by world leaders, and was even awarded the Nobel Prize for Peace in 1979. The contrast between this tiny, aged woman who knew God and the worldly heads of state was striking. On one occasion, she had the courage to speak unvarnished truth to a pro-abortion American president: Abortion, the killing of the unborn child, causes a deep spiritual poverty, making America a truly poor country.[1] Mother Teresa taught the world what it means to love and what it means to follow Jesus. She followed God's lead with total trust, even as she battled for years a dryness and suffocating dark night of the soul. Her life is an example that true joy comes from our relationship with God, not from the world, nor even from our emotions.

Like Francis and many other saints, she stood against the hedonistic, secular world of power and pleasure. Instead of opposing faceless "poverty" as a social condition, her ministry was to real people who were poor and dying, as individual persons created by God. Mother Teresa's way was in contradiction to the ways of liberation theology or governmental anti-poverty programs — she acted in love, recognizing the dignity of each individual person. She was so committed to following Jesus that the world has had a difficult time ignoring her. She made the Church's message of faith and love resonate in this postmodern era. She was small. She was humble. In an ironic twist of providence, she was the most famous Albanian in the world. In her day, Albania was arguably the world's most atheistic country.

In this "postmodern" world, what Pope Benedict XVI called "the dictatorship of relativism" now reigns in world thought and culture. If nothing is true, there is no higher morality to live up to. One can reject gender, sexual restraint, religion, and even demand that others approve of such rejections. The idea of a natural law, so deeply entrenched in human existence, has been discarded.

Into this growing situation stepped our final saint, Karol Wojtyła: a Polish man, cardinal of Krakow, and the one saint whose life reached into the twenty-first century, **Pope St. John Paul II** (1920–2005; r. 1978–2005). He had endured both Nazism after Germany occupied Poland in 1939, and communism when the Soviets took control of Poland after World War II. Wojtyła worked stealthily to keep Polish culture alive during these occupations and worked quietly as a priest. He was an intellectual and an expert in the philosophy of personalism, which acknowledges the dignity of the individual person. He was a pioneer in sexual ethics. His book, *Love and Responsibility*, is a classic explanation of the Christian vision for sex and marriage. He conducted many youth retreats in the Polish mountains, encouraging young singles and couples to embrace the Catholic vision of marriage and family life. And he stood against the Communists in power as much as he could.

Then, in 1978, Karol Wojtyła became pope — a stunning choice. For four hundred years the cardinals had chosen Italians as popes. No one in

1978 expected anything else. Yet this Cardinal from outside the Vatican bureaucracy became arguably the most significant pope in modern times. He stood up fearlessly against postmodern forces in the West, against the brutal Communist regime that heavily kept Catholic Eastern Europe in its vise, and against the secularizing forces within the Church herself. His first words upon becoming pope were "Be not afraid." The first of many encyclicals, which set the tone of his pontificate, was *Redemptor Hominis*, the Redeemer of Man. He sought to focus attention directly on Jesus Christ and the reality of God's love as the remedy to what ails the world.

But the many things he accomplished nearly did not come to pass. Just over two years into his pontificate, on May 13, 1981, an assassin shot him at point-blank range in Saint Peter's Square. John Paul survived, but suffered a long road to recovery. His assassin, the Turkish agent Ali Ağca — who, according to many historians, acted under Soviet auspices — still cannot understand how he failed to kill the pope. John Paul knew why: the day he was shot was the anniversary of Mary's first apparition at Fátima. John Paul, who had always had a devotion to the Blessed Mother, attributed Mary's intercession to sparing his life. The following May 13, he traveled to Fátima to offer public thanks to Mary for her intercession. Many have considered this assassination attempt to be the realization of the "Third Secret of Fátima," entrusted to the young seers in 1917.

His life spared, John Paul II embarked upon one of the longest and most powerful papal reigns Church history has seen. In response to Mary's request during an apparition at Fátima, as reported by Sister Lúcia, in 1984 he consecrated Russia and the world to Mary. Twice he visited Poland, drawing massive crowds and encouraging the Poles to have hope in the Lord. He fearlessly supported the Polish Solidarity labor movement in the 1980s. These acts — in the teeth of Soviet communism — emboldened a massive force within Poland and elsewhere in Eastern Europe for deliverance from communism.

The most stunning geopolitical development of the century was the fall of communism and the Soviet Empire, and it would not have happened but for the relentless efforts of Pope John Paul II. He collaborated with US President Ronald Reagan and British Prime Minister Margaret Thatcher to pressure the Soviets to release their hold on Poland and other countries. They were aided by the surprising openness of Soviet Premier Mikhail Gorbachev. Heartened, the Polish people succeeded in pushing the Communists out of power in 1989. This wave of freedom spread throughout central and Eastern Europe as one Communist regime after another in the erstwhile Soviet Bloc crumbled in the late 1980s and into the early 1990s. The Berlin Wall came down, the peaceful "Velvet Revolution" freed Czechoslovakia, and by 1991, the Soviet Union itself collapsed and the Communists were out of power.

Virtually no one thought this was possible. Pope John Paul II did, and he saw it as God working in history. Although many had a hand in fostering the fall of the Soviet Empire and crumbling of the "Iron Curtain," no one had a more significant role than he. Soviet dictator Joseph Stalin once quipped, "How many divisions has the pope got?" John Paul's answer was that courage, prayer, grace, and an emboldened human spirit — not military action — can bring down one of the most powerful empires in world history.

Using all his intellectual and pastoral skills, Pope John Paul fought for theological clarification in the Church so that she could move forward for the salvation of souls. His task, as he saw it, was to reorient the Church away from secularizing trends and back to a full focus on God, on Jesus Christ, the Redeemer. This was his vision of the Second Vatican Council and he worked with vigor to implement the tenets of this council. In an effort to lead the Catholic faithful to a deeper understanding of their Faith in these secular times, he implemented the now widely used *Catechism of the Catholic Church* in 1992, the first such papal-sponsored catechism since the Catechism of Trent over four hundred years earlier. In his introduction to the *Catechism*, he noted its link to the Vatican II: "The principal task presented to the council by Pope John XXIII was to guard and present better the precious deposit of Christian doctrine in order to make it more accessible to the Christian faithful and to all people of good will."[2]

John Paul traveled more extensively than any pope before him, preaching the Gospel in every corner of the world. He sponsored numerous World Youth Days, usually in cities chosen for their dire need to hear the Gospel. These often drew over a million young people and had discernable impacts on the host cities. Among his many encyclicals and apostolic letters were *Veritatis Splendor*, a defense of the Catholic vision of morality, *Evangelium Vitae*, a defense of life, including a theological case against abortion, *Mulieris Dignitatum*, an affirmation of the dignity of women, and *Fides et Ratio*, an explanation how faith and reason are compatible and together necessary to reach the truth.

Perhaps his most significant spiritual and theological contribution was his *Theology of the Body*, a synthesis of the Christian vision of human sexuality. He explained how human persons, created in God's image as the Book of Genesis describes, reflect God's love. He showed how, as male and female, we reflect the complementarity among the Persons within the Trinity, and how love in marriage, mirroring the love within the Trinity, creates new life. Human sexuality is an echo of the Trinity itself, he explained. This is a powerful word in direct opposition to the tenets of the sexual revolution, and may, in time, provide human civilization the way back from whence it has come.

John Paul altered the perspective of the papacy. He was more an evangelist than a manager. He was more pastoral than bureaucratic. The popes before him had been nudging the papacy in this direction, but John Paul, with his spiritual and personal gifts, brought the spirit of evangelization to the heart of the papacy and sought to bring it to the heart of all the Church. His vision for the Church was to bring Christ to the world.

His health deteriorated in his last years, particularly from Parkinson's disease. He bore it well, and in his final days in the spring of 2005, he kept his eyes on God. It is too early to tell the full nature of Pope St. John Paul II's legacy, but only a few popes have had as much spiritual and temporal impact on the Church and the world, and only a few have left us with such a treasury of theological and spiritual writing that points to God in such a godless time.

44
TOWARD THE FUTURE

Our walk through the two thousand–year history of the Catholic Church and her saints has come to an end. Much of this history has been crisis, conflict, and weakness. Despite her failings, however, the Church has made tremendous contributions to the world. In addition to her saints, the Church has generated countless millions of disciples over the centuries who have served faithfully in the name of Jesus, spreading love, handing down the Faith, and leavening society. Their impact is immeasurable.

The Catholic Church is primarily responsible for the development of Western civilization — which, despite modern attacks on all things of the West, is arguably the greatest civilization in world history. Openness to human achievement, seasoned by the ethic of Christian love of God and neighbor, has fostered literature and learning, the growth of cities, science, the arts, technology, commerce and industry, and the foundations for democratic governments. Christianity cultivated the growth and development of marriage and family as a foundation for productive society. Great art, great music, great architecture, great learning, great cathedrals, and great ideas of freedom and justice all flowed from the Christian worldview. Some historians have observed that, had many of the heresies or non-Christian perspectives prevailed over Christianity in the Middle Ages, civilization would have retreated into social upheaval, sensuality, or even barbarism. Just as the Church deserves blame for her failures, she deserves credit for the great civilization she fostered as well. This is our heritage as we look to the future, and the saints were at the heart of creating this rich heritage.

The history of saints in the twentieth and twenty-first centuries is still being written. The process of identifying and formally canonizing holy men and women of God in modern times is and will be ongoing for many years. The last three popes, including Pope Francis, have accelerated the pace of beatifications and canonizations of new saints, whose stories we are just beginning to hear. Many recent and current stalwarts of faith will likely attain the title of "saint" in future years. Some of them may include Dorothy Day, the devout and tenacious American lay convert who overcame many obstacles to faith, gave her life for the poor, and founded the Catholic Worker Movement; Hans Urs von Balthasar, the brilliant Swiss theologian who, like Aquinas, always kept his eyes fixed on God; and Joseph Ratzinger, Pope Benedict XVI, a man of deep faith and a brilliant theologian and writer with extraordinary insight into eternal truths.

Among Protestant spiritual giants in the modern era are Billy Graham, the great American Evangelical preacher who stirred millions to deeper faith, and C. S. Lewis, the British-Anglican scholar and writer whose reflections on the Christian faith both in fiction (*The Chronicles of Narnia*) and apologetics (*Mere Christianity, The Screwtape Letters*) have had enormous impact in strengthening and spreading the Faith throughout the world. Lewis's writings have been responsible for as many conversions to Christianity as anyone's in the last century. Countless others, many without renown or fame, will come to light in the years ahead and their stories will be told as well.

To be sure, we will not see or fully understand the true picture of the Church and world in our present times until enough time has passed for us — or our children — to gain perspective. But it is clear that the Church is moving through fast-changing, turbulent times. The world is vastly different than even in the recent past. At this point, two thousand years since the Ascension of Jesus, the Catholic Church is now, for the first time, truly global. The Catholic presence is on every continent, in every part of the world. Over one billion people identify as Catholic. Her reach, her ministries, and her efforts for evangelization are in place, despite the Church's weaknesses and the challenges of this world so often hostile to the Faith.

The future of the Church is likely to be the era of the lay person. It may well be that the main body of saints of the future will be lay people whose tasks will include evangelizing cultures, institutions, family, friends, neighbors, and leaders in secular societies.

Many have envisioned that the Church will become smaller in the West and see growth in the Third World, that a fierce battle for souls will intensify, and that the Holy Spirit, in ways that we cannot predict, will ignite a massive wave of evangelism and conversion.

This may also be a time of sainthood by martyrdom. The blood of future martyrs — whether or not they are canonized — will be the seeds for the Church in the future.

Whatever the future holds, the Church needs saints and those who would nurture them. Many are already in our midst. Some, like Thérèse of Lisieux, may be hidden now, yet may come to inspire the world in the days ahead. History tells us that God will continue to raise them up. And God is calling us all to this same sainthood as well.

AFTERWORD

In these pages, we have walked through two thousand years of history, from the hills of Palestine to the ends of the earth. We have passed through various epochs, cultures, and lands. We have met scores of extraordinary men and women of faith, from eyewitnesses of Jesus to modern-day disciples. To what end?

My hope is that this book may lead us to reflect on the significance of the saints — both for the Church and for us. In these last few pages, I will offer five themes for consideration. They have already been raised during the course of this book, and I pull them together now for your reflection.

JESUS CHRIST IS THE LORD OF HISTORY

This reality bears repeating: The Church is the Body of Christ, and Jesus Christ is her founder and head. Just as Jesus is divine and human, so is the Church divine and human, as she moves through history between the first and Second Comings of Jesus. It is vital for the Christian to read Church history from this perspective. Historian Christopher Dawson said it well: "It is impossible for us to understand the Church if we regard her as subject to the limitations of human culture. For she is essentially a supernatural organism which transcends human cultures and transforms them to her own ends."[1]

God is intimately involved in the Church's movement through history. He raises up saints and inspires his sons and daughters to help him draw all people to be with him in eternity. It is for this only that the Catholic Church exists. Although I have referred to *the Church* throughout this book, this term creates a danger of deemphasizing the supernatural reality and presenting the Church as a mere human "organization." She is not.

God is the Lord of history. This world is his world; the Catholic Church is his Church. Jesus promised to be with us until the end of the world. He has and continues to keep this promise. This is why we have seen, time and again, the providential hand of God in the history of the Church.

At first glance, it may seem that much of the Church's history is shrouded in darkness and sin. There is truth to that. Original sin — and the actual sin that flows from it — is a powerful force in history. But it is not the only force, nor the strongest. God's grace and power supersede the power of sin and Satan. As we have seen, each time the Church has encountered a crisis, God has provided a way through.

To be sure, each crisis has exacted a toll. God never puts the Church back at the same spot as she was before a crisis. Sin damages the Church. But God has always kept the Church alive by each time creating something new. Theologians call this *divine accommodation*. As God did with the Hebrew people in Old Testament times, giving them new starts each time they broke his covenants, so God does today under the New Covenant in Christ. God loves his people too much to abandon the Church. He will not let her die.

The Church is on a divine mission. Jesus assured Peter that the gates of hell will not prevail against the Church (see Mt 16:18). Many Christian commentators have noted that we tend to look at this as if the Church will always be able to withstand the attacks of evil. While this is true, Jesus said it is the "gates" of hell that will not prevail — not the forces or the attacks or the weapons of hell. Gates don't attack. Jesus was prophesying that the Church will be on the *offensive* against the forces of hell, and hell will be on the defensive against the power of Church, which will break through hell's gates and prevail.

When the Roman emperors persecuted the early Christians and threw them to the lions, God went on the offensive, and astonishingly, the emperor himself converted to Christianity. In short order much of the empire became Christian. When corruption in the Church and the attacks of the Protestant reformers seemed to put the Catholic Church on the brink of collapse, God went on the offensive. He raised up a host of remarkable saints, spreading holiness and renewal. Amazingly, the Church did not collapse but, though smaller, became stronger and healthier.

And so with any crisis now or in the future. The power of God's grace will lead the Church on an offensive against hell's gates and create a new day for the Church. Those Christians who have lived and who will live during crises may not always see the victory in their lifetimes, but it will come, in God's providential time, hastened by the prayers of the faithful. Ultimate victory is at the end of time when Christ returns. God indeed is the Lord of history.

THE LESSON OF HOPE

Christ's lordship over his Church and history gives us every reason — even a duty — to hope. By all rights, the Church should have collapsed and died off numerous times in her history, as so often predicted by her enemies. But she never has. The very existence of modern saints gives witness to this. After two thousand years, men and women today are still drawing from the same well of grace, preaching the same Gospel and spiritual wisdom, and rising up as committed disciples of Jesus. We can ask ourselves, "Where do all these saints come from?" Christ's Church is the garden which grows saints — as much today as at Pentecost. As Saint Paul observed, "Hope does not disappoint" (Rom 5:5).

Despite many crises, failures, and human weaknesses, the Church has never collapsed. Throughout the centuries, in dark times and in good, millions of faithful believers filled the churches, preserved and passed on the Faith, pushed for reform, spread the love of God among their neighbors, and nurtured saints. They built churches and monasteries and peopled them. They kept the Gospel message alive in every circumstance. The Holy Spirit was alive in them.

This may be the most profound lesson from our walk through history. God does triumph. God does save and protect. God does raise up saints and leaders to lead his people out of the dark times. God does offer salvation to all his faithful who are mired in a time of darkness. God is always present, no matter the times. Renewal does flow from darkness. His saints are witnesses to this hope. In this hope, we too can have the conviction to be disciples of Jesus. And as we see the crises in the Church and the world around us, we can take up the call to pray that God raise up great saints for our own time, in our own midst.

THE LEGACY OF THE SAINTS

I have sought to portray the saints as a body, so that we can see their collective influence on history and the example they provide for us. Just as we have much to learn from each individual saint, we can also learn from what all the saints have in common. Their lives show that God acts in time and through people. Together, by their lives, they create a portrait of Jesus himself.

Through hard times and major obstacles, one thing is clear: *The saints never aimed low*. They were men and women of prayer who excelled at blending prayer into a life of service. They stand as examples of virtue under fire. Among their most prominent characteristics were courage, tenacity, perseverance, and trust in God. Saint Athanasius never quit the struggle against the Arians, despite being forced out of his bishopric multiple times. Saint Francis did not wilt under the extreme pressure of his father to rejoin polite society. St. Thomas More faced down the King of England, refusing to assent to his claim of authority over the Church, though it cost him his life. St. Frances Cabrini blew through logistical obstacles that daunted those around her and founded institutions all over the Americas and Europe, so strong was her trust in God's providence.

Sometimes the saints were successful by human standards; often they were not. Yet they sought to follow Jesus whether or not they saw the results of their life's work. Mother Teresa's famous observation bears repeating: "God calls us to be faithful, not successful." The saints kept their eyes on God, with a holy confidence that his ways transcend apparent human success. This hope was their secret. It inspired their unwavering commitment to the work of the Gospel, no matter the obstacles.

Above all, the saints loved. Their concern and care for the people in their lives, no matter the nature of their ministry, was unmistakable. We have met many saints whose life's work was charity — Mother Teresa, Vincent de Paul, and Martin de Porres among them. But it is clear that saints in other ministries also had a heart for the poor and needy. They did not hide in an ivory tower. Love of God leads to love of neighbor. In every saint, if we look behind their ministries of teaching, preaching, or leading, we will also see an active concern for neighbor.

The saints are signs of contradiction. The world teaches self-assurance; the saints teach reliance on God. The world teaches the primacy of science and reason; the saints teach the reality of God and his love. The world teaches the quest for power; the saints teach the power of humility. The world exudes a fear of death; countless saints have given their lives in martyrdom. And, as history has shown time and again, in the midst of trial and travail, the saints called the faithful back to holiness, back to Jesus. On this earth, they point to heaven. In a real sense, they are prophets, witnessing to the reality of God and eternity.

THE COMMUNION OF SAINTS

The saints throughout history — from Mary Magdalene to John Paul II — now stand before the throne of grace and intercede for us. We can look to them for help and inspiration.

The work of the saints on behalf of the Church did not end with their deaths. The very definition of a saint is one who has won the crown of salvation and resides with God in heaven. In most instances, two verified miracles after petition to a deceased saint are required for canonization. Just as Jesus "always lives to make intercession for [us]" (Heb 7:25), the saints in heaven join with Jesus in a ministry of intercession for those of us on earth until the end of time. This is the Communion of Saints in action. St. Thérèse of Lisieux expressed this best: "I will spend my Heaven doing good upon the earth."[2] The saints are not confined to history. They remain with us. We are invited, even urged, to call upon our brothers and sisters who stand before the throne of grace, for their help in this "valley of tears." And led by the Blessed Virgin Mary, Queen of Saints, they will answer. The saints who no longer walk this earth are still affecting the Church's history.

OUR CALL TO DISCIPLESHIP

Beyond their place in history, the saints also stand as examples for us to emulate. As Pope St. John XXIII said, "God desires us to follow the example of the saints." As with the men and women we have encountered throughout this book, God created each of us for our particular moment in time. We all share in the making of history. No soul, no event is too small for the kingdom of God — even if our lives remain unknown to posterity. God gives us our own place, our own role, in salvation history. Like all the saints, we are called to holiness. The virtues we have seen in the saints on these pages are ours to pursue as well. Their focus on prayer, on love of God and of neighbor, is ours to pursue, too. Their devotion to Jesus and spreading the Gospel is also for us. As St. Teresa of Ávila noted, the Devil tries to get us to think that saints are only for our admiration, not for our inspiration.[3] The New Testament's Letter to the Hebrews says it well: "Therefore, since we are surrounded by so great a cloud of witnesses, let us also lay aside every weight, and sin which clings so closely, and let us run with perseverance the race that is set before us" (Heb 12:1).

How we respond to grace affects every friend, neighbor, or family member in our lives in the same way the saints affected those around them. Most canonized saints would be quick to point out that simply doing the ordinary, daily things in life, one step, one day at a time, is the secret to effective ministry. That is what they sought to do. We can as well — whether we have a ministry that is global or simply in our little corner of the world.

We are also called to support, encourage, and nurture those around us. We may never know how significant our role might be in nurturing a saint-to-be who will have a major impact on history. Note well St. Thérèse of Lisieux's parents who gave her the gift of faith, St. John Vianney's mentor who got him into seminary, or Saint Monica, who relentlessly sought her son Augustine's conversion. They did not know that they were nurturing future saints.

Jesus has not yet returned to bring an end to history. Until then, God's plan of salvation — Church history — will continue to unfold. God acts through us to bring his plan to fruition — just as he has through the saints, great and small, canonized or not, known or obscure. Whether our own ministry is on a stage large or small, we are called, like the saints, to follow Jesus, and thereby join those saints for eternity in heaven, beyond the end of history.

ACKNOWLEDGMENTS

I will be forever grateful to the many people who have supported me in writing this, my first book.

In memory of Sister M. Georgia, CSC, my high school English teacher, who died recently at age 99, having served 81 years as a Holy Cross Sister. I am thankful for the inspiration of her resolute faith in God, for introducing me to *The Chronicles of Narnia* and to the genius of Shakespeare, and for helping me to become a better writer. She is a shining example of the thousands of nuns who served with dedication throughout the history of the Catholic Church.

Thank you to the many friends who have encouraged me, always asking how the book is coming along, asking when it will be published so they can read it. I cannot tell you how much that meant.

My thanks to Dr. Alan Schreck, whose courses on Church history at Franciscan University of Steubenville, taught with great scholarship and with the eyes of faith, stirred me to become a student of Church history.

Thank you to those hearty souls who braved cold and snowy roads to attend my winter 2019 saints and history series, from which this book came to be, and for my fellow writers at Rev. Peter Stravinskas's Catholic Writers Retreat in June 2019, who, when I confided that I was thinking of writing this book, said, "Go, do it!" Your encouragement gave me the confidence to forge ahead and write this book.

Many thanks to my good friend, Jim Garland, who first steered me to the wonderful people at Our Sunday Visitor.

Profound thanks to the fabulous editors at OSV: Mary Beth Giltner, who believed that this project had merit, and Rebecca Martin, who through her erudite editing and knowledge of history, fostered innumerable improvements to the text.

My heartfelt gratitude to my beloved wife Elizabeth, who read and critiqued my text with her great skill as an English teacher, offered constant reassurance, encouraged me to stop revising and seek a publisher, and who came to my rescue at those times of angst when my computer (surely descended from HAL of *2001: A Space Odyssey*) launched its surprise attacks at this tech-challenged writer.

And above all, thanks be to God!

QUESTIONS FOR REFLECTION AND DISCUSSION

I – THE EARLY CHURCH

1. What would have happened to Saint Paul and his ministry if Saint Barnabas had not convinced the apostles that Paul's conversion was authentic? What was at stake for the Church? What does this say about the significance of Barnabas to Church history?

2. Why did Peter end up in Rome? Could Peter's successors have moved to Jerusalem or Antioch instead? Did they succeed Peter only, or Peter as head of the entire Church? Why did Rome end up as the site of the head of the Church?

3. How did the Church survive after the deaths of Saint Paul and the apostles? Who were the key leaders and what were the key developments that saw the Church forward?

4. Do you think that the early Christians who stood up heroically during the persecutions were "better" Christians than we are today? Why or why not?

5. Who, in your assessment, were the two or three most significant saints after the apostles, up to the year 312? Why?

II — FROM CONSTANTINE TO CHARLEMAGNE

1. At one point in the fourth century, over half of the bishops were Arian. How did this happen? How did the Holy Spirit assist the Church in getting out of this situation?

2. Picture Saint Athanasius exiled in the Sahara, defeated, most likely discouraged. How does he motivate himself to keep up the fight? What's at stake in his response?

3. Saint Augustine, Saint Jerome, and Saint Ambrose were towering intellectual giants. How important is intellect and scholarship in the Church? What is its proper place? The philosopher or the peasant — who is more important in the kingdom of God?

4. The Muslims defeated the Christians at Yarmouk in 636. The Christians defeated the Muslims at Tours in 732. What impact did these two battles have on the history of the Church? Picture the Church if these battles had gone the other way.

5. Who, in your assessment, were the two or three most significant saints in the period from 313 to 800? Why?

III — CHRISTENDOM

1. Was the Church better or worse off after Charlemagne and the emergence of "Christendom"? Why or why not?

2. Was the Great Schism of 1054 avoidable? How? In what ways might saints have either helped to avoid the Schism or helped to heal it in the aftermath? Is reconciliation possible even today? What would it take?

3. Was the Black Plague a punishment from God? Why or why not? What significance, if any, is the fact that it occurred during the Avignon Papacy? Or that Rome was mostly spared?

4. Is St. Francis of Assisi overrated? Is his influence on the Church through the centuries based more upon sentiment or genuine contributions to the Faith? If the latter, what are his significant contributions?

5. This era saw some of the most prominent saints in Church history, including Bernard, Gregory VII, Francis, Clare, Dominic, Albert, Bonaventure, Thomas Aquinas, Catherine, and Joan of Arc. Who are the most significant, and why?

IV — REFORMATION, REFORM, AND RENAISSANCE

1. Was the Protestant Reformation avoidable? Why or why not? If it could have been avoided, how? How might history have been different if it had been avoided?

2. Might God have called Martin Luther to lead and inspire a genuine, Holy Spirit–directed reform of the Catholic Church? If so, what happened that caused the reform movement to "go off the rails" and end up dividing the Church?

Where does fault lie? What might the Church have looked like in, say, 1600 if Luther, Calvin, and the other reformers had not led their movements or had been stifled — or had become saints?

3. Compare the state of religious liberty as it affected Catholic England at the time of St. Thomas More to America today. Are we close to a period of similar persecution, or heading in that direction, or do we still have sufficient safeguards? Why or why not?

4. Vienna (and likely Christian Europe) was spared at the last moment from falling to the Ottomans in the siege of 1683. One key reason is that heavy rains in the Balkans prevented the Ottoman army from getting its artillery up the roads to Vienna. Providence? A lucky break? Just the way things were? Discuss.

5. Who, in your assessment, were the most vital Counter-Reformation saints, and why?

V — ENLIGHTENMENT AND MODERNISM

1. Why did the most influential intellectuals of the eighteenth century mostly reject the Church and even stray from belief in God? Why did this happen at this time, and not at other times in the previous one thousand five hundred years?

2. The great Christian but Jansenist scholar Blaise Pascal was perhaps the strongest eighteenth-century intellectual opponent of the Enlightenment scholars. Does God use those who are not fully orthodox Catholics to defend the Church? Why?

3. Compare and evaluate the methods and approaches of St. John Vianney and St. Thérèse of Lisieux on the one hand, and St. Pius X and St. John Newman on the other, in standing against the forces of the Enlightenment and modernism.

4. Arguably, two of the most consequential apparitions of Mary in all of Church history occurred at Lourdes and Fátima, in this era, only fifty-nine years apart. They remain consequential to this day. Their messages of prayer for conversion of the world are similar. Why so close in time? What does this say about the urgency of the times?

5. Who, in your assessment, were the two or three most significant saints in this era of "Enlightenment"?

VI – THE CHURCH IN MODERN TIMES

1. The last century has seen the greatest number of martyrs in all of Church history. Why? Why now? Do you see this getting better or worse in the years ahead? How might persecution affect your children or grandchildren who hold onto the Faith?

2. If the Second Vatican Council had not taken place, what would the Catholic Church look like today? How many of the changes in the Church are attributable to Vatican II vs. the larger movements in society, particularly the 1960s?

3. Japanese Catholic convert Dr. Takashi Nagai, a survivor of the atomic blast at Nagasaki, has proposed the controversial theory that the Catholic community of Nagasaki, which was at ground zero, was a "sacrificial peace offering." Many say this is preposterous. What do you think? Was the American decision to bypass the intended target city due to heavy

cloud cover and drop the bomb on Nagasaki instead, above the Catholic cathedral, providential, a circumstance without meaning, or something else?

4. Some view Pope St. John Paul II as worthy of the title "John Paul the Great." Others say not so fast, that he had flaws and made key mistakes during his pontificate. What do you think? Why?

5. What signs of renewal and hope do you see in the Church today? Do you see exemplary Catholics in the world today who might one day be canonized as saints? Who comes to mind?

NOTES

INTRODUCTION

1. From a 1968 letter to a conscientious objector, quoted in Dorothy Day, *All the Way to Heaven: The Selected Letters of Dorothy Day*, ed. Robert Ellsberg (Milwaukee, WI: Marquette University Press, 2010), 351.

CHAPTER 1: THE CONDITIONS WERE RIGHT

1. These are approximations. Demographers' estimates vary on the population of the Roman Empire and the number of Christians at various points in time.

2. Cardinal Joseph Ratzinger, *Introduction to Christianity*, trans. J. R. Foster and Michael J. Miller (rev. ed., San Francisco: Ignatius Press, 2004), 221–222.

CHAPTER 3: THE NEXT GENERATIONS

1. Irenaeus of Lyons, *Against Heresies*, 3, 3, 3. See also Pope Benedict XVI, *Church Fathers: From Clement of Rome to Augustine* (San Francisco: Ignatius Press, 2008), 23.

CHAPTER 4: THE ORIGINS OF THE SACRAMENTS

1. The Church is rich with theological and pastoral literature on the sacraments. Perhaps the best starting place is the *Catechism of the Catholic Church*. Part 2 is devoted specifically to the liturgy and sacraments. Sections 1212–1666 provide a detailed discussion of each of the seven sacraments.

2. See Herbert Vorgrimler, *Sacramental Theology* (Collegeville, MN: Liturgical Press, 1992), 107–108.

3. Ignatius of Antioch, *Letter to the Ephesians*, 20, in *Early Christian Writings: The Apostolic Fathers*, trans. Maxwell Staniforth (New York: Penguin Books, 1968), 82.

4. Ignatius of Antioch, *Letter to the Romans*, 7, in *Early Christian Writings: The Apostolic Fathers*, 106.

5. Ibid., *Letter to the Smyrnaeans*, 8, in *Early Christian Writings: The Apostolic Fathers*, 121.

6. Clement, *Letter to the Corinthians,* 44, in *Early Christian Writings: The Apostolic Fathers*, 46.

7. Ignatius of Antioch, *Letter to the Church at Philadelphia*, 1.

8. See Vorgrimler, *Sacramental Theology*, 208–209.

9. Ignatius of Antioch, *Letter to Polycarp*, 5.

CHAPTER 5: THE BIRTH OF THE NEW TESTAMENT AND THE CHRISTIAN BIBLE

1. Joseph Lienhard, *The Bible, the Church, and Authority* (Collegeville, MN: Liturgical Press, 1995), 20.

2. See Lienhard, *The Bible and the Church*, 34, 37, 40; Henry Chadwick, *The Early Church* (New York: Penguin Books, 1967), 43–44.

3. Lienhard, *The Bible and the Church*, 27.

4. Ibid., 25; Chadwick, *The Early Church*, 81.

5. Ibid., 33.

6. Justin Martyr, *Apology*, 67, quoted in Jimmy Akin, *The Bible is a Catholic Book* (El Cajon, CA: Catholic Answers Press, 2019), 134.

CHAPTER 6: FATHERS OF THE CHURCH

1. Lienhard, *The Bible and the Church*, 34; Chadwick, *The Early Church*, 43.

CHAPTER 7: PERSECUTION

1. Tacitus, *The Annals*, bk. 15, 44–45, in *Complete Works of Tacitus*, ed. Moses Hadas (New York: Random House, 1942), 376–381.

2. John Vidmar, OP, *The Catholic Church Through the Ages,* 2nd ed. (Mahwah, NJ: Paulist Press, 2014), 45.

CHAPTER 9: WAS JESUS DIVINE? ATHANASIUS AND THE ARIAN CONTROVERSY

1. Jerome, *Dialogue Against the Luciferians,* 19.

CHAPTER 11: A BRIDGE FROM ANTIQUITY: AUGUSTINE AND HIS CONTEMPORARIES

1. Quoted in *Butler's Lives of the Saints*, new concise edition, ed. Paul Burns (Collegeville, MN: Liturgical Press, 2003), 456.

2. From Jerome, *Letter 195,* as quoted in Augustine, *Confessions*, ed. David Vincent Meconi, SJ, Ignatius Critical Edition (San Francisco: Ignatius Press, 2012), 297, n. 78.

3. Pope Benedict XVI, General Audience, January 9, 2008, in *Church Fathers*, 120.

4. Ambrose, *Commentary on Twelve Psalms of David*, 40:30.

CHAPTER 12: THE EMPIRE COLLAPSES; THE CHURCH FILLS THE VOID

1. Janet Burton and Karen Stober, eds., *Women in the Medieval Monastic World* (Turnhout, Belgium: Brepols Publishers, 2015), 16, 53, 186, 190, and 195.

2. Thomas Cahill, *How the Irish Saved Civilization* (New York: Anchor Books, 1995), 192.

CHAPTER 13: THE CHURCH IN THE EAST AND THE RISE OF ISLAM

1. Quoted in Jules Leroy, *Monks and Monasteries of the Near East*, trans. Peter Collin (London: George G. Harrap and Co., 1963), 81.

2. Jules Leroy, *Monks and Monasteries of the Near East* (Piscataway, NJ: Gorgias Press, 2004), 93–94.

CHAPTER 16: THE MIDDLE AGES

1. Pope Benedict XVI, General Audience, November 18, 2009, in *Church Fathers*, 27.

CHAPTER 17: THE CRUSADES

1. Vidmar, *The Catholic Church Through the Ages*, 125.

2. Ibid., 134.

3. Ibid., 134.

CHAPTER 18: A RESURGENCE OF CHRISTIAN FAITH AND CULTURE

1. Quoted in *Butler's Lives of the Saints: Concise, Modernized Edition*, ed. Bernard Bangley, (Brewster, MA: Paraclete Press, 2005), 22.

CHAPTER 21: THE BLACK DEATH

1. Demographers vary in their estimates of the population of Europe in 1347. Estimates range from eighty million to well over one hundred million. Estimates on the percentage of deaths vary as well, from about one-third to over half.

2. Dorsey Armstrong, Ph.D., *The Black Death*, The Great Courses Lecture Series, (Chantilly, VA: The Teaching Company, 2016), lecture 2. See also Sigrid Undset, *Catherine of Siena* (San Francisco: Ignatius Press, 2009), 167.

3. Armstrong, *The Black Death*, lecture 5.

4. Christopher Dawson, *The Dividing of Christendom* (repr., San Francisco: Ignatius Press, 2009), 143.

5. Quoted in *The Trial of Jean d'Arc*, ed. W. P. Barrett, trans. Coley Banks Taylor, Pierre Champion, Ruth Hamilton Kerr, et al. (New York: Gotham House, 1932), 52.

6. Edward Wagenknecht, *Mark Twain: The Man and His Work* (Norman, OK: University of Oklahoma Press, 1961), 60, as cited by Andrew Tadie in the introduction to Mark Twain, *Joan of Arc* (San Francisco: Ignatius Press, 1989), 15.

CHAPTER 24: MARTIN LUTHER AND THE PROTESTANT REFORMATION

1. See the *Catechism of the Catholic Church* 150–155, and 1987–2005.

2. Christopher Dawson, *The Dividing of Christendom*, 120.

CHAPTER 25: THE INQUISITION

1. Vidmar, *The Catholic Church Through the Ages*, 157.

CHAPTER 26: CATHOLIC COUNTER-REFORMATION

1. Dawson, *The Dividing of Christendom*, 149.

2. Teresa of Ávila, *The Book of Her Life*, 24, 3, in *The Collected Works of St. Teresa of Ávila*, vol. 1, trans. Kieran Kavanaugh, OCD and Otilio Rodriguez, OCD (Washington, D.C.: ICS Publications, 1976), 159–160.

3. Teresa of Ávila, *The Book of Her Life*, 8, 5, in *The Collected Works*, 67.

4. Thomas Bokenkotter, *A Concise History of the Catholic Church* (New York: Image Books, 1979), 253.

CHAPTER 29: SCIENCE AND THE RENAISSANCE

1. Bokenkotter, *A Concise History of the Catholic Church*, 268.

CHAPTER 30: THE OTTOMAN THREAT AND THE SIEGE OF VIENNA

1. Kenneth Harl, Ph.D., *The Ottomans*, The Great Courses Lecture Series (Chantilly, VA: The Teaching Company, 2017), lecture 19.

CHAPTER 31: ENLIGHTENMENT PHILOSOPHERS

1. Bokenkotter, *A Concise History of the Catholic Church*, 276.

CHAPTER 32: EUROPEAN SAINTS IN ENLIGHTENMENT TIMES

1. John Henry Newman, *An Essay on the Development of Christian Doctrine*, 5.

2. Louis Bouyer, *Newman: His Life and Spirituality*, trans. J. Lewis May (San Francisco: Ignatius Press, 2011), 192, quoting Fr. Przyara.

CHAPTER 33: SAINTS IN AMERICA, ASIA, AND AFRICA

1. Gregory Orfalea, *Journey to the Sun* (New York: Charles Scribner's Sons, 2014), 252.

2. John Delaney, *Pocket Dictionary of Saints*, abridged edition (New York: Image Books, 1983), 494.

CHAPTER 34: THE BATTLE AGAINST MODERNISM: FROM VATICAN I TO PIUS X

1. For example, Delaney, *Pocket Dictionary of Saints*, 219.

2. Rupert Matthews, *The Popes: Every Question Answered* (San Diego: Thunder Bay Press, 2014), 285.

CHAPTER 35: COUNTER-ENLIGHTENMENT

1. Thérèse of Lisieux, *The Story of a Soul* (Charlotte, NC: TAN Books,

1997), 84.

    2. Ibid., 188.

CHAPTER 38: MARTYRS IN WAR

    1. Ronald Rychlak, *Hitler, the War, and the Pope* (Huntington, IN: Our Sunday Visitor, 2010) is a thorough account of Pope Pius XII's opposition to the Nazi regime and defense of the Jewish people.

CHAPTER 39: A BRIDGE TO THE PRESENT DAY — MID-TWENTIETH-CENTURY SAINTS

    1. Pope John Paul II, Homily, Green Square, Khartoum, Sudan, February 10, 1993, vatican.va, par. 8.

    2. Quote from Joel Schorn, *God's Doorkeepers* (Cincinnati, OH: Franciscan Media, 2006), 91.

CHAPTER 41: THE CHALLENGE FOR SAINTS TODAY

    1. A "prophecy" spoken by Ralph Martin, a Catholic evangelist, at an ecumenical gathering of charismatic Christians in Kansas City, MO in July, 1977.

CHAPTER 42: TWO POPES AND A COUNCIL

    1. Pope John XXIII, Address to Open the Second Vatican Council, October 11, 1962.

CHAPTER 43: MOTHER TERESA AND POPE JOHN PAUL II

    1. Speech given at the National Prayer Breakfast, February 3, 1994, in Washington, D.C., with President Bill Clinton and First Lady Hillary Clinton in attendance.

    2. Quoting from Pope John Paul II, *On the Publication of the Catechism of the Catholic Church*, in *Catechism of the Catholic Church* (New York: Doubleday, 1995), 1.

AFTERWORD

    1. Christopher Dawson, "Is the Church Too Western to Satisfy the Aspirations of the Modern World?," in *World Crisis and the Catholic*, ed. Vittorino Veronese (New York: Sheed and Ward, Inc., 1958), 166.

    2. Thérèse of Lisieux, *The Story of a Soul*, 213.

3. Teresa of Ávila, *The Book of Her Life*, in *The Collected Works of St. Teresa of Ávila*, vol. 1 (Washington, D.C.: ICS Publications, 1976), 90.

RECOMMENDED READING

From the various sources I drew upon to write this book, both academic and popular, the following may be useful to the reader interested in further study.

GENERAL CHURCH HISTORIES

Bokenkotter, Thomas. *A Concise History of the Catholic Church*. New York: Image Books, 1979.

Schreck, Alan. *The Compact History of the Catholic Church*. Cincinnati, OH: Servant, 2009.

Vidmar, John, OP. *The Catholic Church Through the Ages*. Mahwah, NJ: Paulist Press, 2014.

Weidenkopf, Steve. *Timeless: A History of the Catholic Church*. Huntington, IN: Our Sunday Visitor, 2019.

TOPICS IN CHURCH HISTORY

Akin, Jimmy. *The Fathers Know Best*. El Cajon, CA: Catholic Answers, 2010.

Aquilina, Mike. *The Mass of the Early Christians*. Huntington, IN: Our Sunday Visitor, 2001.

Robert Barron. *Catholicism*. New York: Image Books, 2011.

Cahill, Thomas. *How the Irish Saved Civilization*. New York: Anchor Books, 1995.

Chadwick, Henry. *The Early Church*. London: Pelican Books, 1980.

Dawson, Christopher. *The Dividing of Christendom*. Reprint, San Francisco: Ignatius Press, 2009.

———. *The Dynamics of World History*. Wilmington, DE: ISI Books, 2002.

Glynn, Paul. *A Song for Nagasaki*. San Francisco: Ignatius Press, 1988.

Ibrahim, Raymond. *Sword and Scimitar*. Cambridge, MA: Da Capo Press, 2018.

Lienhard, Joseph. *The Bible, the Church, and Authority*. Collegeville, MN: The Liturgical Press, 1995.

Matthews, Rupert. *The Popes: Every Question Answered*. San Diego: Thunder Bay Press, 2014.

Odell, Catherine. *Those Who Saw Her: Apparitions of Mary*. Revised edition, Huntington, IN: Our Sunday Visitor, 2010.

Pope Benedict XVI. *Church Fathers: From Clement of Rome to Augustine*. San Francisco: Ignatius Press, 2008.

———. *Great Teachers*. Huntington, IN: Our Sunday Visitor, 2011.

Royal, Robert. *Columbus and the Crisis of the West*. Nashua, NH: Sophia Institute Press, 2020.

Rychlak, Ronald. *Hitler, the War, and the Pope*. Huntington, IN: Our Sunday Visitor, 2010.

Staniforth, Maxwell, ed. *Early Christian Writings*. New York: Penguin Books, 1968.

Stark, Rodney. *God's Battalions: The Case for the Crusades*. New York: Harper One, 2009.

Woods Jr., Thomas E. *How the Catholic Church Built Western Civilization*. Washington, D.C.: Regnery Publishing, Inc., 2005.

"QUICK REFERENCE" SAINT BOOKS

Bangley, Bernard, ed. *Butler's Lives of the Saints: Concise, Modernized Edition*. Brewster, MA: Paraclete Press, 2005.

Delaney, John. *Pocket Dictionary of Saints*. New York: Image Books, 1983.

Farmer, David. *Oxford Dictionary of Saints*. Oxford: Oxford University Press, 1997.

Ghezzi, Bert. *Voices of the Saints*. New York: Image Books, 2002.

One Hundred Saints: Their Lives and Likenesses Drawn from Butler's Lives of the Saints *and Great Works of Western Art (Illustrated)*. New York: Bulfinch Press, 1993.

BIOGRAPHIES AND WRITINGS OF SAINTS

Augustine. *Confessions*. Ignatius Critical Edition. San Francisco: Ignatius Press, 2012.

Bouyer, Louis. *Newman: His Life and Spirituality*. San Francisco: Ignatius Press, 2011.

Chesterton, G. K. *St. Thomas Aquinas/Saint Francis of Assisi*. San Francisco: Ignatius Press, 1986.

di Donato, Pietro. *Immigrant Saint: The Life of Mother Cabrini*. New York: McGraw Hill, 1960.

de Mattei, Roberto. *Saint Pius V*. Nashua, NH: Sophia Institute Press, 2021.

Orfalea, Gregory. *Journey to the Sun* [Life of St. Junípero Serra]. New York: Charles Scribner's Sons, 2014.

Schorn, Joel. *God's Doorkeepers — Padre Pio, Solanus Casey & Andre Bessette*. Cincinnati, OH: Franciscan Media, 2006.

Teresa of Ávila. *The Collected Works of Saint Teresa of Ávila*. Washington, D.C.: ICS Publications, 1976.

Thérèse of Lisieux. *The Story of a Soul*. Charlotte, NC: TAN Books, 1997.

Twain, Mark. *Joan of Arc*. San Francisco: Ignatius Press, 1989. First published 1896.

Undset, Sigrid. *Catherine of Siena*. Translated by Kate Austin-Lund. San Francisco: Ignatius Press, 2009.

Weigel, George. *Witness to Hope: The Biography of Pope John Paul II*. New York: HarperCollins, 1999.

INDEX OF SAINTS

Page numbers in bold refer to the primary entry on the saint.

ABOUT THE AUTHOR

Randall Petrides, a lifelong Catholic, is retired after forty years of practice as a lawyer. He holds degrees from the University of Michigan and Notre Dame Law School and a masters in theology from Franciscan University of Steubenville. He resides in Michigan with Elizabeth, his wife of forty-three years, where they raised their five children. They have sixteen grandchildren.